YORK

YORK

THE HISTORY AND HERITAGE OF A CITY

R. K. BOOTH

BARRIE & JENKINS
LONDON

First published in Great Britain in 1990 by
Barrie & Jenkins Ltd
20 Vauxhall Bridge Road, London SW1V 2SA

British Library Cataloguing in Publication Data
Booth, R. K.
  York: the history and heritage of a city. — (Cities)
  1. North Yorkshire.York, history
  I. Title   II. Series
  942.8'43

ISBN 0-7126-3590-4

Typeset by DP Photosetting, Aylesbury, Bucks
Printed and bound in Great Britain by
Butler & Tanner Ltd, Frome and London

CONTENTS

For Cathy

LIST OF ILLUSTRATIONS

PHOTOGRAPHIC CREDITS

J. B. Morrell Library, University of York: 6b, 8; York City Art Gallery:
1–3b, 5a, 5b, 6a, 10a–15, 16b, page 148; York Minster Library: 4, 7, 9,
16a; The Yorkshire Museum: page 84.

CHAPTER ONE

THE HISTORY OF THE CITY OF YORK

The Roman Ninth Legion marched into Yorkshire in AD 71, twenty-eight years after their army of conquest had landed on the shores of southern England. Led by the governor of the province of Britain, the able commander Quintus Petillius Cerialis, their first task was to establish a legionary base in the north. Around the site Cerialis chose was to grow the city now known as York.

With three other legions, the Ninth had landed in Britain in AD 43 with the purpose of imposing political stability on the quarrelling factions which then presided over southern England. Their motive was more than simple expansionism. They hoped to ensure the continuation of the centuries old trade with Britain which had proved to be of value to the Empire.

Although a significant quantity of that trade, particularly in metals such as lead, iron and tin, was with the Celtic tribes of what was to become Northumbria (the land north of the Humber) the people of northern England initially showed little active hostility towards their new neighbours, and the earliest governors of the new province saw little advantage in taking on the burden of heavily garrisoning north of a line joining Chester and Lincoln.

The dominant northern Celtic tribe were the Brigantes, who occupied most of what is now Yorkshire, Durham and Northumberland. During the decade from AD 60 onwards the Brigantes were beset by internal power struggles which culminated in one of their leaders, Venutius, a man bitterly opposed to the Roman presence in Britain, rising in revolt and expelling their rightful ruler — his wife, Cartimandua. When Cartimandua fled south to Roman protection, Cerialis decided that the time had arrived to annex northern England to the Empire.

Of the four legions then stationed in Britain, Cerialis chose for his invasion of the hostile wild land of Northumbria the Ninth. Ten years earlier a part of the Ninth Legion had been ambushed near Cambridge during the rebellion led by the famous Iceni queen, Boudicca. They had been caught by surprise and were heavily defeated, but not before showing their skill and bravery as a fighting force. Their commander at the battle had been Cerialis, and he and the Ninth continued to share a mutual respect.

Leaving their former base at Lincoln, the Ninth Legion marched north, crossing the Humber at Brough and proceeding along the ridge of the Yorkshire Wolds.

The site Cerialis chose for the legion's new headquarters is a fine location for a military town. Firstly, it is the junction of two rivers, the Ouse and the Foss. The triangle of land between the rivers offered a naturally defended site ideal for a fort. Further, both rivers are navigable and were then tidal as far inland as York.

Secondly, while the land around York is both low and flat, York itself stands on a glacial moraine, and is thus somewhat protected from the dangers of frequent flooding which plagued the lands around. This raised ridge extends west to the Pennine hills and east to the Wolds. In so doing it creates a route above the surrounding boggy ground of the Vale of York, to and from other centres of population.

Thirdly, the area around York was rich in raw materials. The Vale of York itself was thickly wooded, providing a ready supply of timber, while a local source of limestone ideal for building existed a few miles to the south-west in the quarries around Tadcaster, from where cut stone could easily be transported by river to York. Further, the nearby Yorkshire Dales were rich in minerals, including iron and lead ores, and the grain prairies of East Anglia were also within easy reach by water.

The first Roman fort consisted of a collection of buildings for garrisoning the legionary troops, laid out around an administrative building, the *Principia*. The *Principia* itself stood partly on the site today occupied by the Minster. The fort, an area of about fifty acres, was enclosed by a strong wooden stockade standing on a mound of earth. This in turn was surrounded by the ditch created by the digging of the mound. (Further details of the site and walls of the fort can be found in Chapter Four.)

The first fort was built in some haste, as the Brigantes were an ever-present threat. Shortly after its construction, Cerialis took the Ninth Legion north and, near what is now Scotch Corner on the A1, engaged and defeated the Brigantean army. With the establishment of their superiority, time could be taken to strengthen the fort at York and about ten years after the Romans first came to Northumbria a second, stronger fort was built on the site of the first. This was also of wood — it was not until the end of the first decade of the second century AD, when the Roman settlement was about forty years old, that the wooden defences were replaced with stone.

The Romans built the first known bridge over the Ouse. This was not where any of the modern bridges today span the river. It stood immediately outside the main entrance to the fort, close to the site of the present Guildhall.

Shortly after AD 120 the Ninth Legion were replaced in York by the Sixth, who were brought from Germany. There is a mystery about what happened to the Ninth Legion after they left York. They were one of the most respected of the Roman legions, and had become famous during campaigns in Spain before they were brought to Britain. To serve with the Ninth was considered an honour of which any Roman soldier would have been proud. Yet after they left York they were never heard of again. Presumably they were disbanded, but the reason why is not known. Perhaps they suffered an extreme military disgrace.

A Roman legion was composed of about five thousand regular soldiers, together with many more auxiliary troops, administrators, servants, slaves and other persons. Such a large settlement soon attracted traders and their families, anxious to supply the Romans with all their material needs. During the period that the Romans occupied York (about the same as the length of time from the accession of Charles I, in 1625, to the present day) a sizeable town grew up on the north bank of the Ouse, around the legionary fort.

Although the street plan inside the fort was laid out in a strictly rectangular grid, the streets did not run north–south and east–west. Rather, the whole fortress was built facing to the south-west, so as to front squarely onto the Ouse. Consequently, as the adjacent town grew outwards from the walls of the fortress, so the streets of the town were constructed running north–west to south–east, and north–east to south–west. To this day this portion of the city of York retains this street plan — a plan which confuses visitors as it is not that of the Minster which, aligned conventionally east–west, dominates the site of the former Roman fort and trading settlement.

Many remnants of Roman buildings have been found under York, and no doubt far more remain to be unearthed. Just to the north of St Sampson's Square the remains of a Roman hot bath-house can be seen in the cellar of a public house. Close by, a Roman sewer remains intact, and another Roman sewer is still functioning under the Minster, keeping the great church, a thousand years younger than itself, dry. During repair work in the late 1960s part of the interior of the Minster had to be excavated. Many remains of Roman buildings were unearthed, including part of the *Principia* building mentioned above. (These are described in the section on the Minster Foundations in Chapter Two.)

The settlement which grew up around the fort was dominated by the military presence, and stood on land which was owned by the fort. On the south bank of the Ouse another quite different settlement evolved. The town on the south of the river was completely civilian and the people who lived there were merchants, retired soldiers, civil servants and people engaged in a variety of manufacturing trades (some of which were of expensive luxury goods such as jewellery, suggesting a wealthy town). In addition there would have been an army of servants and slaves.

This southern settlement, almost a separate town from that on the opposite bank of the Ouse, was granted a charter from Rome giving it independence from the administration of the fort, and the right to set up its own bodies for local government, law enforcement and justice. A *forum*, stood in the North Street–Rougier Street area. The *forum* would have been a square which served as a market place, enclosed by local government buildings. It provided a general meeting place and a centre for the town. The courts of law would also have been part of the *forum*. Close by would have stood the *basilica* — the official residence of the governor of the province. Although its site has not been found, it is suspected that the *basilica* stood close to where All Saints' Church on North Street stands today.

This civilian town was also protected by a defensive wall, and between Micklegate and Lendal Bridge the medieval wall largely follows the line of the Roman wall, standing in places on Roman foundations. The civilian town would have grown up around the main road to the south from the fort. This ran from the south end of the bridge, opposite the present Guildhall, along the line of the medieval Tanner Row and Toft Green, to a gate in the wall at the south end of Toft Green, a few yards north-west of the medieval gate — Micklegate Bar.

Above Skeldergate, the buildings of modern York stand on a huge river terrace, built by the Romans to protect their town from the ravages of the frequent flooding of the Ouse. The terrace can best by seen from the north bank of the river. It is a considerable achievement of civil engineering.

The Romans adapted the local Celtic name for the site of their new fort and settlements, naming it *Eboracum*, meaning the place where the yew trees grow. There is a widely told legend that the city took its name from a man called Eburos, said to be a descendant of one of the refugees who fled from defeated Troy. The legend originated in the twelfth century. Similarly, the association of York with a boar is a mistranslation or misinterpretation of the original form of the name.

During the period of Roman occupation, York became an important town of significance beyond the shores of England. The province of Britain was divided into two, and York was made the capital of *Britannia Inferior*, the northern province. Invasions by the Celtic peoples of unoccupied Scotland (referred to by the Romans as 'Picts' or painted people) twice led to the administration of the Roman Empire being overseen from York. In 208, the Emperor Severus moved his entire court to the town from Rome and ruled from the city until his death three years later. Severus' remains are buried at Acomb, now a suburb of the modern town.

A century later the Emperor Constantius Chlorus again brought the Roman court to the city. On his death in the city in 306, his son was declared his successor and was instated as Emperor Constantine I in the city. Later to become known as Constantine the Great, he was the first emperor to officially adopt Christianity.

The Romans stayed in York until the first decade of the fifth century, when the break up of their Empire on the European mainland forced the withdrawal of all Roman troops from Britain. Over the period of Roman rule York had become highly cosmopolitan and populated by people originating from all corners of the Empire and beyond. Attracted by a city which had become an important political centre and a prosperous trading town, many would have come as merchants. Others would have been soldiers with their families who had become established in the city and who had chosen to remain when they retired from military service.

Some would have been slaves set free by their masters, or freed on their masters' deaths. With the withdrawal of the army to the Continent, most of the civilian population of the city probably chose to remain in the town which had become their home. The cosmopolitan nature of *Eboracum* is confirmed by the variety of deities associated with cultures other than that of Rome who had temples or shrines built to them in the town.

The major reason for the withdrawal of the Romans from Britain was the sweeping across Europe of tribes of nomadic warriors from Asia. Just as centuries before the Celts had ruthlessly swept aside the previous Europeans, so the Germanic peoples, Goths, Vandals, Visigoths, Franks, and many more, pushed the Celtic nations into the sea, leaving wreckage and ruin behind them. The once great city of Rome was in military and political turmoil. With ominous times threatening from over the North Sea, England was abandoned to fend for herself.

AFTER THE ROMANS

For almost two centuries following the departure of the Romans very little is known about life in York. In part this is because, in the absence of an organised bureaucracy like that of the Empire, written records ceased to be kept, or at least have not survived. The Germanic peoples whom we now collectively refer to as the 'Anglo-Saxons' had started to come to Britain long before the Romans abandoned these islands. Indeed, many had come as soldiers with the Roman army. The influx of non-Christian Anglo-Saxons seems to have completely overwhelmed the Celts. However, contrary to what used to be believed, it seems likely that the the Romano-Celtic Britons were not completely driven out of England.

With the collapse of Roman administration, England as a political unit under a central government disappeared, to be replaced by a number of city states and small kingdoms, each of which governed itself. York would have been one of these. Such small, independent communities could not survive the onslaught of the invaders, and unable to mount effective, combined and organized opposition to the Anglo-Saxons, England was rapidly over-run.

This is the period of the 'Dark Ages', the age of shadowy figures and legends, such as those of the Celtic King Arthur and his knights. If, as seems probable, the Arthurian legends are based on an element of historical fact, then Arthur himself would have lived around the end of the fifth century AD — perhaps the last of the Christian British fighting the invading pagans. One of the Arthurian legends describes the fall of British rule in York at a great battle in which Sir Percival, the Romano-Celtic lord ruling over Northumbria, was killed.

From a little before AD 600 we have a continuous history of York to the present day. By that time England was completely dominated by the Anglo-Saxons and was ruled by a handful of royal families. The area now known as Yorkshire roughly corresponds to the Anglo-Saxon kingdom of Deira. Deira means the country of the waters, from the large number of rivers which drain the Pennine fells. North of Deira was the country of Bernicia which today is Northumberland. During the early years of its existence Deira had several 'capitals', the country being governed from wherever the king happened to be living or visiting. York was but one of the more important towns of Deira, but not the most important. Twenty miles to the east of York, Goodmanham, in the Yorkshire Wolds, seems to have been the cultural and political focus of the Anglo-Saxon settlements of Deira, being the site of the most important Anglo-Saxon temple in the kingdom.

Bernicia and Deira were neighbours and enemies. In 603 King Aethelfrith of Bernicia invaded and defeated Deira, uniting the two and creating the Anglo-Saxon kingdom of Northumbria. The King of Deira was killed in the battle, but many of the rest of his family, including his youngest brother, Edwin, fled to the protection of the Celtic kingdom of Gwynedd in North Wales. Edwin was eighteen when he was forced to flee. After spending some years in Wales he moved to the court of the East Anglian king, Raedwald. Aethelfrith sent a threat to Raedwald for harbouring his enemy, and in 616 Raedwald responded by assisting Edwin to invade Northumbria. Aethelfrith was defeated and Edwin became the second king of the new Anglo-Saxon country.

To the south-west of York two villages still bear the name of the last of the Celtic kingdoms of northern England — Sherburn-in-Elmet and Barwick-in-Elmet. Shortly after his defeat of Aethelfrith, Edwin defeated King Cerdic of Elmet and Elmet was absorbed into Northumbria. Edwin now ruled over a united Northumbria covering the same area as the former Roman province of *Britannia Inferior*.

Of the kings of the Anglo-Saxon countries, some were more powerful than others. The most powerful was the over-lord of all the kingdoms — the *bretwalda* or 'wide ruler of Britain'. From the time of the defeat of Aethelfrith by Raedwald and Edwin, Raedwald was undisputed *bretwalda*. He died in the early 620s. (His grave is probably that of the famous Sutton Hoo ship burial in Suffolk.) On the death of Raedwald, the *bretwaldaship* passed to Edwin and, in consequence, Northumbria once again became the focus of power and rule in England.

In 625 Edwin married a Christian, the daughter of King Aethelbert of Kent, Princess Aethelburga. When Aethelburga moved to Northumberland following her marriage, she brought with her Paulinus her chaplain, who became the first Bishop of York, and her deacon, James. Over the next eighteen months Aethelburga and Paulinus converted Edwin to Christianity. On his conversion, many of his nobles and pagan priests also adopted Christianity. His former chief priest, a man called Coifi, rode to Goodmanham and burnt the temple, and Edwin adopted York as his permanent political and religious centre. (The present parish church at Goodmanham stands on the site of the former temple.)

The king decided that he would be baptised on Easter Saturday, 627. For the baptism, which he shared with many of his nobles, Edwin had built a small wooden church — the forerunner of the present York Minster. Tradition has it that a well, today in the crypt of the present Minster, was the actual spot where Edwin was baptised.

Less than six years after his baptism, Edwin was defeated and killed in battle by a combined army under Penda, the pagan King of Mercia (the Anglo-Saxon country of the English midlands) and King Cadwallon of Gwynedd, at whose court Edwin had previously found hospitality and protection. Cadwallon now felt deep animosity towards Edwin. His court had given Edwin refuge when his life had been in danger, only to have Edwin enforce over-lordship over Gwynedd when he became *bretwalda*. He was determined to wreak his revenge on Edwin's people. Bede, a monk based at Jarrow and writing almost a hundred years later, tells us that things were so bad following the overrunning of Northumbria that for a year after Edwin's death no-one could bring themselves to record anything of the terrible events besetting the kingdom. Queen Aethelburga and her children escaped and, together with Paulinus, fled back to Kent. James the deacon bravely stayed in York. He survived and continued to preach the Christian faith in the north.

A year after Edwin's defeat, the pendulum of Northumbria's fortunes swung again. One of the many murdered by Cadwallon was Eanfrith, a son of Aethelfrith. Eanfrith had been visiting the Welsh king in peace, with only a dozen companions. His brother, Oswald, determined to avenge his death assembled an army in the family's old stronghold of Bernicia. Towards the end of 634 Cadwallon was defeated and killed by Oswald, who then declared himself as king in York and *bretwalda* over the other Anglo-Saxon kings.

The declaration was, however, backed neither by true power nor by the influence needed to restore stability to the strife-torn north. The struggle for control of Northumbria continued and in 642 Oswald himself was killed by Penda. He was succeeded by his younger brother, Oswy, who eventually defeated Penda in 655. Oswy united the old royal houses of Bernicia and Deira by marrying Edwin's daughter, and peace, Christianity and civilization once again returned to York. Oswy was now in the position of being the first undisputed King of Northumbria since Edwin's death twenty-two years earlier. With stability came power and once again the king in York was able to exert true *bretwaldaship* over the other Anglo-Saxon kings of England. York was restored to its position as the centre of influence and the effective capital city of Anglo-Saxon England.

EARLY CHRISTIAN YORK

During what for England had been the 'Dark Ages', Christianity had been taken to Ireland by a Romanised Briton, St Patrick, and had evolved there to become a mainly monastic faith. On the defeat of Aethelfrith by Edwin, Aethelfrith's family had fled from York to the protection of the great Irish monastery on the island of

Iona. The Irish style of Christianity differed from that of Rome, brought to York from Kent, in several fundamental ways. As a result of their upbringing on Iona, Oswald and Oswy brought with them to York the Irish style of Christianity. In 635, shortly after his defeat of Cadwallon, Oswald sent to Iona to invite the monastery to found a daughter house in Northumbria. Iona sent a delegation of monks under St Aidan, who founded an island monastery in the style of that on Iona, on Lindisfarne, off the coast of Northumbria.

The differing schools of Christianity met, politically and geographically, at York. The outward discussion focused on when Easter should be celebrated, and the shape into which the monks should shave their tonsures. In fact these were but the outward manifestations of much deeper philosophical differences — perhaps comparable to the present day differences between the Church of Rome and evangelical Baptism. It was clear that it would be very difficult for the two schools to continue to co-exist in York. In 664, or possibly during the autumn of 663, Oswy summoned the major theological figures of northern England. They met, not in York, but on the more neutral ground of the abbey at Whitby, which had recently been founded by St Hilda, Edwin's great-niece.

At the centre of the debate was St Wilfrid. Wilfrid had been educated at Lindisfarne and might have been expected to have been an adherent to the Celtic school of Christianity. However, he had been persuaded of the superiority of the Roman theology during a visit to Rome, and argued vociferously for the Roman liturgy. Oswy might also have been expected to have sided with the Celts, having been educated on Iona. Oswy, however, chose to rule in favour of Rome. It is arguable that, as Oswy was *bretwalda* of England, the adoption of the doctrines of the Church of Rome by York ensured that the rest of England remained or became a part of the European Church. Certainly it united England into one school of Christianity. It was not, however, a universally popular decision, and dozens of monks left Northumbria for Iona and Ireland.

Shortly before his victory over the Celtic Church, Oswy had instated Wilfrid as Bishop of York. At the time of his death, Edwin was in the process of rebuilding his wooden church in stone. On his defeat, the work stopped and the church seems to have remained in this half built state for over thirty years. On his enthronement as bishop, Wilfrid had this second Minster finished (see Chapter Two). He also had built the first cathedral at Ripon, parts of which survive to this day. Wilfrid founded the Cathedral School in York. St Peter's School continues to thrive and is the oldest school in Britain.

Wilfrid was one of the memorable figures of Anglo-Saxon York. Not lacking in a sense of his own importance, he seems to have courted unpopularity by wielding considerable power. The queen took a dislike to him, not least because his retinue at public occasions out-competed that of the *bretwalda* himself in size and splendour. Given his strength of personality it is unsurprising that it was not long before he clashed with the Church of Rome itself. This was precipitated by

Wilfrid's declaration of independence from Canterbury, which had been the principal church in England since its establishment by Augustine's mission. Wilfrid set out for Rome to try to persuade the Pope of the necessity of York's independence. This he did, but on his arrival back in England, Oswy's successor as King of Northumbria, Eogfrith, had Wilfrid thrown into prison.

The saint escaped, and when Eogfrith died, his successor, King Aldfrith, allowed Wilfrid to return to his See at York. Five years later, no doubt having come to know Wilfrid's personality better, Aldfrith dismissed Wilfrid for the second time, but on Aldfrith's death, Wilfrid was allowed to return. This time he was not allowed back to the See of York, but was given the lesser posts of Bishop of Ripon and of Hexham. These he managed to keep until his death in 709.

Wilfrid's Minster was severely damaged by fire in 741. It was a time of prosperity for York and the church was rapidly rebuilt. It seems probable that the fire damaged much of the town. The city of York has been plagued by fires over the centuries — a second fire destroyed the town in 763.

In 674, four years after the death of Oswy, Northumbria lost its suzerainty over the other Anglo-Saxon kingdoms when Eogfrith was defeated by a Mercian army. Pictish raids across the Scottish border would maintain insecurity in Northumbria and York would never again be the political capital of all England. Yet from the time of Oswy and Bishop Wilfrid, York in particular and Northumbria in general became and remained one of the great centres of learning of the Western world. The Minster, with its considerable library and St Peter's School, flourished and in 735 the See of York was elevated to the status of archiepiscopancy.

In 782 the powerful Frankish king, the Holy Roman Emperor Charlemagne, sent to York for a tutor-in-residence to his court at Aix-la-Chapelle. The call was answered by Alcuin, formerly Minster librarian and head of St Peter's School, whom Charlemagne had met previously when Alcuin had undertaken a visit to Rome. When Alcuin left York he took with him to France the use of ecclesiastical Latin, reintroducing to Europe the scholastic role of Latin as the universal language of learning. (Latin had fallen out of use in Europe during the previous dark centuries.)

The eighth century was a time of peace and civilization when York flourished both as a scholastic focus and as a trading centre. Archaeological excavations carried out in York during the 1980s revealed pottery of types manufactured in the Rhineland and in France. Millstones imported from Germany were also found. The evidence suggests that there was extensive trading with the European mainland and there emerges a picture of eighth-century York as a prosperous and busy town, with much shipping and bustling quaysides. Other finds show there was extensive manufacturing of various goods being carried out in the town. Perhaps the most spectacular find was a splendid warrior's helmet, tooled to the highest standards. One other similar helmet has been found — at Uppsala, the Anglo-Saxon capital of Sweden — adding to a now considerable body of evidence suggesting a close connection between the royal houses of Anglo-Saxon York and southern Sweden at this period.

THE VIKINGS

The age of peace, learning and prosperity ended during the following century. The first Viking raid suffered by Northumbria was on the monastery at Lindisfarne. The year was 793 and those monks who survived fled with the few treasures that they could gather. The age of the Scandinavian pirates was about to commence.

For almost two decades following the raid on Lindisfarne, the Vikings harried the shores of Britain. The coastal monasteries of the north were particularly vulnerable and Iona itself was sacked three times. Towards the end of the first decade of the ninth century, as suddenly as they had started, the raids stopped and for nearly a quarter of a century Britain was free of the menace of the pirates. (The Old English word *viking* means nothing more than 'pirate'.) The raids started again in the 830s and continued as a disturbing problem for thirty years more, during which the Vikings were a source of much disquiet and no little affliction. However, they posed no serious threat to the stability of the Anglo-Saxon civilization of Northumbria until the ominous arrival in 865 of a huge Viking army — perhaps as many as a thousand ships.

One of the more colourful of the chiefs of Viking legend was a Dane known as Ragnar Hairybreeks. In his time, Ragnar was said to have been famous and feared throughout the maritime settlements of northern Europe, having plundered around their coastlines for several decades, even making extensive incursions into their hinterlands. On a raid into Northumbria, Ragnar was captured by an army under the command of Aella, a Northumbrian nobleman. Aella ordered his death, according to legend, by having him thrown into a pit of snakes. As he was about to die, Ragnar is said to have uttered prophetically, 'The piglets would be grunting if they knew the plight of the boar!' The 'piglets' subsequently arrived, in the forms of Ragnar's sons, Ubbi, Halfdan and the splendidly named Ivar the Boneless, determined to avenge their father's death. With their lust for revenge came a change in the nature of Scandinavian piracy which was in turn to change York for all time.

The brothers assembled a huge army in Denmark, no doubt drawn by promises of the bounty that would be reaped by those who joined the expedition. Throughout the summer of 865 they raided far and wide across southern England, and for the first time they stayed throughout the winter. In the autumn of 866 the Viking army sailed up the Ouse.

In Northumbria, civil war had broken out between descendants of the old royal houses of Bernicia and Deira. Aella, who had killed Ragnar Hairybreeks, was descended from the Bernician house. His rival, the rightful King of Northumbria, Osbert, controlled his family's lands in southern Northumbria (the old Deira) and was under threat of being overthrown by Aella. When news reached the rivals of the approach of the great Viking hoard, pragmatism forced Osbert and Aella to forget their differences and rapidly form a combined army to repel the invaders. However, the delay caused by the civil turmoil meant that they were too late to save York. The Viking army entered the poorly defended city on 1st November, 866.

Having easily overrun the town, the Viking army spent the winter of 866–7 strengthening York's defences. The earthen rampart was heightened and topped with a strong, new palisade. York, the brothers decided, with its fine access to the eastern coast of Britain, would make an ideal town for a permanent Danish settlement in England. The Vikings had come to stay.

It must have been a terrible time for the scholastic Anglo-Saxons who had to watch their way of life collapse and vanish overnight. Many of the most respected and learned men of the town were killed in the battle or subsequently murdered. Civilization itself must have seemed to have been at an end and, indeed, the arrival of the Vikings in York was to punctuate the tradition of the schoolmen of the city with a sterile period which would last several decades into the tenth century. The arrival of the Danes was also to determine the nature and culture of the whole of northern England, certainly for many centuries and, to a degree, to the present day.

The Anglo-Saxon army, under the joint command of Aella and Osbert, attacked Viking-occupied York on 21st March, 867. They almost succeeded and, when the Viking palisade gave way under their onslaught, they must have thought that the town was recaptured. They had not accounted for the Vikings' experience in hand-to-hand fighting. The Anglo-Saxon slaughter was terrible and the Viking victory supreme. It is not known what happened to Osbert, but Aella was captured and, in a terrible ceremony known as the 'Blood Eagle', was sacrificed to Odin, the Viking god of war and most powerful of the Scandinavian deities.

Having strengthened the city to their own satisfaction, the Danes installed a puppet king in York, an Anglo-Saxon called Egbert, before setting out south once again to occupy themselves with the extortion of money in return for peace. They returned to York for the winter, and the following year attacked East Anglia. By 869 they were ready to take on the most powerful of the Anglo-Saxon kingdoms of ninth-century England — Wessex.

Repeated defeats of the Wessex army by the Danes forced their young king, Alfred, to concede successive payments of money — each payment larger than the one before. The Vikings did not return to York that winter and remained in the south the following year, and the year after that. In 872 the people of York rebelled against the few Danes left in the city, and exiled Egbert. The Danish army immediately abandoned Wessex and hurried back to their base. In York an agreement seems to have been reached over the following winter, which the Danes spent in the town. The Anglo-Saxons were allowed to choose their own king (they instated a man called Ricsige) in return for peace with the Vikings and allowing

11

the Danes to treat York as their home in England. A compromise in Northumbria having been reached, the great army again set out for Wessex and the wealth the rich southern country offered.

The following year Mercia, the wealthy country of central England, collapsed, unable to field any further resistance to the Viking army. Only Wessex now stood in the way of the Danes' uncontested domination of the whole of England. At this point, however, a split occurred in the Viking forces. Half, under Halfdan, the only surviving son of Ragnar Hairybreeks, returned north to settle first in Northumbria and, later, in Ireland. The remainder, under a leader called Guthrum, remained in the south.

Wessex seemed to have succumbed to Scandinavian domination when Alfred started to defeat the Danes in a series of lightning guerrilla attacks, carried out by small groups who had remained loyal to the all but defeated king. With these small but significant successes, supporters who had abandoned Alfred when times looked hopeless began to drift back. Further, with the departure of Halfdan, the Danish army found themselves much reduced in numbers. By the spring of 878 Alfred had assembled an army large enough to confront the Danes directly and, at Edington in Wiltshire, on 13th May, the Anglo-Saxons under his command put the Vikings to flight.

Alfred and Guthrum reached an acceptable compromise. Guthrum agreed to be baptized a Christian, and he and Alfred exchanged clothes and gifts. It was agreed that north of a line roughly from Essex to Cheshire would become a Viking province, ruled from York according to Danish law — and northern England became known as the 'Danelaw'. South of the line would remain Anglo-Saxon. Guthrum and his followers returned to settle permanently and in peace in the city.

The Roman name for the town we now know as York, *Eboracum*, had become Celticized on the departure of the legions, to become *Caer Ebrauc* — the castle at *Ebrauc*. The Anglo-Saxons added a suffix, calling their town *Evorwic*, or *Eoforwic*, a *wic* being a market or trading town. Under Danish pronunciation, *Eoforwic* became *Jorvik* — and in later centuries *Jorvik* became York.

The extent of influence of the Viking civilization is often forgotten, and their way of life is often misleadingly thought of as one dedicated to destruction and robbery. In fact those Vikings who raided around the shores of Britain, and later landed and settled in York, were part of a culture whose fingers of influence spread as far as North America in the west and, by way of the great rivers and seas of Europe and western Asia, to Samarkand and possibly beyond. Jorvik, which had been an important trading post since the time of its founding by the Romans, continued to flourish as a Viking capital, and under the rule of their part-nautical, part-agrarian trading culture, grew in size and prosperity. One might speculate that the Vikings who raided the shores of Britain were very probably those who possessed no land of their own, or possibly younger sons who would inherit little or nothing. Such men set out with others in similar positions to make their own fortunes at the expense of whoever they could dispossess.

The Vikings who initially settled in York were of Danish origin. Later, Norsemen of Norwegian roots colonized the Scottish islands, the Isle of Man and eastern Ireland, and eventually came to the Yorkshire Dales by way of Lancashire and Cumbria. To this day the settlements of the Lake District and the upper parts of the Dales, where the harsh climate had meant the Danes were less attracted to establish farms, have Norse rather than Danish or Anglo-Saxon names. The Norsemen seem to have been less gregarious than their southern cousins, and tended to keep to the isolation of the fell country ('fell' itself being a Norse word).

The city of York rapidly developed a distinctive, mixed Anglo-Saxon – Danish culture, adopting the strongest elements of the two, very different societies. To this day the people of Yorkshire retain a deep sense of their own particular identity and are fiercely independent of the Anglo-Saxon counties of southern England. It is said that when the soldiers of a Yorkshire regiment landed in northern Norway during the Second World War, the strength of their dialect meant there was little real barrier to communication between the Yorkshiremen and the Norwegians.

In inner York itself the streets are named 'gate' rather than street (the Scandinavian word for street being *gata*). In fact, only three streets in York (Blake Street, Coney Street and North Street) retain names from a time before the arrival of the Vikings. Around outer York many of the suburbs have names with the suffix *thorpe*, a Danish word meaning a village. Such *thorpes* are an indication of the prosperity of the period of Anglo-Danish rule in the town, and the expansion of the city by 'ribbon development' during the ninth and tenth centuries. The essential nature of York under the Danes remained very much as it had been in Anglo-Saxon times, an important trading town with bustling staiths and busy markets.

The thought of the annexation of the rest of England remained in the minds of the Danes of York for a number of decades after the battle of Edington. When Alfred died and was succeeded by his son, Edward, Alfred's nephew, Aethelwold, attempted a *coup d'état*. Rapidly defeated and driven from Wessex, Aethelwold was welcomed in York as a potential ally. During the first decade of the tenth century and under his leadership the Northumbrian Danes repeatedly invaded southern England. In 909, Edward responded by sending an army into the Danelaw and sacked much of Yorkshire. The following year the Danes rode in force into the English midlands, where they were confronted and defeated by Edward's forces. The battle marked the end of the period of total independence of the Danelaw. From 910 the Anglo-Danish culture of York and the rest of Viking England would retain independent self-government only at the sufferance of the Anglo-Saxon king in Winchester.

This is not to say that York ceased to be self-governing. On the contrary, a variety of Viking kings came and went in York until the middle of the tenth

13

century. They were not, however, allowed to display too much power, or present any threat to the House of Wessex. In 927, a conspiracy between the King of Scotland and the King of York to rid the north of subservience to the south was quickly suppressed by Athelstan, and as a result, Scotland joined Northumbria under Anglo-Saxon subjugation.

Ten years later a similar plot again brought Athelstan to York. On this occasion the great Wessex king stayed long enough to dismantle the castle. Where exactly this stood is unclear, although many think it may have been the old Roman gatehouse, still standing in King's Square. Before leaving York in 937, Athelstan founded a hospital, attached to the Minster (see St Leonard's Hospital, Chapter Five).

The last, and perhaps the most colourful King of Viking Jorvik was Erik Bloodaxe. Erik had been King of Norway, but had fled his homeland after a family squabble during which he murdered two of his brothers. After a few years as a wandering pirate, Erik found himself in York late in 947. The effective leader of Anglo-Danish Northumbria was, at that time, the Archbishop of York, a man called Wulfstan. Wulfstan nursed a smouldering desire for York's independence and on Erik's arrival the archbishop greeted him as the leader they had been looking for. Erik was enthroned in his second kingdom.

The following year, the King of Wessex, Eadred, responded by invading Northumbria. Erik's army was defeated. Erik fled and spent the following four years pursuing his alternative career of piracy. In 952, Erik once again sailed into the Humber and was once again instated as king in York. Eadred's army invaded, but this time it was Erik who defeated the Saxons. Northumbria under Erik seemed to have regained its independence from Wessex. It was a period of independence that was to be short-lived. Towards the end of 954 Erik was killed in a battle with Norsemen from Ireland, on Stainmore, between Swaledale and Teesdale, and with the passing of Erik went the old independent kingdom of Northumbria. An ancient cross, known as the Reay or Royal Cross, stands on the high moorland close to where the last king fell.

Erik Bloodaxe was one of the last of the old pirate warriors of the Viking tradition who, with a relatively small band of supporters, carved out a kingdom for themselves on whatever foreign shore appealed to them. He has been described as 'cruel, elusive and silent', and was clearly popular with the Anglo-Danes of the York of his day. One of the Norse sagas records a story which gives an insight into the character of the last King of York. It seems that Egil Skalagrimsson, a long-time enemy of Erik's, carelessly shipwrecked himself on the Yorkshire coast. Unsure about how to proceed, he sought out a long-lost friend who lived in Erik's York, a man named Arinbjörn. Arinbjörn was horrified to see Egil at his door, but waited until after sunset before presenting him to Erik.

In spite of his fury, Erik could do nothing until the morning as, under Viking law, one could not slay a man (even an enemy) after dark. Arinbjörn was ordered to keep Egil in custody and to return with him in the morning. Under Arinbjörn's encouragement, Egil spent the night composing a poem in Erik's praise, managing to ignore the distractions of a singing bird which, Egil explained, was Erik's wife, who was a witch, come in disguise to try to prevent him completing the verse. Arinbjörn's ploy worked. Erik was sufficiently flattered to allow Egil to depart, no doubt hoping that Egil's verse would be heard far and wide. (It was and survives to this day as part of 'Egil's Saga'.)

From the mid-980s, England outside the Danelaw, under Aethelred of Wessex, came increasingly under attack from Danish and Norwegian Vikings extorting ransom for peace. One of the leaders of these raids was the King of Denmark himself, Swein Forkbeard. The situation continued after Swein's death in 1014, under the leadership of his son, Cnut. Following the death of Aethelred and his son, Edmund Ironside, both during 1016, England found herself under the undisputed rule of a Dane — King Cnut.

Cnut is today remembered as a wise ruler. One of his first acts was to partition England into four administrative units — Wessex, Mercia, East Anglia and Northumbria, each to be governed in proxy by an earl. The Earl of Northumbria appointed by Cnut to rule from York was Erik of Hlathir, a Viking of his father's generation who had helped Swein gain the Danish throne, and had later orchestrated Cnut's conquest of England.

The Danish earls ruled from their stronghold in the city of York — a 'castle' which stood outside and to the north-west of the area of the ancient Roman fortifications, where St Mary's Abbey would later be built. The castle was known as *Earlsburh* and was most probably a fortified enclosure, designed for the defence of all members of the community in the days before feudal castles with keeps for the protection of the aristocracy and their personal staff alone. (See Earlsborough Terrace, Chapter Six.) Today the site of the former *Earlsburh* is the home of the Yorkshire Museum Gardens.

A wise and able man, Erik of Hlathir proved to be a fair and just governor — unusual attributes in a Viking of his time, without which he might easily have found himself ruling over a kingdom entirely of his own. He was succeeded (perhaps not directly) by Earl Siward, one of the great figures of York's history and the last of his breed of independent Viking warriors. Although a Dane from overseas (by now quite distinct from the Anglo-Danish culture of York) Siward rapidly became popular with the people of his city. His marriage to a Yorkshire princess did his public image no harm. At once feared, respected and liked, Siward ruled from the town for nearly three decades until his death in 1055.

The great earl was the same Siward who appears in Shakespeare's *Macbeth*, although the truth of the events covered by the play was very different from Shakespeare's tale. Macbeth rose to power as a Celt, attempting to rid Scotland of subservience to the English throne which had been imposed by Athelstan in 927. Macbeth probably did kill King Duncan in 1040, but almost certainly in fair fight. Duncan was little more than a 'puppet king' and had been installed on the Scots throne by Siward in order to extend the earl's suzerainty over the Scots. On his death, Duncan's sons were taken to York where they grew up as part of Siward's family, and in 1054 Siward left York with a Northumbrian army of invasion and marched north to instate Malcolm Canmore, the dead king's eldest son and now the earl's own stepson, on the throne of Scotland. The attempt succeeded, although the cost to Siward was the loss of his own eldest son — a loss which was to lead to troubled times for York in the following decade. (Macbeth himself remained in control of the Scottish highlands until his death three years later.)

At his stronghold of *Earlsburh*, Siward founded the Church of St Olave's, now on Marygate (see Chapter Three). Olave is a medieval English spelling of the Scandinavian name Olaf, and the dedication is to his friend, King Olaf of Norway. The two men had come to know each other when fighting as enemies. Siward was a commander with Cnut's army during the struggle to overthrow Aethelred, for whom Olaf was fighting as a mercenary. Olaf was murdered by his own guard during an uprising in 1030, and canonized only two years later for introducing Christianity to Norway.

As Siward himself lay dying he called his servants to his bedside and asked that they help him into his battledress. To die peacefully of the ravages of age, rather than in battle, the old man felt to be ignoble. He asked that his body be buried outside the city. His body is said to lie beneath a mound above the University of York, now known as Siward's Howe — all except his heart. He asked that his heart be buried beneath the altar of St Olave's Church.

With Siward's death in 1055, the age of the Viking warrior ruling alone or as governor over an independent Northumbria was at an end. While York would remain the focus of secular government in the north for many centuries, and remains today the centre of ecclesiastical administration in northern Britain, the days of York's status as the capital of an independent Northumbria were over for ever.

Had he not been killed in Scotland two years before, the elder of Siward's two sons would have been expected to follow his father. Siward's younger son, Waltheof, was still a child (destined to enter the politics of the city in the following decade). The earldom, together with those of Mercia and Wessex, commanded a power in the kingdom second only to that of the king himself. Against the counsel of many, Edward the Confessor took the advice of the powerful Earl of Wessex, Harold Godwinson (who virtually ran England on the king's behalf), and appointed Harold's unpopular and unsuitable younger brother, Tostig.

York was destined to suffer a decade of incompetence, maladministration and injustice from Tostig Godwinson. The city was finally driven to rebellion following the murder, at Tostig's instigation, of a prince of the old Northumbrian royal family. Taking advantage of an absence of the Anglo-Saxon earl from York, in 1065 the town rose against Tostig's garrison. Following the rebellion in York, an *ad hoc* army of Yorkshiremen marched on the south. King Edward sent his brother-in-law, Harold Godwinson, Tostig's brother, to meet the Yorkshiremen at Oxford. Harold had governed England on Edward's behalf since the role fell to him on the death of his father in 1053.

Harold had presumably hoped to negotiate a reconciliation between his brother and the peoples of York and the rest of Northumbria, but things had gone too far. In the end Tostig and his second, Copsi, were banished from England and the Yorkshire army returned peacefully to their homelands, perhaps a little less suspicious of the Saxon earl, Harold. In his place, York found itself under the governorship of a new earl, Morcar.

On 5th January, 1066, only a few weeks after the uprising, Edward the Confessor died. The following day the childless king's funeral was followed by the coronation of Harold Godwinson as his successor. Harold Godwinson was chosen by the Witan, the parliament of the day. He had no familial claim to the throne, but had led England successfully for the past thirteen years. William, the Duke of Normandy and the cousin of the late king, had what appeared to be a far better claim to the English crown. In addition to being the closest male relative of Edward, William also claimed that the late king had promised that he would succeed and had deliberately avoided having children of his own in order that the succession should not be disputed. Another of the late king's cousins, Edgar, also had claims to the throne lodged on his behalf, although he was then still only twelve years of age.

The Kings of Norway and Denmark, Harald Hardrada and Swein Estrithson, also claimed the right to govern England, mainly because they saw the English succession in disarray, and to an eleventh-century Viking this was more than reason enough to embark on an invasion. It was in Hardrada's court that Tostig and Copsi took refuge, determined to avenge their deposition from York.

York might have been expected to be wary of Harold Godwinson, Saxon as he was. (The Saxons were not highly respected in Danish York.) Yet Harold had found in favour of the north against his own brother only the year before. The newly crowned Harold came to the city in May 1066 to try and consolidate his following in Northumbria. While not rejected openly, he was nevertheless treated coolly by the people of York. During his visit to the town, a comet, later named Halley's comet, appeared in the sky. It is perhaps a measure of underlying feelings that while in France the comet was taken to be a sign of William's impending success, in England it was taken to be an omen of ill fortune. Harold departed south to spend the summer awaiting the arrival of William's invasion fleet on the shores of southern England.

Which force attacked first was, in the end, determined as much by the weather as by politics. In the late summer of 1066 a strong north-easterly wind kept

William pinned in the Channel ports of northern France, but brought Hardrada, accompanied by Tostig, Copsi and a fleet of over three hundred ships, across the North Sea and, after plundering Scarborough, up the Ouse to Riccall, eight miles south of York.

With Harold and the army he had raised to defend his realm encamped in the south, the defence of York from Hardrada fell to the people of Northumbria alone. However, the Norwegians' attack on Scarborough had been a mistake. It alerted Earl Morcar of the impending danger and allowed him to assemble an army. As Hardrada marched towards York along the east bank of the Ouse on the morning of Wednesday, 20th September, 1066, they were met by an army of significant size, led by Earl Morcar of Northumbria and his brother, Edwin, Earl of Mercia.

Hardrada was a warrior of long experience, having first wielded a sword in anger nearly four decades before. The same was true of his brother Tostig. Not so the two earls. Edwin, the elder, could not have been more than twenty-four years of age. Morcar was then not yet twenty. Neither had ever seen a battle. The armies met at Fulford, two miles south of York. It was a terrible defeat for the English — thousands died, including many of York's clergy. It seems that lack of experience led to misunderstandings of commands. Without experience of battlefield tactics Morcar seems to have assumed that when the Danes withdrew to regroup they were actually running away. He led a charge against them, was cut off from behind and trapped. The English were routed and fled. Unfortunately, there was nowhere for them to flee. To the west was the Ouse. To the east and behind them, apart from a narrow road to the city, was marshy ground (since drained and now known as Walmgate Stray and Heslington Common). The two earls escaped to the protection of York's walls, but thousands of English died in the marshes, mostly by drowning, and it was said that after the battle (known as the Battle of Gate Fulford — meaning Fulford on the road) one could walk across the marshes from the Ouse to Heslington dry shod, by hopping from body to body.

After such a victory, a Viking army would normally plunder the undefended city. Hardrada, however, had come not to plunder but to seize the Crown of an intact and wealthy nation. His troops withdrew to their boats at Riccall, having made an agreement with Morcar to meet the nobles of York on the morning of the following Monday, when York would formally surrender and pay homage to Hardrada as their king. The meeting was to take place at Stamford Bridge, where the road east from York crosses the River Derwent eight miles away.

Meanwhile news of the coastal raids had reached Harold, probably by means of a chain of beacons. Assembling a small cohort of elite full-time specialists — his *housecarls* (perhaps best compared to the Special Air and Boat Services of today), Harold rode north with an impressive speed which has never been fully explained. He arrived at Tadcaster, eight miles south-west of York, on Sunday, 24th

18

September — the day before the arranged meeting between Morcar and Hardrada.

It was around this time that the cold north-easterly wind which had pinned William in the Channel ports changed to a south-westerly. On the morning of the following day, as William made his preparations to sail from France, the weather in York was warm and humid. Many of Hardrada's army consequently left their heavy battle armour at their boats in Riccall when they marched to meet the English for the formalities at Stamford Bridge. Their surprise must have been immense when what they saw riding towards them from York was not a subservient delegation but what was later described by a Norwegian present that day as 'an ice-field of steel'.

The battle of Stamford Bridge was hard fought and gruesome. It lasted the whole of the day and on several occasions either side could have succumbed. In the end, the evening of 25th September, 1066, saw Harold, Morcar and Edwin victorious, and Hardrada and Tostig slain. On the morning of the following Wednesday Duke William set sail from Dives-sur-Mer to claim his new kingdom. Harold fell at Hastings three weeks later, after a battle much smaller than that of his victory at Stamford Bridge. William, Duke of Normandy, was crowned King of England on Christmas Day.

Few in England were happy about being ruled by William. In 1068, several towns staged rebellions, including York. However, when William arrived at the gates of the city, the men of York apologised without even a token of defiance. To ensure against further insurgence, William ordered the building of a castle (the site of which is now known as Baile Hill) and stationed a garrison in the town. In January 1069, a second rebellion started in Teesdale, and quickly spread to York where the people of the town, humiliated by their previous defeat, were determined to get their revenge. Again it came to nothing, collapsing on William's arrival. He ordered a second castle to be erected (on the site of the present Clifford's Tower) and installed a larger garrison. The creation of a moat around the second castle, by damming the Foss, flooded 120 acres of prime arable land in the Layerthorpe area, and created a lake which became known as the King's Fishpool.

The third revolt in York, on 19th September, 1069, succeeded. Jointly led by Edwin, Waltheof (the surviving son of Earl Siward), Prince Edgar (cousin of Edward the Confessor) and Swein Estrithson (the opportunistic Danish king) the rebellion looked almost certain to succeed, and possibly drive William from the English throne. Both castles in York were overrun and every Norman in the city, save three, was killed. In panic the Normans made a desperate attempt to create a diversion by starting a fire (a recognized tactic of the time). It spread and was soon beyond control. Most of the city, including the Minster, was destroyed.

The rebellion collapsed for two main reasons. Firstly, lack of proper leadership prevented the uprising from grasping the opportunities created by their initial success. Instead their indecision allowed William to organize a counter-offensive.

Secondly, the Danish army, who were pursuing the spoils of war rather than the Crown, allowed William to buy them off, and deserted their English allies.

William's patience had expired and he decided upon punishment, not just of the city of York, but of the whole of northern England as far south as Derbyshire and Cheshire. Towards the end of the year his men rode over Northumbria, killing whoever they encountered, and putting to the torch every building and food store in their path. The destruction was pursued relentlessly, apart from a short break while William celebrated Christmas in York, until the whole of the north was laid waste. The effects on the population were terrible and are still evidenced today in the low population density of much of northern England. Most perished not by the Norman sword, but as a result of starvation the following winter — their seed grain burnt, there was no harvest in the north in 1070. The destruction wrought by William's troops during the winter of 1070-71 became known as 'the harrying of the north'. York never rebelled again.

THE MIDDLE AGES

The following centuries were, for York, on the whole peaceful and, as a result, prosperous. The city was rebuilt from the ashes of the fire which accompanied the rebellion of the summer of 1069, only to be burnt down again by Swein Estrithson's Danish army which plundered the city in 1075. York was again rebuilt, and again destroyed by yet another fire on the night of 4th June, 1137. This seems to have been the most destructive of all York's fires. It swept through the city on both sides of the Ouse, destroying the whole city, including the Minster, two great monasteries, and thirty-nine parish churches.

The years of civil war which accompanied the reign of King Stephen largely passed York by, but for one incident. In the spring of 1138 the Scots king, David I, invaded England hoping to take advantage of the political chaos in the south to extend the Scots border to York. Under the administrative direction of Archbishop Thurstan an army set out from York and pursued the Scots from an abandoned siege of the town, catching up with them at Cowton Moor, some thirty miles to the north, on 22nd August. The resounding victory for the men of Northumbria in what became known as the Battle of the Standard (from a huge battle standard, carrying a pyx containing the consecrated host, which the York army carried before it) ended David's expansionist plans.

On the 16th March, 1190, there occurred perhaps the most shameful event in the post-Conquest history of the city. At that time it was forbidden for Christians to lend money at interest. The banking activities essential for an expanding economy therefore fell exclusively to the Jewish community, who, as a result, were envied and hated, particularly by those who owed them money. With anti-Middle-Eastern feelings running high as Richard I embarked on the Third Crusade to the Holy Land, riots started in London and spread to several other cities.

The anti-Jewish riot in York, while not nearly as bad as many in continental Europe, was the worst in England. It was started by a group of landowners who owed money to Jewish bankers in the city. It ended when those Jews who had survived the initial rioting took refuge in the king's castle and were besieged. Rather than surrender and endure enforced baptism and probable death, they took their own lives. Not a single Jew is believed to have survived (out of a population of several hundred). Only one non-Jew died — a fanatical monk, killed by a piece of falling masonry. Those who incited the riots did so to clear their debts. Ironically, although they destroyed their debtors' records, the shrewd Jewish bankers had lodged a second set with the Minster, and the debts were transferred to the Crown. However, not one person was prosecuted for involvement in this terrible episode.

York again escaped lightly during the chaos of the civil war of the 1260s, in spite of changing hands twice. The worst that was witnessed was when, in 1267, a small band of Scots opportunists, claiming loyalty to the now defeated Simon de Montfort, invaded the town and a small battle was fought out on Ouse Bridge.

Throughout the medieval centuries York maintained its position as the political centre of the north, and on a number of occasions Parliament was held in the city. During Edward I's wars with Scotland, when York became the king's base, the entire Treasury and Exchequer was moved to the town, the Minster Chapter House serving as the king's Council Chamber. From 1287 until 1337, when war with Scotland gave way to war with France, York was frequently the base of king and government, and played a more important role in national politics than at any other time in the post-Conquest history of the city.

It was during the wars with Scotland that one of York's greater military disasters took place. In the late summer of 1319, a Scots army crossed the Solway and headed for the Yorkshire Dales hoping to take the city. Archbishop William Melton, no doubt remembering the Battle of the Standard, assembled an army largely composed of clergy and set out to engage the Scots. The two armies met nine miles north of York at Myton-on-Swale, on 10th October. For Melton's army the encounter was a disaster. His army was destroyed and the city's and Minster's treasures (taken only out of pride) lost. The day is remembered as the Battle of the White, from the robes of the hundreds of priests slain.

The Peasants' Revolt of 1381, while not passing the city by, was of a different flavour in York. While in the south-east the revolt was chiefly against the introduction of the poll-tax, in York the turmoil elsewhere was used as a 'backdrop' and an excuse to express in violence the differences and rivalries between the craft and merchant guilds. Both sides raised small armies and for a while the craft guilds, having taken the Guildhall (the seat of local government in the city) by force, established a commune. A subsequent investigation by the Crown, unable to elicit a consistent set of facts as to the events which had occurred in York, fined the entire city 1000 marks.

Throughout this period the wealth of the city grew, mainly as a result of trade, chiefly through the export of the large quantities of wool produced on the fell sides of the Yorkshire Dales by the powerful monasteries which had established themselves in northern Yorkshire. By 1379, two-thirds of all wool being exported to the Continent from England was passing through York. With the growth of trade-generated wealth, so grew the power of the medieval institutions known as the guilds or hanses (and particularly the power of two guilds — those of the Merchant Adventurers, and the Company of the Staple, which for a while held a monopoly in the trade in wool). With the power of the guilds behind it, the city itself was able to gain increasing independence. The office of mayor was in existence in York by the middle of the twelfth century, and in 1212 King John granted York a Charter giving the city autonomy in matters of its own government, and allowing the city to raise its own taxes — in effect, the guilds' representatives, presided over by the mayor, taxed themselves in return for payment of a fixed annual fee to the Crown. In 1396, in a ceremony at which the sword of the city was presented, Richard II elevated the status of the mayor to that of Lord Mayor (second only in seniority to the Lord Mayor of London). The office of Sheriff of the City was created at the same time.

York's fortunes began to change as early as the end of the thirteenth century as a result of a number of factors, the most important of which was probably the disruption caused in the north by the war with Scotland. Subsequent war with France did not help the recovery of York's export trade to the Continent. Further, changes in manufacturing and trading practices and laws meant that much of the weaving previously carried out in York gave way to the cottage weavers who were beginning to establish themselves in the Pennine hills of the West Riding, beyond the reach of the restrictive practices of the guilds.

By the beginning of the fifteenth century York's golden age was past. Poverty, rather than prosperity now characterized what was becoming an increasingly run-down city, and the Lord Mayor was forced to appeal to the king for charity. This decline continued throughout the Tudor and Stuart periods, at the end of which York had the reputation for being decidedly unfashionable: rather unpleasant, dirty, derelict and squalid. The town did not even possess the money to replace ageing and outmoded buildings — the buildings which today give York much of its charm (and which were mostly destroyed in the more prosperous towns of England).

Political troubles returned to York with the fifteenth century, the first decade of which saw Archbishop le Scrope executed by Henry IV for joining a rebellion (inspired by loyalty to the cause of Richard II) protesting against unfair taxation of the people. (Richard le Scrope is the only archbishop to have been executed to date.) The city itself Henry threatened with complete destruction if the citizens did not 'come to heel'.

Throughout the fifteenth century, York was to play a central role in the political and personal fortunes of the country and its leaders, and never less so than during the Wars of the Roses — the three decades of struggle for the monarchy between the Royal House of Lancaster, whose emblem was a red rose, and the Royal House of York, whose emblem was a white rose. The events of the civil wars which we now remember as the Wars of the Roses are too complex and convoluted to detail in the space available here. In brief, when Henry VI was mentally incapacitated, Richard Plantagenet, Duke of York, was appointed protector. In fact, doubly descended from Edward III, Richard's claim to the throne was not only legitimate but stronger than that of the king. On Henry's recovery, in 1455, Richard challenged Henry's power and took the king prisoner at St Albans. It was the first of twelve battles which were to culminate in the ascension of the House of Tudor to the monarchy.

In September 1460, York made his claim for the throne, only to be defeated and killed at Wakefield the following December. His head was brought to York, topped mockingly with a paper crown, and placed on a spike, first on Ouse Bridge and then on top of Micklegate Bar (the main gate into the city), 'so that York may overlook the town of York', in Shakespeare's words. His mother and youngest son, later to be Richard III, were imprisoned.

Fortunes, however, changed fast in those violent and troubled times and York's eldest surviving son secured his claim as Edward IV in one of the bloodiest battles English soil has ever seen. It took place on 29th March, 1461, between the villages of Saxton and Towton, ten miles south-west of York. In a letter to his mother following the battle, the king estimated that 28,000 men lay dead at the end of the battle. Following Edward's death in 1483, his brother Richard assumed the throne, usurping Edward's sons, who subsequently disappeared and were never seen again. (The fate of the two 'princes in the Tower' remains a matter of speculation and debate, and Richard was by no means the only person to whom their existence was a political impediment.)

Richard III is thought by many to be one of the most maligned characters in English history. In York he is a local hero. All his life he had close connections with the town, having grown up in, and succeeded to the estates of his maternal grandfather, Ralph Neville, Earl of Westmorland, on the death of his cousin, Richard Neville ('Warwick the Kingmaker'). The seat of the Neville family, which became that of Richard, was at Middleham Castle, sited where Wensley-dale opens into the Vale of York. Richard was a member of the city's prestigious Corpus Christi Guild and championed York in a number of disputes with the king over such matters as the town's independence in matters of local government.

The picture of Richard we have today, that of the cruel hunchback (which he was not), is largely that painted by the man who defeated and killed him at Bosworth on 22nd August, 1485. Henry Tudor's claim to the throne was exceedingly tenuous and, as Henry VII, he launched an effective propaganda campaign against Richard which persists to this day, largely through William

Shakespeare's portrayal. (Shakespeare was, after all, writing at a time when the ruling monarch was the granddaughter of Henry Tudor, and the rights or otherwise of the Tudor claim to the throne perhaps still not quite forgotten.)

An important legacy bequeathed by Richard to Northumbria was the King's Council of the North. Together with Lord Percy, the Earl of Northumberland, Richard had ruled over the north on behalf of his brother, the king. He understood the fierce independence of Northumbrians, and recognized that much was to be gained by establishing a separate parliamentary assembly for northern England, with administrative, legislative and judicial powers. When he became king, Richard created the Council, which first sat on 14th July, 1484, at Richard's castle in Sheriff Hutton, ten miles north of the city. For over a century and a half the Council of the North exercised jurisdiction over the whole of northern England, from as far south as Nottinghamshire to the Scottish border (excluding Lancashire, Cheshire and Lincolnshire). In York, however, the independence of the city frequently led to a conflict of authority, and the power of the Council of the North remained very limited within the town itself until the city's independence was compromised by the failure of the Pilgrimage of Grace.

In 1536, a mass rising of peoples of all classes, largely drawn from Lincolnshire, Yorkshire and Lancashire, protested to the king against his recent split with the Church of Rome, and in support of the many, now destitute Roman Catholic clergy. (At least this is what the majority of those who joined the movement believed. In fact, the Pilgrimage was a manipulation of the mass of its supporters by a handful of London-based nobility with political ambitions.) Its leader emerged as a one-eyed Yorkshire lawyer, Robert Aske, and the majority of the people of the city of York joined in supporting the rising. The city became the centre of the movement and a Great Council of the Pilgrimage was held in the town.

On being promised a full pardon, together with a parliament to be held in York to consider their grievances, the Pilgrimage of Grace disbanded. However, a further outbreak of sporadic violence gave Henry VIII an excuse for revenge. Aske was seized and hung in chains from Clifford's Tower until he died. Intimidated by Henry and without organization and leadership, the movement collapsed.

With the failure of the Pilgrimage of Grace, the status of the city of York as a town permitted to exercise autonomous government in local matters came to an end. The town, fearful of the punishment Henry might inflict in retribution for York's central part in the rising, quietly acquiesced to the authority of the king in all matters both ecclesiastical and secular. It was the end of the city's independence, but not the end of its position of central importance to the history of the north of England.

In the aftermath of the Pilgrimage it was decided, partly in order to emphasize the new relationship between the city and the king, that the Council of the North would be moved from Sheriff Hutton into York itself. A number of sites were considered and in 1539 the Council of the North took up residence in the former house of the abbot of the recently dissolved St Mary's Abbey. (The house is now known as King's Manor — see Chapter Five.) The movement of the Council to the city effectively marks the end of the right of self-government enjoyed by York since the days of King John. (Indeed, the superior power of the Council over the corporation of the city was emphasized when on one occasion the Lord President of the Council had the mayor imprisoned in the castle.) It also marks the final period, ending with the abolition of the Council by the 'Long Parliament' in 1641, during which York again served in the role of the secular administrative centre of the north of England. (See also under King's Manor in Chapter Five.)

York once more found itself in a central position in national politics when the relationship between Charles I and his Parliament deteriorated. In January 1642, distrustful of the people of London, Charles moved to York, where he felt sure of loyalty. For five months the king governed the country from the town. He set up his mint and a printing press in the city, and proceeded to amass funds to finance a possible armed conflict with his Parliament, and to issue propaganda illustrating his case. During his stay he bestowed upon his younger son, James, the title of Duke of York, since which time the dukedom has been reserved for the second son of the monarch, granted not automatically, but as a personal gift.

Charles left York for Nottingham on 16th August. Within a week of his departure, the country found itself in a state of civil war. (It is said that the king would have raised his standard in York, but was dissuaded from doing so by the Royalists of the city who could well imagine the horrors of a civil war.) By the end of 1643 the two sides had reached an impasse. In south and west Yorkshire, the Marquis of Newcastle was inflicting small but demoralizing defeats on a Parliamentarian army led by Lord Fairfax and his son, Sir Thomas Fairfax, when the apparent deadlock was broken by the crossing into England of a Scots army led by Lord Leven, to fight for the Parliamentarian cause. The Marquis was forced to leave Yorkshire and hurry to Durham to meet and engage the Scots.

The Royalist garrison at York early in 1644 was about 4,000 men strong, under the command of Colonel John Bellais. Bellais gained intelligence that the Fairfaxes were to rendezvous and recombine their forces at Selby, ten miles south of York, and saw his opportunity. On 11th April he left York with 3,000 of the garrison and rode for Selby. His army was badly defeated and Bellais was himself captured. When the news reached Newcastle at Durham the Marquis realized that York, the key to the north, was essentially undefended. Newcastle force-marched his army south, closely pursued by the Scots, and re-entered the city on 16th April.

The Earl of Leven established a base for the Scots army at Middlethorpe Manor, on the west bank of the Ouse. Lord Fairfax positioned his forces to the east of both the Ouse and the Foss, with his headquarters at Heslington Hall. On 22nd April the two armies moved to within a mile of the city walls. The great siege of York had begun. It was to last three months, and the scars in the city's defences can be seen to this day (see Chapter Four).

The two armies were insufficient to completely surround the city, and for the first six weeks of the siege the area to the north, bounded by the Ouse in the west and the Foss in the east, remained unoccupied, presumably allowing access to and from the town. The encirclement of York was completed at the beginning of June when the Earl of Manchester arrived from East Anglia with a third army. The garrison and citizens of York prepared to sit and wait for the rescuing Royalist forces, commanded by Prince Rupert, which since the end of April had been rumoured to have been arriving within days. The delay was due to Prince Rupert ensuring that Lancashire was in Royalist hands before embarking on a Yorkshire campaign. His army finally arrived in sight of York on the last day of June.

At this point the situation became somewhat bizarre. The Marquis of Newcastle and his second-in-command, Lord Eythin, both had personal grievances with Prince Rupert, and when the order came to join forces, those inside the city refused. Rupert's forces were left to face the three Parliamentarian armies without the aid of the garrison who had awaited their help! The two sides met eight miles west of York on Marston Moor on Tuesday, 2nd July. Not only was the battle of Marston Moor the biggest ever fought on British soil and the most far-reaching in consequence of any in the Civil War (as it resulted in the fall of the north), it need never have taken place. By the time Newcastle's men did reach Marston Moor the day was all but lost for the Royalists. The bedraggled remains of their army made its way back to York that night and the siege resumed on the Thursday, but with the garrison reduced from about 4,000 before the battle to less than 1,000 after (the majority considering it prudent not to return to the city). With no hope of a second rescue by Prince Rupert, all York could hope for was honourable terms of surrender from the besieging armies.

That York in general, and the Minster in particular, suffered little in the subsequent occupation of the city by the Puritan forces was due to the actions of Sir Thomas and Lord Fairfax. Their home city, both father and son took steps to ensure that looting was prevented by pain of the most severe penalties. No doubt prevailed upon by the Fairfaxes, the terms of surrender of the city to which the Parliamentarian commander-in-chief, Lord Leven, agreed, were magnanimous in the extreme. The Royalist defenders were to be allowed to leave the city, fully armed with colours flying and in no disgrace. The city of York itself was forgiven its loyalties outright. The surrender terms were agreed on 15th July and the Royalist garrison left the following day. For York, the Civil War was all but over.

FROM THE 18TH CENTURY TO THE PRESENT DAY
The eighteenth century saw the town become, once again, a blossoming and fashionable focus. The *York Mercury*, the city's first newspaper, appeared in 1719, and the Theatre Royal in 1769, having been granted a patent by George III (see St

Leonard's Place, Chapter Five). Acquiring a status only rivalled outside London itself by the city of Bath, the influx of 'society' saw many fine Georgian town houses erected, of which some of the best survive to this day, designed by several of the most talented architects of their time (most notably John Carr and Richard Boyle). The Assembly Rooms, built specifically to serve as a social centre during the mid-eighteenth century, are considered amongst the finest examples of neo-Palladian architecture in Europe (see Chapter Five).

York ceased to be of any national political importance in the seventeenth century, but throughout the nineteenth and twentieth centuries the town evolved into the bustling and busy modern provincial town of today. The city remained the administrative centre of Yorkshire until 1974, and retains its position as the legal focus of the old county to this day. As a result, the town has seen a number of gruesome public executions, the most famous of which were those of the notorious highwayman Dick Turpin, who was hung on the Knavesmire on 10th April, 1739, and, in January 1813, the public hanging outside the castle of nineteen men found guilty of machine wrecking during the 'Luddite' riots which took place in the West Riding in 1812.

At the beginning of the nineteenth century the population of York was a little less than 17,000, about half of what it had been in its heyday during the thirteenth century. By 1901 this had risen to nearly 70,000, two-thirds of that of today. This growth was due to the arrival in the town of a number of large employers, two industries dominating. Several chocolate and confectionery manufacturers established themselves in the York. Rowntrees in particular brought much more to the city than employment for thousands. The founder of the company, Joseph Rowntree the elder, a Quaker philanthropist and for several decades an influential Liberal councillor, contributed much to the welfare of the people of York, and in 1901 his son, also Joseph, acquired a plot of land to the north of the town and built the 'model village' of New Earswick, to house his workers in cheap but pleasant and sanitary conditions.

The second major industry to establish itself in York was the railway. Throughout the 1830s and 1840s local politics in the city was dominated by the Tory leader, George Hudson. Driven by greed, Hudson, who became known as the 'Railway King', made York the focus of the railways of northern England by establishing the central role of his York and Midland Railway, based in the city. He was three times Lord Mayor and was Member of Parliament for Sunderland, continuing in the latter office for a decade after his fall from power in York. Hudson was neither likeable nor honest. (On one documented occasion he had a family evicted from their home onto snow-covered streets for being but two weeks in arrears with their rent.) Towards the end of the 1840s his corruption came to public notice and his withdrawal from public office in the town resulted in the replacement of an almost exclusively Tory council by a Liberal majority.

Like the Torys, the Liberals were also dominated by a single personality,

George Leeman, who was also Lord Mayor for three terms of office and subsequently Member of Parliament for the city. Following two terrible outbreaks of cholera and a typhus epidemic in the town the Liberal administration under Leeman spent the two decades of the 1850s and 1860s creating a city which was healthy to live in, by laying the first real sewers York had seen since Roman times, and equipping the town with piped clean water. The Foss had become a stagnant and dangerous open sewer and was cleaned up (although for a long time that merely meant diverting raw sewage directly into the Ouse). The lake created when the castle was built had become little more than a cesspool. It was drained and the land reclaimed, creating the Foss Islands area. Sewers, however, do not have the glamour of the railway, and today it is Hudson who is the better remembered of the two dominant figures of nineteenth-century city politics (to the extent that there is a local myth that the statue on Railway Street is not of Leeman, who is now largely forgotten, but actually of Hudson).

The nineteenth century was also a century of enthusiasm for science, philosophy and the arts. The city was home to a number of scientists, most notably the telescope designer and manufacturer Thomas Cooke, the electrical and audio engineer Henry Hummings, and Sir George Caley, who designed a number of aircraft in the days before powered flight was a technical possibility. The Yorkshire Philosophical Society, founded in 1823, became an influential body of national importance. At its meeting held in 1831 the British Association for the Advancement of Science was founded.

Throughout the twentieth century York has continued to expand. Since 1945, there has been a trend for residential accommodation to decline within the centre of the city, with a concomitant increase in the population of the surrounding villages. The nineteenth century pattern of employment continued into and throughout the present century, with the confectionery industry and the railways dominating until very recently. Since 1914, a number of light industries, most notably engineering, have come to the town, creating further employment and introducing some diversity of commerce to the city.

In spite of having little heavy industry, York did not completely escape the bombing raids of the Second World War, which in the city were largely targeted at the railways. Nearly ten thousand houses were destroyed, although less than a hundred people lost their lives. The worst single raid came on the night of 29th April, 1942, when the Church of St Martin-le-Grand and the Guildhall were both burnt out (see Chapters Three and Five).

The lack of any sizeable industrial activity in the city centre has meant that recently it has been possible to exclude much of the motor traffic from the older parts of the town, which retain a disproportionate number of buildings surviving from medieval, Tudor, Stuart and Georgian times. In addition, the lack of any large-scale heavy industry has kept York cleaner than many towns of comparable size. Particularly since 1970, visitors to the city have become increasingly important to York's economy. Tourism has surpassed chocolate manufacturing as the town's major source of income, and York now receives more visitors than any other town in Britain with the exception of London (and far more in proportion to its population than the capital). The most important industry in late-twentieth-century York is the town's past.

An ancient seal used by the chapter of York and engraved by the Society of Antiquaries.

CHAPTER TWO

YORK MINSTER

THE CATHEDRAL AND METROPOLITAN CHURCH OF ST PETER IN YORK

In AD 306, in York, following the death of his father in the city, Constantine was proclaimed Roman Emperor in the West. He was the first Roman Emperor to openly adopt Christianity, and York became firmly Christian. Eight years later there are records of a Bishop of York being one of three bishops representing England at a synod, held at Arles, called by Constantine to formalize the government of the Western Church. With the coming of the fifth century and the pagan Anglo-Saxons (who seem to have suppressed almost all of the native Romano-Celtic culture and religion) Christianity effectively vanished from England. Its return to the north was the work of a Roman monk, Paulinus, and his influence over the Northumbrian king, Edwin, in the seventh century.

The Anglo-Saxon Edwin, who had been pagan in his beliefs, was persuaded into the Christian faith through associations with the Royal House of Kent. The King of Kent, Aethelbert, had been converted by the mission of St Augustine of Canterbury. Augustine was sent to England by Pope Gregory I who, the story goes, had seen some fair Anglo-Saxon children being sold as slaves in the market in Rome. Struck by their beauty, Gregory is supposed to have asked who they were and, on being told they were Angles, made a Latin pun about their being not Angles but Angels, and resolved to bring their country into the Church. Accompanied by forty monks, Augustine established his See in Canterbury in 597. Paulinus joined the mission four years later.

It was a condition of the marriage of Edwin to Aethelbert's daughter, Aethelburga, that Edwin respect his wife's religion. When Aethelberga came to York in 625 she brought Paulinus with her as her priest. Before he left Canterbury, Paulinus was consecrated as the first of the modern line of Bishops of York, by Justus, the successor to Augustine as leader of the Roman mission to Britain. The strong association between York and Rome is reflected today in the dedication of the Minster to St Peter. In the middle of the west wall of the present cathedral, below the great west window and between the two doors, stands the statue of St Peter, at the foot of his church.

The ancestral church of the present Minster was presumably a place of worship built, or perhaps converted from a temple of pagan dedication, by Constantine. No trace of such a Roman church had been found. The first building that can be

31

thought of as a forerunner of the present Minster was a small wooden church constructed for the baptism of Edwin (along with thirty of his nobles) which took place the day before Easter in 627. The tradition of Edwin's conversion to Christianity is that while in exile in East Anglia during his youth, a stranger appeared and promised Edwin his kingdom and deliverance from peril in return for a promise that when, in the future, a stranger appeared and asked for obedience, Edwin must give it. A decade later Edwin had regained his kingdom and had been living in peace for eight years when Paulinus arrived in York and, divinely inspired, reminded Edwin of his promise. (It is even possible that it was Paulinus himself, on one of his missionary journeys, who had spoken to Edwin in East Anglia.) Edwin recognized Paulinus as the prophesied stranger and was duly converted to the Christian faith.

Where Edwin's church was situated is not known, but it was probably on or not far from the site of the present Minster. However, it has been suggested, very reasonably, that it may have been on the other side of the Ouse, in the Bishophill area of the town. The site upon which the Church of St Michael-le-Belfry now stands has also been suggested (see Chapter Three).

Recent excavations under the Minster (see the Foundations, p. 47) failed to reveal any trace of Edwin's church, although this does not tell us very much. Edwin's original building was little more than a small wooden hall, and only a small part of the site of the present Minster has been excavated. What we do know is that a great deal of the ground area of the Minster was occupied by the remains of the Roman *Principia*, which were still standing when Edwin's church was built. Under the south transept a Saxon burial ground was found. This could easily have adjoined a Saxon church. The burial ground was just outside the Roman building, with the Roman alignment, rather than that of the present Minster.

A widely believed local tradition is that the position of a font which stands over an ancient well in the crypt of the Minster, below the high altar in the present choir, is the place where the actual baptism took place. While a well is the most likely place for a baptism, it should be noted that other ancient wells under the present Minster have been found.

Edwin subsequently set about having his church rebuilt in stone, but work seems to have stopped following his death in 632, rule in the city having been seized by the pagan King Penda of Mercia and Cadwallon of Gwynedd. Edwin's church was finally finished in the late 660s, by King Oswy and St Wilfrid, and featured glass windows. (Wilfrid became Bishop of York in 663.)

On Sunday, 23rd April, 741, after an exceptionally dry winter and spring, fire broke out in the city and devastated much of the town. The Minster was badly damaged or destroyed. A new stone building was subsequently built, the work being presided over in the later stages by the great York scholar Alcuin. The new Minster, which was constructed over a period of fifteen years, was significantly larger than Wilfrid's church and contained thirty altars as well as a number of side chapels and galleries.

Alcuin's Minster was in turn destroyed, together with its irreplaceable library, in the great fire which swept through York during the besieging of the Norman garrison in the town during the autumn of 1069. (It is widely believed that if the Minster library had not been destroyed in 1069, the famous Minster school would today be the oldest university in Britain.)

Following the Conquest, William instigated a major reformation of the Church in England to bring it into line with the continental Church with which the Normans were more familiar. This included a programme of building which encompassed the advances in church architecture being made in the eleventh century, chiefly in northern Italy and southern France, as a result of an increasing understanding of the engineering principles governing building in stone. From the Conquest onwards, throughout the country, the Saxon diocesan churches were gradually replaced by great cathedrals in the modern Romanesque style.

Masterminded by William's half-brother, Odo, Bishop of Bayeux and the Earl of Kent (the sponsor of the Bayeux Tapestry) the reforms started with the appointment of Lanfranc, Prior of the Abbey of Caen, to the See of Canterbury, and of Thomas, a canon of Bayeux, to the See of York. Thomas of Bayeux arrived in York at the beginning of 1071 and set about reorganizing the government of the Church. (See also the Treasurer's House in Chapter Five.) Of the Minster itself, Thomas found only the ruins left by the destruction some fifteen months before.

It appears that work was started to patch up what remained of the burnt-out building, but four years later a Danish army again set fire to the church, following which Archbishop Thomas ordered the construction of a completely new cathedral in the new Romanesque style. The Minster of Archbishop Thomas was one of the first to be started in England, begun in the late 1070s.

In 1137, another great fire swept through York and once again extensively damaged the Minster (see p. 37). In the years that followed the Minster was rebuilt, including a new choir and crypt, begun in 1154 under Archbishop Roger Pont L'Evêque.

The Minster of Archbishops Thomas and Roger, which was aisleless, was 360 feet long, with a central tower sixty-five feet square — in its time the largest cathedral in northern Europe. It was also the direct structural ancestor of the present church and parts of the original building survive today, incorporated into the present Minster (mostly in places out of sight, such as in the triforium of the nave, where part of the late eleventh-century tower still carries its decorated plaster rendering).

The present Minster was started in 1220, under Archbishop Walter de Gray, one of York's most influential Archbishops. It was not completed until the end of the fifteenth century, taking over two hundred and fifty years to build and representing, as a result, all styles of medieval ecclesiastical architecture.

John Maynard Keynes once suggested that there was an economic drive to the building of the great medieval churches of Europe, in that they may have represented public spending encouraged as an answer to the problem of unemployment. Certainly the amount of time and labour that went into building a structure as immense as the Minster, in an age of machines no more complex than levers and pulleys, must have accounted for a significant proportion of the workforce of the surrounding area, particularly when it is remembered that St Mary's Abbey and many York churches were also being built at the same time. The population of the York area at the beginning of the fourteenth century was about thirty thousand. The ravages of plague meant that by the beginning of the fifteenth century this had fallen to about ten thousand, yet this marked the period of the most intensive building, not only of the Minster but of churches throughout the city.

The stone of which the Minster is built (as is much of the rest of York) is an oolitic magnesium limestone. It is almost white when newly cut, but subsequently weathers to an attractive light honey colour as a result of the oxidation of the traces of iron minerals it contains. The stone was cut in quarries near Tadcaster, about ten miles west of York, and brought by barges by way of the rivers Wharfe and Ouse to York. On reaching the city it was unloaded at staiths close to the site of the Victorian Lendal Bridge, only 300 yards from the Minster. Generally it has withstood the centuries well, but during the past 150 years the stone's susceptibility to acidity has meant rain-water has taken its toll and much of the exterior stonework of the Minster is in need of urgent repair or replacement.

The completed Minster is the largest cathedral in Britain and is second only to Seville as the largest medieval cathedral anywhere. It is 486 feet long, and 223 feet across the transepts, with a tower at the crossing 184 feet high. It is not the highest medieval cathedral in Britain (that honour goes to Salisbury) nor even that with the highest nave (Westminster Abbey) but, for collectors of records, that with the largest volume. This is accounted for by the unusually large width of the nave and choir. The width was achieved by having wooden rather than stone roofs, although the roofs of the aisles have traditional stone vaulting.

The width of the nave, together with the light colour of the stone (cleaned during the mid-1980s) gives the cathedral its particularly light and airy feel. It is also one of the most beautiful of medieval cathedrals, and it is the grace and ratios of its various proportions which perhaps betray its true size from close by. What really makes the interior of the Minster so attractive in comparison with other cathedrals is the relative lack of clutter, particularly in the nave, found in other cathedrals in the form of tombs, chapels, statues and memorials. Many of the fittings of the nave were destroyed when the present marble floor was laid in the 1730s (under the supervision of either Lord Burlington or, more probably, his assistant William Kent). This was accompanied by a directive from the Dean and Chapter that no new graves be placed in the nave. Since then, various fires have played their part in clearing the church of much in the way of fittings.

The transepts are the oldest rooms of any significance in the present cathedral, and are in the architectural style now referred to as Early English. They were first built as additions to the smaller transepts of the Norman Minster. The south transept was completed first, in 1241, and the north transept around 1260. They were significantly rebuilt by Archbishop John Romeyn between 1286 and 1296.

The nave, chapter house vestibule and chapter house were the next parts of the present Minster to be built, started in that order. The foundation stone of the nave was laid in April 1291 and the building was ready for the roof to be added by 1334. The chapter house was completed in the 1360s. All this part of the Minster is in the Decorated style and is as fine as any in England. That the chapter house (unlike chapter houses in other cathedrals) does not have a central pillar makes it particularly attractive. This was achieved, as in the nave, by making the roof not of stone, as was traditional, but of wood. Sixty-six and a half feet high and sixty-three feet across, the use of a wooden roof allowed the construction of the largest chapter house of any medieval cathedral.

Edward I's need for an administrative building in York, from which to command his war with Scotland, was the incentive to commence the building of the chapter house. It was subsequently used by the royal court, on which occasions England was governed from York. The chapter house of a cathedral was used by the Dean and Chapter, the management and government committee of a cathedral, as the room where their business was conducted, and as such is the only part of the cathedral which is not consecrated ground. It is particularly important that the acoustic properties of a chapter house be good enough for the Chapter (together about thirty persons) to hold a discussion with ease. Sound in a circular chapter house travels by reflection around the walls and the members of the cathedral Chapter could be easily heard throughout the room without the necessity of raising their voices, merely by addressing themselves to their neighbours.

The two towers at the west end of the nave, originally completed at about the same time as the chapter house, are today about eighteen inches higher than the later central tower. Initially, they were the same height as the gable of the west end. However, they were heightened to house the Minster bells following the collapse of the central tower, the home of the original peal (see p. 36). In their present forms they were completed, but for a few details, by 1485. The south-west tower houses the peal of twelve bells. The present bells were recast in 1926 from their predecessors, given to the Minster in 1844 (the original bells having been destroyed when they fell during a fire in the tower in 1840, see p. 38). The north-west tower houses the mammoth 'Great Peter', a bell of almost eleven tons in weight dating from 1845. In the York Arms Hotel, close to the west end of the Minster, are two interesting photographs of Great Peter as it was being transported through the streets of the town on its way to be rehung following recasting in 1927. Great Peter is rung each day at midday.

The final parts of the Minster to be built, the choir and central tower, were started shortly after the completion of the nave and chapter house. Throughout the Middle Ages, masons steadily learned how to build stronger halls using less stone. The choir represents the pinnacle of these achievements being in the Perpendicular style of the fifteenth century. The ability to support a cathedral with less stone meant fewer and narrower pillars and more delicate tracery in the windows. This in turn meant a lighter and more open interior (and a more elegant exterior). Unlike many cathedrals, the architects of the Minster choir showed a sensitivity to the earlier limitations to the designs of the nave and transepts. The architecture of the choir utilizes the advantages of the techniques of Perpendicular design without creating a building that failed to match the style of the nave.

The tower which originally stood at the crossing of the church collapsed in strong winds in 1407. In fact, there have been recurrent problems with this tower, resulting mainly from its foundations being inferior to those used by the Normans. The tower foundations consisted of stone laid on rubble. The Norman foundations of the Minster were based on a pontoon of whole oak trunks which supported the stone structure built above it for the hundred years or so needed for lime mortar to harden to full strength. Buried deep in the ground, the carbon dioxide needed for the hardening process takes a considerable time to diffuse. (Lime mortar, all that was available in Yorkshire for the Minster masons, is both softer and takes longer to harden than the mortars available to the Italian builders and the Romans before them.)

From the relative dimensions of the central tower it appears that the original intention was that it would carry a spire. It seems probable that, following a series of collapses of churches in both England and France, the masons decided that perhaps prudence should be heeded. The replacement tower was paid for in large part by Walter de Skirlaw, Bishop of Durham, who also met, out of his private purse, the considerable cost of the Great East Window.

It was decided that the new tower would be a lantern tower, rather than a bell tower, and that the bells would be moved to the two west-end towers, which were to be heightened to accommodate belfries (a decision which was to create problems with the foundations of the west end of the Minster in the middle of the present century). Why the bells were not replaced in the central tower is not clear. It is commonly supposed that it was to further reduce the weight of the tower, but this is improbable. A peal of twelve sizeable bells, complete with their mechanisms, would probably weigh, at a very generous maximum, fifty tons. This is less than one per cent of the 16,000 tons or more of masonry supported in the central tower. It seems more feasible that the engineers were concerned about the damage caused by resonance when the bells were rung. It cannot have been an easy decision to take. The modifications to the west end were not only expensive but somewhat spoiled the proportions of the building.

On 3rd July, 1472, a ceremony formally dedicating the church was held, 252 years after work started on the transepts of what was to become the present Minster. The final small touches completed the fabric of the Minster in the 1490s.

Of course, the Minster has not remained unchanged since the end of the fifteenth century. Much has been added to the church; a little has been removed. The interior of the church was not bare stonework, but painted bright blue and red. The outside was painted white, with red lines to give the impression of brickwork. There have been numerous restorations and refittings of various parts, most drastically those following the three major fires the building has suffered over the last two centuries.

The Minster has acquired a reputation for attracting fires. Edwin's original church was severely damaged by fire in the seventh century and the replacement church, built by St Wilfrid, also fell victim to fire in 741, when it was probably beyond repair. Alcuin's Minster was gutted in 1069 when fires lit as a diversion by besieged Normans got out of control. Under Thomas of Bayeux, restoration following this fire was underway when, in 1075, a Danish army, who had been living in England and causing intermittent trouble for several years, set fire to the Minster and apparently destroyed it beyond restoration.

The cathedral built by Thomas as a replacement was itself severely damaged by a fire on 4th June, 1137, which destroyed not just the Minster, but most of the town on both sides of the Ouse, including St Mary's Abbey, St Leonard's Hospital and much of Holy Trinity Priory. Thirty-nine other churches in the town were razed during that single night. In 1202 the Minster bought up the land outside the west end of the church to prevent it being built upon, in order to reduce the risk of another fire.

A fire broke out in the Lady Chapel on 11th March, 1464. The extent of the damage is not known, although it can be inferred to have been substantial from the manner in which it was recorded. (This fire is said to have been extinguished by water taken from the well over which Edwin is claimed to have been baptized.) There was another fire in the choir in 1711, and in 1753 fire badly damaged the roof of the south transept. This time the fire was caused by a brazier being used by workmen to melt lead to repair a leak in the roof. (The roofs of the Minster are all clad in lead, except that of the north transept which is copper.) As a result of this fire, the Dean spent £25. 19s. 6d. on fire-fighting equipment bought in London.

Two fires in the last century badly damaged the choir and the nave. A fire in 1829 was started deliberately by a religious extremist called Jonathan Martin. Martin belonged to an antinomian sect known as the Ranters. (The Ranters had risen to become a political force to be reckoned with in the seventeenth century, comparable to the better known Diggers. By the nineteenth century, however, the handful of followers of the movement were characterized more by their fervour rather than by their faith.)

Believing that he had been inspired by God to destroy the Minster, the symbol of the Anglican Church which he believed was an instrument of the Devil, Martin hid when the cathedral was closed up on the night of Sunday, 1st February, 1829, behind the tomb of Archbishop Greenfield in the St Nicholas Chapel (which, incidentally, carries the only engraved brass effigy in the Minster). When all was quiet he emerged and climbed over the iron gates into the choir. There he gathered into two piles all the hassocks and prayer-books he could find. He made an exception of the crimson curtains around the archbishop's throne — deciding these would make a splendid cloak, he took them with him when he fled, along with a small Bible he found.

All of the wooden fittings of the east end of the Minster were destroyed, including the organ, the medieval roof and the dozens of chantry chapels which had accumulated over the years in the choir aisles. Nevertheless, many of the prayer-books in one of the two piles that Martin had made and ignited were saved. They came to be much sought after as souvenirs.

One outcome of Martin's actions was the formation of the Minster police, who patrol the church to this day. Some of the glass crazed by the heat from the fire of 1829 can still be seen in some of the windows of the choir.

The fire which started on the evening of 20th May, 1840, was caused accidentally. Shortly before nine o'clock flames were spotted by passers by. The fire rapidly spread across the wooden roof of the nave to the north-west tower, and the whole of the west end of the Minster was badly damaged. The crowds which the fire drew were so large that troops were called out to control them. (It is said that the entire population of York turned out hoping to help fight the blaze in some way. Most would remember the fire of 1829, the subsequent repairs not yet complete.) All the bells came down and were destroyed, but the fabric of the Minster was again saved, this time with the help of fire engines brought from Leeds and Tadcaster by the new railway.

We now know the fire was caused by a neglected candle left in the south-west tower by the man who looked after the clock. Blowing in the wind, a curtain probably kindled what grew into a large conflagration. At the official enquiry the poor fellow denied having taken anything into the tower that could cause a fire. The enquiry found otherwise but, knowing him to be of good character and a lover of the Minster, absolved him of any blame. Some years later he admitted that he had, against the explicit orders of the Dean, taken a candle into the south-west tower on the evening of the fire, and forgotten to extinguish it when he left.

The fire in 1829 destroyed the choir and during the restoration work an unsuspected and long hidden extension to the crypt was found under the west end of the choir. Today this part of the crypt is a private chapel, dedicated to St William (see p. 47). St William's Chapel is now used ecumenically and is connected to the Minster Treasury, part of the recently created foundations.

The latest fire started during the early hours of the morning of 9th July, 1984. The official report states that there was an eighty per cent chance that the fire was started by a freak lightning strike. It rapidly spread through the age-dried wood of the roof of the south transept. The damage was remarkably slight. The only part of the Minster outside the south transept that suffered was the apex of the arch separating the transept from the crossing. Standing in the crossing and looking up at the south tower arch, it is possible to see the new stone replacing that affected by the lapping flames. Without the support of any one of the four arches, the tower would fall. Had the fire progressed any further before being brought under control by the fire brigade, the central tower itself might have been threatened, and with it the whole structure of the Minster. That the Rose Window in the south transept survived is quite remarkable.

Without probing too deeply, there are interesting circumstances surrounding the fire of 1984. It occurred the day after the enthronement in the Minster of the bishop of a local diocese. The particular incumbent was not (and is not) particularly well liked by all quarters of the Church. His theological views force people to think in a way to which they are unaccustomed, and when, in the early hours of the following morning, the Minster was supposedly struck by a single isolated bolt of lightning from a clear sky, more than one person saw it as a Divine comment.

Yet the meteorological office insisted there was no lightning in the York area on the night in question, and indeed no-one in the town seems to have seen any lightning or heard any thunder (although it is possible to have large electrical currents induced by atmospheric electrical fields, without the violence of a sudden discharge). Furthermore, the extremely sensitive smoke detectors did not function, and this, in connection with which other suspicious circumstances, make it difficult to rule out deliberate destruction.

Something worthwhile nevertheless came out of the fire of 1984. In the days following the news of the disaster, contributions of money flooded in from all quarters. Volunteers worked in shifts to clear up the mess. Asda supermarket set up a table and gave drinks and snacks to the workers. Yet, as the money poured in, it became clear that the cost of necessary restoration work would after all be met by the Minster's insurance. The Dean and Chapter decided to use the extra money donated by well-wishers to clean the whole of the interior of the Minster, which was done in less than six months just using scrubbing-brushes and plain water. This is the reason why the inside of York Minster looks so pristine today.

That the windows of the Minster have survived the various fires throughout its history is a fortuitous result of the wooden, rather than stone, vaulting of the nave, choir and transepts (unusual in large medieval buildings). When, during each fire, the roof has burned and collapsed, the flames are then drawn upwards, away from the windows, not only reducing the heat to which their leading is exposed, but also releasing the pressure on them from hot gases, which would otherwise (as has happened during major fires in other cathedrals) cause the windows to blow out.

A SHORT GUIDE TO THE INTERIOR OF YORK MINSTER

Listed here are some of the interesting places and objects in the Minster. They are arranged in a clockwise order, starting in the nave and continuing to the crypt and finally, the Foundations.

THE DRAGON

About halfway along the north wall of the nave, high up protruding from the triforium, there is a curious dragon mounted on a pivot, apparently staring at the ceiling. Its origins are long forgotten but are certainly pagan. Why it is there, nobody now knows. The widespread belief that it is the prow of a Viking ship is almost certainly wrong. It has been suggested that for a while it held a hoist pulley for a rope lifting the cover of a font which stood below (a hole where a pulley could have been attached can be seen on the lower side of the dragon's neck) although there is no record of a font having been sited in the nave below the dragon. It has also been suggested that it might have something to do with the small statue on the south wall of the nave, opposite the dragon, which is of St George (lacking a right arm).

It is said in York that each night, on the stroke of midnight, the dragon bows three times to St George opposite, in reverence. It is also added, as a corollary, that as the Minster is closed to all but the Minster police at that time of night, nobody except the police know if this is true — and they will not tell.

THE ASTRONOMICAL CLOCK

This stands in a tiny chantry at the entrance to the chapter-house vestibule, but is prominent because of its size. It was placed in the Minster in 1955 in remembrance of the airmen based at aerodromes in north-east England, who died during the Second World War. The clock displays many different aspects of the time, most of which are essential to navigation whether by sea or by air. It is sometimes forgotten that the primary impetus behind the invention of clockwork mechanisms was to reproduce the movements of the heavenly bodies, rather than to give information as to the time of day (which all such mechanisms do incidentally).

The clock has two major faces, on the west and the east sides (i.e. there is a face at the 'back'), and six smaller dials at the bottom of the west side of the clock. The six small dials at the bottom show both solar time (that is 'ordinary time', shown by the three dials on the right) and sidereal time (the time with respect to the stars, shown by the three small dials on the left). Because the apparent position of the sun against the background of the 'fixed' stars moves gradually throughout the Zodiac as the year progresses, solar time drifts when compared to sidereal time (by about four minutes each day). The large blue west face shows the present time, the present position of the sun in the sky over York, its height and direction in the sky at the present date and time (including the points on the horizon where the sun rises and sets at the present date) and the positions of the stars in the sky at the present moment (even if they are not visible because of daylight). The large blue dial on the east side (the 'back') simply shows the present positions in the sky of those stars around the Pole Star which are visible from York whatever the season, together with the present sidereal time, shown by a pointer at the top of the dial.

The workings of the clock were designed by Dr Robert D'Escourt Atkinson of the Royal Greenwich Observatory, and the clock was built by Dr Atkinson, his engineer Mr A.C.S. Wescott, and their staff at the R.G.O.'s workshop. It is extremely accurate — much more so than the majority of mechanical clocks, retaining over extended periods an accuracy such as that which would be required by airmen relying upon the sun and stars for navigation.

Mechanical clocks of such accuracy are no longer built and the art of the master clockmaker is dying rapidly. With the advent of microelectronics, it is easier, simpler, quicker, far less cumbersome and far cheaper to program a microcomputer to continuously display all the information shown on this astronomical clock. This is one of the last astronomical clocks of its kind to have been made, and as a consequence its mechanism is already of some historical interest and importance — an importance which will undoubtedly grow rapidly as the years pass.

A Book of Honour stands in front of the Memorial, recording the names of 18,000 airmen who fell during that war. It also contains accurate drawings of all the types of aircraft they flew — twenty-five in all. Since many of these are no longer in existence, the Book of Honour has additional historical value.

On the wall behind the astronomical clock a little of the original blue and white paint work of the Minster can be seen in the memorial to the prisoners of war who died in the Far East during the 1939–45 war.

THE NORTH TRANSEPT CLOCK

This interesting clock is something of a hybrid. The mechanism dates from 1752 and was made by John Hindley. It was placed in its present position in 1883 and the rather splendid dial dates from its installation here.

The figures (described as 'men-at-arms') who strike the quarter hours are much older. They were made in 1528 and, while their hammers are iron, their bodies are carved oak. They are believed to be statues of Gog and Magog and are unique in English churches (although statues of Gog and Magog can be found in the Guildhall in London). Like the dragon above the nave, their place in a major church of God is interesting, if questionable.

FIFTEEN KINGS (BENEATH THE CENTRAL TOWER)

Along the pulpitum (that is, the screen which divides the nave from the choir, under the central tower) are a distinguished-looking collection of statues of the fifteen kings of England who followed the Conquest, running in chronological sequence with William I at the north end and Henry VI at the south. The first fourteen, seven on either side of the early eighteenth-century wrought-iron gates to the choir, are all medieval, and are contemporary with the completion of the choir. They are thought to be by William Hyndeley, but may be earlier. Their style is very much that of stately authority. The fifteenth statue spoils the symmetry of the screen — a consequence of a misalignment of the choir itself, rather than of the pulpitum.

The first fourteen statues date from some years after the murder of Henry VI in 1471. Henry came to be revered as a saint and, as such, his statue was removed at the Reformation. It was replaced in 1810 by the present statue by Michael Taylor in a style rather different from his fourteen predecessors.

THE TOMB OF PRINCE WILLIAM (IN THE NORTH AISLE OF THE CHOIR)

Prince William of Hatfield (his birthplace) was the third child of Edward III and his queen, Philippa of Hainault. He was only ten years of age when he died in 1344.

Edward was just fourteen at the time of his father's abdication and subsequent murder. Because of his minority, the country was governed by a council led by his mother. It was soon decided that he should have a wife and the Bishop of Lichfield was assigned to find him a suitable bride. Towards the end of the year the royal retinue was in York, composed of despised foreigners, mostly mercenaries his French mother had gathered around her. The daughter of one caught the attention of the bishop, and so it was that Edward came to be married in York Minster to a Dutch girl, the daughter of John, Lord Beaumont of Hainault. Edward continued to have close associations with the Minster for the rest of his life. The grave of the young prince (at the west end of the north aisle of the choir) is the only royal tomb in the Minster, chosen by Edward and Philippa as the place for their son's funeral because of their personal affection for the church.

The alabaster effigy of William is now once again in its original position in the Minster, having resided in a number of locations around the church over the centuries.

THE CHOIR STALLS, THRONE AND PULPIT

When Jonathan Martin set fire to the Minster in 1829 he destroyed the fittings of the choir, including the elaborately carved choir stalls, pulpit and cathedra. (The cathedra is the archbishop's throne of office and stands within the choir. A church which houses a cathedra is referred to as a cathedral.) Restoration work started almost immediately and Sir Robert Smirke was commissioned to design the replacement woodwork. (Smirke was known both as a painter and an architect. His best-known buildings include the British Museum and the Royal

Opera House in Covent Garden.) He set about attempting to re-create, as closely as he could, the choir stalls, pulpit and throne which had been destroyed. He made an excellent job of his task of the designing and justice was done to his designs by the York carver, John Wolstenholme, who transformed them into reality. The canopies are by another artist, Robert Hulme. The teak was donated by the Royal Navy from its own plantations.

THE TOMB OF ARCHBISHOP RICHARD LE SCROPE (IN THE LADY CHAPEL)

This simple marble tomb stands between the Lady Chapel and St Stephen's Chapel to its north, below the Great East Window. The tomb itself is not of notable artistic merit — in fact, to modern eyes, its attraction lies in the simplicity of its plain marble. It is Richard le Scrope himself who is interesting. He has the unique privilege of being the only Archbishop of York to have been executed — by Henry IV, in 1405 (see Chapter One). A man of great intellectual power, from a family of no little influence (their seat was Castle Bolton in Wensleydale) Archbishop Richard was condemned for joining a 'conspiracy' led by the Earl of Northumberland, in protest against high taxes, both secular and ecclesiastical, and mal-government of the country. In the north his execution was viewed as the murder of a local hero and Richard le Scrope is considered a martyr. The people of York came to regard him as a saint. His coat of arms was added by his family in 1972. (See also the Great East Window, p. 54.)

THE TOMB OF ARCHBISHOP JOHN DOLBEN

At the north-eastern end of the south choir transept is a tomb and memorial to Archbishop John Dolben, his effigy looking slightly amused, recumbent on his right arm. The carving is by Grinling Gibbons. Dolben was one of the more colourful characters in York's history. As a student at Oxford, he joined Charles I's forces and carried the Royalist colour at the battle of Marston Moor. Shot in the shoulder and badly wounded in the battle, he was carried back to the city. After a short recuperation he insisted on joining the defences of the town, whereupon he was badly wounded a second time. The shot which hit him in the leg confined him to his bed for a year, at the end of which the king's cause was lost. Dolben went back to college, and returned to York nearly forty years later as archbishop.

THE TOMB OF ARCHBISHOP WALTER DE GRAY (IN THE SOUTH TRANSEPT)

Megalithic peoples erected monuments in stone to their dead ancestors and leaders. Such rites have continued without break into modern times. Walter de Gray was the archbishop who initiated the building of the present Minster in 1220. He had been a powerful figure in the government of the land since the days of King John, over forty years before his death. When he died, in 1255, a tomb was created for his body, elaborate enough to do justice to a much respected man of intelligence, insight and influence not only in York but throughout the whole country. It stands just inside the entrance to the south transept, on the east side. It is considered the finest monument in the Minster. Indeed it has been described by some as the finest of its type in the country.

THE CRYPT

The description 'crypt' means nothing more than a hiding place, and the crypt of a cathedral often contained the treasures of the church, secreted there in a place of relative safety. The Minster was built on level ground, and the crypt is actually slightly above ground level. Although its descending steps give the impression of a dungeon, one descends less than one ascends on climbing the steps at the entrances to the church.

Today the Minster crypt falls into three distinct parts. The old crypt, under the east end of the choir, dates from the construction of the present building in the fifteenth century. Marked out by studs in the floor are the positions of the inner and outer faces of the apse at the east end of the church built by Archbishops Thomas of Bayeux and Roger Pont L'Eveque — the distance between the two rows of studs shows the thickness of the walls of a medieval cathedral church.

Below the crypt, accessible through a trap-door, are remains of the Roman *Principia* — the plinth of a pillar can be seen beneath a trap-door.

Against the east wall of the crypt are three striking, modern paintings of King Edwin, St Hilda (Edwin's great-niece who founded the great Abbey at Whitby), and James, deacon to Queen Aethelberga, by the Leeds artist Graeme Wilson.

The western part of the original crypt was filled in and forgotten, only to be rediscovered during the fire in February 1829. Today it is referred to as the west crypt and is used as an ecumenical chapel, dedicated to St William (see p. 47). The lower parts of four patterned Norman columns, once part of the Norman Minster, survive intact in the aisles of the west crypt.

Finally there is the western-most part of the crypt, created in the 1970s and referred to as the Foundations (also described on p. 47).

THE SHRINE OF ST WILLIAM (IN THE WEST PART OF THE CRYPT)

William Fitzherbert's place in the history of York has rarely been without ambiguity. Perhaps the most controversial of archbishops, William's appointment caused a scandal throughout England, felt nowhere more fiercely than in the Minster, where the canons were split. As Treasurer of the Minster, William had been extremely popular, known for his love of company and entertaining, rather than piety. When Archbishop Thurstan (one of York's most influential archbishops) died in 1140, William's supporters put him forward as Thurstan's successor.

Of the four senior posts in the government of the Minster (Dean, Chancellor, Precentor and Treasurer) William's was politically the most junior (if fiscally the most powerful). All four had hoped to become archbishop. The rumour was spread of nepotism. William was a nephew of King Stephen. Stephen had first tried to appoint another nephew, and only after he was rejected by the Pope (on the grounds that he was Abbot of a Normandy monastery and was unwilling to resign) did Stephen put William forward. An even stronger accusation of nepotism was levelled against another of William's uncles, Henry of Blois, Bishop of Winchester, who on William's behalf talked to his cousin Stephen, in the right tones and at the right times, in favour of their mutual nephew.

Amongst the people of York, William was as popular as Archbishop elect as he had been as Treasurer, leading a publicly generous, if somewhat extravagant life. William's popularity was not shared by many of the various factions within the Church, particularly the frugal Cistercians, who saw William as representing all that was rotten in England. St Bernard of Clairvaux (the leading Cistercian Father) was furious, and wrote to the Pope, Lucius II, in protest, speaking in most uncharitable terms of Henry of Blois as 'the Whore of Winchester'. It was a complaint which fell on deaf ears — Lucius was no progressive, and no admirer of the Cistercians. The arguing and wrangling went on for three years until, finally, William was appointed to the Archbishopric of York on 26th September, 1143.

A tenuous peace prevailed in York for four years, with William popular in secular circles and with the lower clergy, but with much animosity felt amongst some sections of higher ecclesiastical office. This balanced peace was upset when, in 1147, Lucius died and was succeeded as Pope by Eugenius III, a man much more in sympathy with the Cistercian movement. Under the influence of St Bernard, Eugenius dismissed William (who left York) and replaced him with the Abbot of the Cistercian Abbey of Fountains, Henry Murdac. The popularity of William with the people of York, together with little respect for the Cistercians, led to them barring the city to Murdac for a short time, preventing him from entering to take up his See. (For this act of defiance York was temporarily placed under an interdict by the Pope.)

In 1153, Eugenius, St Bernard and Henry Murdac all died (Murdac shortly after being forcibly expelled from the city by the secularly minded population). A new Pope was enthroned — Anastasius IV, a man with more reactionary views than Eugenius. William, reappointed, returned to York in triumph in 1154, and the populous turned out in jubilant crowds to greet him. In fact, so great was the number of people lining the streets that those crowded onto Ouse Bridge caused its collapse. That none of the people swept away in the flooded spring river (about two hundred in all) were drowned was quite remarkable.

William died only seven months later, under questionable circumstances. He collapsed during Mass and the Cistercian faction in the Minster was suspected of poisoning his communion wine. Their main protagonist, the Archdeacon Osbert, resigned in the scandal. William's body was interred in the nave. (Normally, he would have been buried in the choir, but the choir was being rebuilt at the time following the great fire of 1137.)

Beverley Minster had a saint interred within its precincts (St John of Beverley, the fourth Bishop of York who died in 721), as did Ripon Cathedral (St Wilfrid, see Chapter One). Pilgrims came to both to pay respects, ask for absolution, and lay gifts (hopefully of financial worth) upon the relics. Why not to York? It is probably no coincidence that the appeal for the canonization of William came during the years which followed the start of construction of the present Minster. Yet how could this man of worldly pleasures be put forward as a saint?

The answer came in the form of the events of the day of his return to York from exile. Remembering the collapse of Ouse Bridge with no loss of life, it was argued that surely it must have been a miracle. (Indeed, there is evidence to suggest that the entire story was 'borrowed' from an event which occurred in Pontefract and had nothing to do with William.) Many 'miracles' which were later attributed to William and are illustrated in the St William Window in the Minster are known to have been 'borrowed', particularly from events previously attributed to St John of Beverley. Nevertheless, William was canonized in 1227, just as the building work on the new transepts was reaching its peak, and at its most expensive. (The first recorded appeal for funds for the building of the present Minster is dated 1227.)

A chapel on the new Ouse Bridge, built towards the end of the twelfth century to serve as a civic chapel to the city council was also dedicated to William at this time, remembering the miracle he was believed to have worked there. It remained in use until the bridge was demolished in 1810.

Even after his death William continued to cause controversy. His body has meandered around the Minster over the centuries which have followed. As the years passed, and the pilgrims came to the tomb of St William with their donations and gifts, the Dean and Chapter decided that perhaps William ought to have a shrine more befitting a saint. One was duly constructed behind the high altar, and some, but not all of his remains were moved there in 1284. Now each pilgrim was directed first to William's tomb in the nave. Following worship there, and a suitable financial offering, the pilgrim was told of the shrine behind the altar, with further remains, so demanding a further contribution, the Dean and Chapter profiting twice from one saint.

During the iconoclastic fervour of the republican occupation of the city which followed the siege of York, the shrine to St William was removed. (Parts of it have since been found in Precentor's Court at the west end of the Minster and are now in the Yorkshire Museum.) Back to the nave went William's remains from the shrine, where he was reunited with himself and lay in peace until, in the late 1960s, he was disinterred yet again. This time it was the cathedral itself that had him moved. The central tower was threatening to collapse unless engineers excavated under it and replaced the foundations (see the section about the Foundations, below).

St William's remains were moved to the west end of the crypt under the choir, where a small chapel was created to his dedication. Today this private chapel is used ecumenically. St William's sarcophagus, which sits in his chapel, is probably a reused Roman coffin. To the west of this is a small altar, a gift from the Roman Catholic Bishop of Leeds. The mosaic floor and 'sunburst' tapestry were made by local art students. The floor depicts the swirling Ouse in which no-one was drowned on that fateful day in 1154.

The Feast of St William of York is celebrated each year on 8th June.

THE FONT (IN THE OLD CRYPT)

Against the west wall of the eastern part of the crypt is the only font in the Minster. It dates from the twelfth century, and was brought from the Bedern Chapel — the chapel belonging to the dormitory of St William's College a few yards south-east of the Minster. The cover was made in 1946 by Sir Ninian Comper (who also designed the pulpit in the nave).

The font is sited on top of a well. Tradition has it that it was in this well that Edwin was baptized on 12th April, 627, the day before Easter, so bringing Christianity back to northern England (see Chapter One).

The portraits on the inside show Queen Aethelberga, King Edwin, Paulinus (Aethelberga's, and subsequently Edwin's priest and the first of the modern line of bishops of York), St Hilda, and Paulinus' Deacon, James, who kept the dim flame of Christianity alive in the north following Edwin's death and the return to Kent of Aethelberga and Paulinus, six years later.

THE FOUNDATION (ENTERED FROM THE SOUTH TRANSEPT)

In the 1960s it was discovered that parts of the Minster (notably the central tower and the west end of the nave) were in serious danger of collapse. The foundations of the west end had not been built to support the two bell towers added in the fifteenth century. Originally the towers were the height of the west end gable, but were raised during the mid-fifteenth century, considerably increasing the weight of masonry supported by the foundations of this part of the building.

It seems probable that the fifteenth-century engineers and masons responsible for the erection of the present central tower were never completely confident of its foundations. The art of laying foundations had become partially lost since the days of the Norman builders who erected Archbishop Thomas' Minster in the second half of the eleventh century, 400 years before. The proportions of the central tower (which is built on the same foundations as the tower which collapsed) suggest it was designed to carry a spire, which was never added, probably through worry about the weight the foundations would have to support. By the twentieth century, drainage of the surrounding land had lowered the water table and by the 1960s the threat to the tower meant something had to be done.

The solution was to undermine the tower and place giant hydraulic jacks beneath the foundations. Very slowly, hydraulic fluid restored the tower to equilibrium. The machinery was now replaced by new foundations — huge girdles of concrete, stressed *in situ* by large steel bolts, locking the four modern collars (one round each of the piers at each corner of the tower) to the medieval foundations. If nothing else, a visit to the Foundations is worthwhile just to see the new foundations and be impressed by the skills of the twentieth-century engineers who contributed so importantly to the fabric of the Minster.

It was realized long before the first stone of the floor was removed that a large amount of archaeologically invaluable material would be found under the site, which has been in continuous use for nearly 2,000 years. Still, the actual findings outweighed even optimistic expectations. Close co-operation between the archaeologists and the engineers (who themselves were professionally interested in the history of the site, and rapidly became personally interested in the archaeology) led to a careful uncovering of years of accumulated material as layer after layer of the past was removed.

First, the foundations of Archbishop Thomas' Norman cathedral were uncovered at various places throughout the Foundations, much being reused Roman stone. A well, no doubt used by the Norman Minster, was found just north of what would have been the angle of the nave and the north transept of the Norman cathedral and is today reopened in the Foundations. It became enclosed within the walls of the present nave and buried when the present Minster was built in the thirteenth century.

The next levels were those of Viking York. These contained surprisingly little of significance. Then Anglo-Saxon York was uncovered. Here the most interesting find was a graveyard in the corner of the Foundations, under where the south transept joins the crossing. A number of carved Saxon stones were exposed — more than had been found during modern times in the whole of York. Some of the earlier bodies of the Saxon graves had been buried packed in charcoal as a preservative. Interestingly, the alignment of the Saxon graves was north–east to south–west. This was the alignment of Roman York, and of much of the present town of York, but is not the east–west alignment of the later Minsters.

The lowest levels were those of Roman York. The chambers of the Foundations into which one enters and from which one leaves, stand on what was the most north-westerly room of the Roman *Principia* — the administration building at the heart of the Roman fort. Amongst the Roman finds were fallen columns — one intact, lying as it fell. In 1971 it was re-erected by York Civic Trust outside the door of the south transept of the Minster — mistakenly upside down. One of the most exciting finds of the excavation was a large Roman culvert, still intact and still functioning, today continuing to keep the Minster dry almost two millennia after it was built.

During the course of the excavation of this large hole under the crossing of the transepts, nave and choir, the Dean and Chapter took the inspired decision to create another crypt, rather than refill the excavation (as had originally been envisaged). The western extension to the crypt under the choir (which had been discovered during the restoration work following the fire of 1829) was joined to this new crypt, and is now known as the Foundations. It was turned into a museum of the past history of the Minster and the site upon which it stands.

The Foundations comprise a circular walk, arranged such that one walks through a series of chambers around the piers of the two western pillars of the tower. An additional chamber to the east now houses the Minster Treasury, filled with some of the most valuable and treasured possessions of the church. The new Treasury is in turn joined to the west end of the old crypt, which houses the Shrine of St William (see p. 44). A first visit to the Minster would be incomplete without seeing the Foundations.

A SHORT GUIDE TO THE MINSTER'S STAINED AND PAINTED GLASS

The windows of the churches of York contain more medieval stained glass than is to be found in the whole of the rest of England, and stained and painted glass from every century since the eleventh is represented in the Minster. The Minster contains far too much stained glass to attempt to catalogue here even the major windows. Yet to omit any reference to the windows would be to omit that for which the Minster is most famous. Included here are a few of the most beautiful or interesting windows.

In general, the windows of the Minster are made up of individual panels about three feet square. However, some of these have got mixed up during restoration work over the years. Each of these panels has to be removed and releaded, on average once every 120 years if the glass is not to fall out through deterioration of the lead. In addition, twice this century, during times of war, much of the glass has been removed for safe-keeping. Gradually, through the skill and patience of York Glaziers Trust, and the generosity of the sponsors who are funding the work, all the windows of York Minster are being examined, cleaned, releaded, and returned to their pristine glory.

A surprising proportion of the Minster's stained glass depicts secular themes — perhaps the most whimsical of which is the Bell-founder's Window (see p. 51). The lights in the nave clerestory display the coats of arms of influential York families who took part in the campaigns against the Scots prior to the battle of Bannockburn in 1314. (A booklet, *A Guide and Index to the Windows of York Minster*, published by the Dean and Chapter, catalogues each panel in each of the Minster's windows, and a second booklet, *The Stained and Painted Glass of York Minster* by Peter Gibson, the Superintendent and Secretary of York Glaziers Trust, describes the more interesting glass in some detail.)

The windows are described below in order, moving clockwise around the Minster as viewed from above, starting at the west end of the nave.

The Windows of the West End of the Nave

All three of these windows were installed in 1338 at the time the west end was being finished. The outer two windows were a gift from Thomas de Beneston, a vicar-choral of the Minster, while the Great West Window was paid for personally by Archbishop William Melton at a cost of a hundred marks. It portrays scenes from the life of Christ in the upper part, and past archbishops in the lower. The glass contains much red and gold, creating a warm atmosphere in the nave, particularly with the setting sun falling directly on the window on a fine summer evening. The tracery is curvilinear — a technique which was novel at the time the window was being built. The design of the tracery is unusual, a substantial heart shape dominating the upper part of the window. It is, of course, the Sacred Heart of Christ, symbolic of His love of mankind. However, at the Reformation this was 'reinterpreted' and a number of stories as to what the heart might represent grew up. It has become popularly known as the Heart of Yorkshire.

A Norman Jesse Panel

Most of the second window from the west end of the nave is contemporary with the completion of this part of the cathedral in about 1335. One of the three-foot-square panels, the panel in the centre of the lower row of lights, is, however, from the earlier Minster built by Thomas of Bayeux (that is, the cathedral which preceded the present Minster on this site, see p. 33). The panel shows a king and was taken from a Jesse Window (see the Jesse Window across the nave, described on p. 56). Until recently it was thought to be the oldest stained glass light in Britain. However, a small panel some three centuries older was recently unearthed during archaeological excavations at the site of the great monastery at Jarrow. The Jesse panel is now thought to be the second oldest stained glass in the country.

The Pilgrimage Window (in the north aisle of the nave)

This is the third window from the east end of the north aisle of the nave, next to the Bell-founder's Window. Again it is fourteenth century and contemporary with the building of the nave. On the left and right of the bottom row are a knight and his lady going on a pilgrimage. (The figure in the centre is St Peter.) However, it is perhaps the borders which are particularly interesting. The left of the bottom border depicts monkeys conducting a funeral. The woman with a stick, in the centre panel, chasing a fox with a goose is also curious. (The stick is actually a distaff — the piece of wood that holds the wool during spinning.) The right of the lower border shows a hound being chased by a stag, reversing the normal course of events.

The Bell-founder's Window (in the north aisle of the nave)

This is the second window from the east end of the north aisle of the nave. Most of the medieval stained and painted windows in the cathedrals of Europe were gifts paid for by ecclesiastics. This window is one of the exceptions and was given to the Minster by a local dignitary, Richard Tunnoc, in remembrance of St William, whose tomb once stood nearby. Tunnoc was a bell-founder himself. His foundry was close by in Stonegate. He rose to become one of the most powerful men in the city, eventually becoming Lord Mayor. Full of little gold and silver bells in lozenge-shaped panels, the window commemorates the craft and skills of the bell-maker, and shows various aspects of bell-making such as casting a bell (bottom right — a boy and a girl pumping the bellows of the furnace) and tuning a bell (bottom left). In addition, there are monkeys playing musical instruments.

THE FIVE SISTERS WINDOW (IN THE NORTH TRANSEPT)

The Five Sisters is the best-known window in the Minster, and may even be the best-known window in the world. Built during the 1270s, it contains no pictures and is purely decorative. Built of grisaille (grey-green) glass, the window is too early to contain gold-coloured glass (silver staining was not discovered until the fourteenth century — a hundred years after the Five Sisters Window was built). It does, however, contain yellow. (True gold-coloured glass can be seen in the later window to the west, in the adjacent St John's Chapel, which contains both yellow and gold, together with grisaille glass which could, by the time this window was constructed, be made lighter in colour.) The Five Sisters Window contains patterns of foliage (although much has been jumbled over the centuries).

Strictly, the Five Sisters Window is five separate windows, each a little more than five feet wide and a little over fifty feet high. They are considered the Minster's most valuable amongst so many priceless windows. The upper part of the window is modern, dating from the window's restoration during the 1920s (see below).

The panel at the bottom of the centre window depicts Daniel in the den of lions, being fed by the prophet Habakkuk. This was not part of the original window but is twelfth century and is one of only a few panels of glass in the present church that came originally from the Minster built by Thomas of Bayeux and Roger Pont L'Eveque (see p. 33). It was placed in its present position in the 1970s, having been cleaned and restored.

The window takes its name from the tapestry from which it was said to have been copied, woven by five unmarried sisters, all of whom became nuns. The windows are supposed to be dedicated to St Barbara, St Margaret, St Mary, St Catherine and St Ursula. The story, and hence the name, is no older than the nineteenth century. It was invented by Charles Dickens for the novel *Nicholas Nickleby*.

The window was removed at the outbreak of war in 1914. When it was about to be replaced it was found to be in need of urgent releading and restoration. The £3,000 needed was raised in the form of contributions for a memorial to the women of the Empire who were killed in active service during the First World War (perhaps the most widely known being Edith Cavell). The names of the women to whom this memorial window is dedicated are recorded on the panels to the right of the astronomical clock, to the right of the window. Helen Little, who had the idea of the memorial, left a letter, found after her death in 1933, in which she told how she had experienced a vision of her two sisters, who had died in childhood, in the south transept. She followed them to the north transept where she had another vision of five women working at a tapestry in a beautiful garden, and as a result the idea of a memorial paid for by contributions occurred to her. The restored memorial window was unveiled in 1925 by the Duchess of York (now Queen Elizabeth the Queen Mother).

There is an interesting story concerning the restoration of the Five Sisters Window. In 1539 Henry VIII dissolved the Yorkshire abbeys and monasteries. The exchequer was in dire need of money and the buildings and belongings of the dissolved Church were seen as a legitimate primary source. The monasteries were disbanded and anything of value seized. Rievaulx Abbey, the oldest of Yorkshire's Cistercian abbeys, was one of the first to fall. Its roof and windows were swiftly plundered for their lead, which was melted down into ingots, stamped with the King's seal, and transported to London. One wagon of lead was lost, buried when a roof collapsed. In 1924, Sir Charles Peers discovered this lead during excavations at the abbey. The Earl of Feversham donated the ingots, still carrying Henry VIII's seal, to the Dean and Chapter of the Minster. It is this metal, once part of Rievaulx Abbey, which today holds the Five Sisters Window together.

The glass in the Five Sisters Window came from France. When the Minster was built, many of the windows were at first filled with cheap coloured or plain glass which could be discarded if a rich patron subsequently came forward and endowed a window in its place. The grisaille glass of this most famous of windows was just such glass. Nobody endowed a replacement for any part of the Five Sisters Window, and so the grisaille survives to this day, now one of the country's most valued windows.

THE WINDOWS OF THE CHAPTER HOUSE AND ITS VESTIBULE

All but the window facing the door of the chapter house are contemporary with the building and its vestibule. The glazing of the chapter house itself was carried out between 1300 and about 1307 and that of the vestibule a little later. All have been restored a number of times over the centuries, most recently by the York Glaziers Trust.

In the chapter house itself the windows depict, clockwise from the door, scenes from the life of St Catherine, scenes from the life of St William of York, and scenes from the Gospels. The next window, opposite the chapter house door, is the only window that is not contemporary with the construction of the building. The top half is fifteenth century, showing scenes from the life of Christ, whilst the lower half is sixteenth century and depicts scenes from the life of St Thomas à Becket. The following window shows the life of St Peter, the next the life of St Paul, and the last of the chapter house windows shows St Thomas, St Nicholas, St John the Baptist and St Edmund.

THE ST WILLIAM WINDOW (IN THE NORTH CHOIR TRANSEPT)

The two windows of the choir transepts (the St William Window in the north choir transept and the St Cuthbert Window in the south choir transept) represent the zenith of medieval glass staining and painting. Unfortunately, they are also the most difficult to see clearly, as a result of the nature these locations.

William Fitzherbert, St William of York, played a significant part in the history of the Minster (see p. 44). The window was given in his remembrance in 1422 by the de Ros family (whose seat was Helmsley Castle). It contains over a hundred scenes from William's life, from the marriage of his parents to pilgrims offering gifts at his shrine, and is contemporary with the building of the choir.

The date of this window, like that of the St Cuthbert Window which is somewhat later, together with the sympathy with which their subjects have been treated, suggests that both might have been by students of John Thornton (see the Great East Window, p. 54).

THE ST JAMES WINDOW (IN THE NORTH AISLE OF THE CHOIR)

This is the first window at the east end of this aisle, and shows events surrounding the death of St James, together with the Nativity (a nineteenth-century panel) and the arms of St James (twentieth century). Apart from these two panels, the window dates from the sixteenth century and came from Rouen Cathedral.

THE GREAT EAST WINDOW OF THE CHOIR

This is the largest medieval stained glass window in the world. It is seventy-six feet nine inches high, thirty two feet wide and is often compared in area to a tennis court. (It is, in fact, slightly larger.) The building of the window was started in 1405 by John Thornton, to designs by Hugh Hedon. Thornton's workshop was responsible for much of York's stained glass during a particularly prolific period of ecclesiastical building in York. Thornton was brought from Coventry to glaze the window, which was paid for by Walter Skirlaw, the Bishop of Durham (who also paid for the replacement of the central tower when it fell in 1407, see p. 36). Walter Skirlaw is pictured in the bottom of the centre panel of the window.

Although John Thornton was one of the most famous glass artists of his day (indeed, of all time) it still seems a long way to send to Coventry. Peter Wenham, an historian of Yorkshire, has suggested that there may have been a shortage of craftsmen in York as a result of the plague which killed two-thirds of the population of the city fifty years before, with subsequent outbreaks in the intervening period.

The connection with Coventry was the Archbishop, Richard le Scrope, who had previously been Bishop of Lichfield. Shortly after Thornton arrived in York, Richard le Scrope was executed by Henry IV. (See p. 43.)

It is difficult to get a good view of the Great East Window, and its size is elusive from ground level in the choir or from immediately outside the church. (An impression of its true size is given when one looks at the Minster from several miles east of York.)

Thornton was paid four shillings a week for the window, together with a five pound bonus at the end of each year — a huge sum of money for a craftsman to earn in the fifteenth century. In addition, at the time the work was started the Dean and Chapter offered a ten pound bonus if the window was completed within three years. The window carries, together with John Thornton's monogram, the date of completion — 1408. Thornton received the promised ten pounds.

THE ST CUTHBERT WINDOW (IN THE SOUTH TRANSEPT OF THE CHOIR)
The splendid St Cuthbert Window forms a pair with the slightly earlier St William Window in the north choir transept. It dates from the late 1440s. There are no adequate words to describe the beauty of this pair of magnificent windows.

St Cuthbert is an important figure in the history of early British Christianity, but played a particular part in unifying the Church in the north of England. As the Church of Rome, advancing from Augustine's seat in the south, encroached increasingly upon the Irish school of friars, spreading through northern England from Iona, a disagreement broke out in the newly established Church. Should Christianity be pursued in the Celtic style of wandering friars, perhaps based at particular monasteries, or should churches be established as concrete bases, run by deans, deacons and canons, as decreed by the Church of Rome?

At a Synod held at Whitby in the autumn of 663, walking on tenuous and uncertain ground over the whole style in which the Church should conduct itself, King Oswy ruled in favour of St Wilfrid, the Bishop of York who adhered to the Roman tradition. The rift that followed was healed in 685 when York agreed that Cuthbert, a monk of the Celtic school, should be enthroned as Bishop of Lindisfarne, a monastery modelled on the great Celtic monastery founded by St Columba on Iona, but insisted that elements of the Roman Church be adopted. Where the enthronement took place is not really known. Most think that the ceremony was in York Minster. However, there is a strong local belief that Cuthbert was enthroned in a church which stood on the site which is today All Saints' Church on Pavement. St Cuthbert's Church itself also claims the honour.

The window depicts almost a hundred scenes from St Cuthbert's life.

THE WINDOWS OF THE ZOUCHE CHAPEL
The Zouche Chapel, off the south aisle of the choir, takes its name from its founder, William de la Zouche, Archbishop 1340-52. It is a quiet corner

(reserved for private worship) with a low, rib-vaulted roof, and contains much interesting (if somewhat quirky) glass. A number of small painted panels, many little above eye level, depicting animals and people in amusing poses — a wren about to devour a spider, a man with a muzzled and chained bear, being threatened by a second bear, a windmill, a unicorn, a stork, eagles, a procession of monkeys, a man playing a drum, several oak trees containing birds, a bird in mating display, various fish, numerous flowers and much more. They were placed here having been removed from other windows (in which they had been misplaced) during the restoration of the Minster glass following the Second World War. (The hassocks in the Zouche chapel are covered with tapestries of details from these windows.)

The St Francis Window, the first of the south wall of the chapel, is twentieth-century glass of the highest quality. The left light depicts St Francis with a child, releasing caged birds. That on the right shows St Francis embracing a leper. (Leprosy had disgusted the worldly Francis until his conversion to a life of piety, when one of his first acts was to encompass the sick of Assisi within his ministry.) The window was constructed in 1944 and installed in the chapel during restoration work carried out by the Friends of York Minster to commemorate their fiftieth anniversary in 1977. (Sadly, the artist, Ervin Bossanyi, died in 1975 before he could view the window installed and lit by the southern summer sun.)

THE ROSE WINDOW (IN THE SOUTH TRANSEPT)

This splendid window, twenty-two feet four inches in diameter, high in the south wall of the south transept, escaped the fire which destroyed the roof above it in July 1984, only by extreme good fortune and the skill of the restorers of the York Glaziers Trust who rebuilt it completely. (Had it not been releaded five years before it would almost certainly have been lost in the fire.) This tracery originally held an earlier window dating from the thirteenth century. Following the defeat of Richard III in 1485, the Houses of York and Lancaster were unified by the marriage of Elizabeth of York to Henry Tudor in 1486. The respective emblems of their royal houses, the red rose of Lancaster and the white rose of York, were unified into a single emblem — the red and white Tudor rose. Some time early in the sixteenth century the window was rebuilt by Flemish glaziers who arranged the red rose of the House of Lancaster with the combined red and white rose of the House of Tudor alternately around the twenty-four petals which make up the edge of the rosette (each five feet long and two feet wide).

The other large panels in the south wall of the south transept depict St William of York, St Peter, St Paul and St Wilfrid. They are the work of William Peckitt (who was responsible for much glass restoration in the Minster during the second half of the eighteenth century, particularly in the south aisle of the nave).

THE JESSE WINDOW (IN THE SOUTH AISLE OF THE NAVE)

This window, the third along the south aisle from the west end of the nave, depicts an abridged family tree of Jesus, from the time of Jesse of Bethlehem (of whom King David was the youngest son) shown lying down at the bottom of the window, to Christ himself at the top of the tree. The window dates from early in the fourteenth century, but has been altered over the years. The figures on the branches are the more influential prophets.

The window was restored in 1789 by William Peckitt, and again in 1950 following its removal against possible damage during the Second World War. The border glass is entirely by Peckitt and depicts foliage (a subject for background patterns often found in medieval glass). In these border panels, Peckitt's style anticipates fashions in design which were not to reach their zenith of popularity until the second half of the nineteenth century.

The Jesse Window is a purely Jewish window. Above the tree of Jesse, Peckitt placed the Star of David and motifs of Cabbalistic symbolism.

CHAPTER THREE

THE MEDIEVAL CHURCHES OF YORK

It is a reverend thing to see an ancient castle or building not in decay.
Francis Bacon

Amongst British towns, only London and Norwich are blessed with more medieval churches than York. At the height of the city's prosperity in the thirteenth century there were forty-seven parish churches in York (together with sixteen other chapels). This was far too many for the community to support as the slow but steady decline in the town's economic fortunes through the fourteenth, fifteenth and sixteenth centuries began to take its toll. A number of churches were largely immune from financial pressure, being owned by large and wealthy religious houses. Others were absorbed into adjoining parishes and so became redundant. Many of these fell into structural decay and were eventually demolished (more often than not for their stone). Fourteen of the twenty-six churches which survived in central York to see the Reformation still stand today and these, together with six largely rebuilt medieval churches and one ruined church, are described in this chapter.

Many of York's medieval churches are architecturally atypical of English ecclesiastical buildings of the period. They are rectangular rather than cruciform and have side aisles running the full length of the church. In a surprising number of cases the tower stands within the body of the church. The towers were absorbed as the aisles were extended to the north and south, both aisles and tower being external additions to a simple hall. York's medieval churches tend to be simple in design and to show signs of being built at minimum cost. For example, the walls are often not as thick as is found in churches of the same period built elsewhere, and internal embellishments such as capitals to their columns, or arches structurally dividing the chancel from the nave, are not infrequently absent. Indeed, some are constructed as a single room and do not have a separated chancel at all, being built in the style of earlier Saxon and Celtic churches (a style returned to in the simplicity of design of later nonconformist chapels). A number have drum-like octagonal towers (two topped by fine octagonal stone spires) which is a design that was much favoured by friars, and presumably reflects the influence of the powerful monasteries which established themselves in the town.

Some of the finest of the medieval stained and painted glass in England is in parish churches — gifts from wealthy parishioners. York had its own school of glass painters and many of the medieval windows of the city's parish churches are quite splendid. (Those of All Saints' on North Street and St Denys' on Walmgate are particularly fine.) Much of the medieval stained glass in England was destroyed by the Puritan armies during the Civil Wars of the seventeenth century. This destructive iconoclasm was largely prevented in York by the intervention of Lord Fairfax and his son, after the surrender of the city following the great siege of 1644. To these two men we owe the city's wealth of medieval stained windows.

York's churches are much older in ancestry than their present structures might lead one to suppose. In their present forms the medieval churches of the town date from the height of the wool exporting and manufacturing trades. Prosperity led to older churches being pulled down and replaced by more modern buildings, paid for by prosperous merchants and guilds. York's wealth in medieval churches is a legacy of the city's heyday and the profits accumulated from the export of wool. There are few remaining examples of Saxon or Norman ecclesiastical architecture in the city. Many of the town's churches, although not the original buildings, occupy sites upon which a church with the same dedication stood long before the Norman Conquest. Eight York churches are mentioned in the Domesday Book of 1086, and churches still stand on five of those sites today — All Saints' (Pavement), Holy Trinity (Micklegate), St Cuthbert's, St Mary's (Castlegate) and St Martin-cum-Gregory. Further, the Domesday Book was not comprehensive in this respect and several churches are known to have existed at the time of the Conquest which are not mentioned in the Book (St Olave's, St Michael-le-Belfry and St Mary's on Bishophill Junior, for example) usually because they were owned by religious orders and thereby excluded from the inventory of the possessions which the Crown could claim.

With a few exceptions, the churches of the city have not been maintained by the diocese. Rather they have been the responsibility of the parishioners. Gifts of monuments and windows were frequent, and appeals for money for maintenance rarely went unheard. The endowment of chantries, small chapels within a church in which a priest was paid to say Mass regularly for the soul of the founder and those of his family, were, until the Reformation, a particular source of income. Chantries were usually endowed by gifts of land or the rent from buildings, and the majority of York's churches contained several.

THE MEDIEVAL CHURCHES OF YORK
(IN ALPHABETICAL ORDER OF DEDICATION)

ALL SAINTS' ON NORTH STREET
On the west bank of the Ouse, tucked away from the bustle of the town only a few hundred yards away, All Saints' has an air of tranquillity all of its own. Yet in the fifteenth century it was one of the busiest churches in the town. The area around the church was dominated by the tanning industry, as the names of streets close by still record — Tanner Row, Tanner Street, Tanners' Moat. The present church

dates from the eleventh century, although the first use of the site as a place of worship may be much earlier. In medieval times, with St Martin-cum-Gregory, St Cuthbert's and Christ's Church (now Holy Trinity), All Saints' belonged to Holy Trinity Priory, a Benedictine House of Canons on Micklegate, founded in the middle of the tenth century. Since then, like the majority of medieval churches in York, as elsewhere, it has undergone many extensions and rebuildings.

The original church was a small rectangular hall which stood on the site of the present chancel, as wide as the present building but one, or possibly two bays shorter to the west. In the twelfth century this was extended by the addition of transepts, first on the south side of the church then, towards the end of the century, to the north. Around 1325 a chantry chapel was built, filling in the north-east corner. A corresponding chapel added to the south-east corner in the middle of the fourteenth century restored the symmetry of the church. The church grew to its present size and rectangular shape when, in the fifteenth century, the tower and spire were added to the middle of the west end of the nave, followed by extensions to the west of what had been, two centuries before, the transepts.

During 1866–7 the church was extensively repaired with little sensitivity (including the complete rebuilding of the south wall) by the well-known York architects J.B. and W. Atkinson, and it has been further restored several times, most recently in 1966.

All Saints' has an interesting stone tower and spire. Both are octagonal and the spire, which rises to 120 feet above ground level, is almost as wide as the tower upon which it stands (rather similar to that of St Mary's on Castlegate). Such octagonal spires were particularly popular with friars, and the Dominican Friary, which stood close by in Toft Green, undoubtedly influenced the design. The chancel has a particularly fine fifteenth-century hammer-beam roof, with wooden corbel-hammers depicting angels playing musical instruments, bearing a church, a crown, a shrine and a soul, and, at the east end of the chancel above the altar, the Archangel Gabriel and the Virgin Mary.

It is a much quoted claim of the city that there is more medieval stained and painted glass in York than in the whole of the rest of England. Amongst the finest of all England's parish church glass is that of All Saints'. Of particular note is the scene picturing St Anne teaching the infant Christ to read, in the fifteenth-century east window (a somewhat unusual subject, but found in three of York's parish churches). The kneeling figures in the lower panels of the east window are of two Lord Mayors of the city, Nicholas Blackburn (Lord Mayor of York 1429, d.1448) and his father, Nicholas Blackburn of Richmond (Lord Mayor of York 1412, d.1432) together with their wives (both called Margaret).

The east windows of the aisles are fourteenth-century glass which was originally made from part of the east window of the chancel, together with medieval stained glass from elsewhere in York. They depict St Peter receiving souls into Heaven (north aisle) and Satan receiving the damned into Hell.

The third window from the east in the south wall, depicting the Nine Orders of Angels, was all but hopelessly confused as a result of misplacing pieces of glass following the restorations of the lead of the window, required every 100 to 150 years. It was splendidly restored when the church was renovated in 1965–6, following the discovery of a drawing of the window, made in 1670, in the Bodleian Library. The panels show (bottom left to top right) virtues, archangels, angels, dominations, princedoms, powers, seraphim, cherubim and thrones. Interestingly, a figure in the lower right-hand panel (the angels panel) is wearing spectacles, which is most unusual in medieval art. (One earlier example is known, in the Church of Notre Dame in Spezet.)

The finest windows of all are the first and second from the east in the north wall. The first depicts, bottom left to top right, 'The Last Fifteen Days of the World', described in a fourteenth-century poem 'The Pricke of Conscience' (inspired by the Golden Legend and the *Historia Scolastica*), and was probably glazed by John Thornton, considered the finest glass artist of his age (see Chapter Two). The narration runs from bottom left to top right, the panels depicting the rising of the sea, the fall of the sea, the end of the flood, monsters rising from the ocean, the sea ablaze, trees ablaze (with fruit falling to the ground), the church spire crashing in an earthquake, the earth devouring rocks, people attempting to shelter, the earth reduced to only land and sky, praying for mercy, death awaiting, the sky falling, death arrived, and the end of the universe. The sponsors of the window (nine in all) are shown kneeling in the lower panels. The date, 1861, is of a restoration.

The window next to 'The Last Fifteen Days', the second from the east, shows six of the seven Acts of Mercy from the Gospel according to St Matthew, and is almost certainly also by Thornton. The top row depicts feeding the hungry, giving drink to the thirsty, giving hospitality to a stranger, and the second row clothing the naked, visiting the sick and visiting prisoners. (The missing Act is the last, the burial of the dead.) The window may have been paid for by Nicholas Blackburn the younger, as a memorial to his father.

The central west window is also interesting. Created in 1977 from fragments of medieval glass the three arms are those of the Crown, the Terry family (who have generously supported the church) and the emblem of York Civic Trust (formerly used as a silver mark by the York Assay office).

There is a curious modern addition to the south-west corner of this church. The small room, about six feet above the ground and reached by means of a short staircase, was until the mid-1960s the home of a solitary lay brother who attached himself to All Saints'. It is built on the site of a cell occupied in antiquity by an anchoress. The building is of reinforced concrete (and is claimed to be the earliest use in York of shuttered concrete as a building material — a claim also made by the Tempest Anderson Hall of the Yorkshire Museum). There is a 'squint' (now blocked up) in the south-west corner of the church which would have been used by the inhabitant of the building to observe the consecration of the host during Mass. (See also Holy Trinity Church, Goodramgate, p. 63.)

It is widely believed that All Saints' may be built on or very near to the site of the old Roman palace built by the Emperor Severus at the beginning of the third century AD.

ALL SAINTS', ON PAVEMENT (OUSEGATE)

There has been a church on this site since well before the Norman Conquest and All Saints' is one of eight York churches mentioned in the Domesday Book, when it was owned by the Bishop of Durham who received it as a gift from William I. Later, in the twelfth century, it was given to Durham Cathedral Priory.

A York tradition has St Cuthbert consecrated Bishop of Lindisfarne in All Saints' in 685 which, it is said, was built especially for the ceremony. The anonymous biographer of the saint tells us that King Ecgfrith and Archbishop Theodore gave Cuthbert the area of the city inside the Anglo-Saxon walls and to the south-west of the Minster. This would seem to mean the parishes of All Saints' and St Peter-the-Little (which stood opposite All Saints', on Peter Lane, and was united with the parish of All Saints' in 1548).

All Saints' has long been one of the wealthiest of the city's parishes (thirty-nine Lord Mayors of the city are said to be buried in the church or its grounds) and was the parish church used by and patronized by the guilds combined. The south wall still carries the arms of a few of the guilds which were the most important to the town. In the fifteenth century the church was even used for meetings of the town council. Traditionally it is also the church used by visitors to the city. At the Dissolution, All Saints' passed from Durham Priory to the Crown who retained the advowson until 1868 when it was given to the archbishop.

The present building dates from the late fourteenth and early fifteenth centuries. Like most of York's churches, All Saints' has undergone considerable changes over the centuries of its existence. The small Norman church developed into a medieval cruciform. The clerestory was added at the end of the fifteenth century. In the eighteenth century the chancel had fallen into disrepair and there were calls for its demolition to accommodate ever-increasing traffic in the streets around.

The food market used to be held in the square which occupied the area where Coppergate, Ousegate, Pavement, Piccadilly and Parliament Streets now meet. In order to meet the demand for the space needed by the increasingly busy market, in 1782 the church garden was taken over, the east end demolished and a new east wall built, seven feet back from the old wall. This pragmatic destruction has continued into modern times, the latest demolition being in 1963 when a widening of Coppergate was deemed necessary and the organ chapel was removed.

The present west window of All Saints' came from St Saviour's Church, when the parish of St Saviour's was amalgamated with that of All Saints' and St Crux in 1954. (The Church of St Crux itself, mentioned in the Domesday Book and described as one of the finest in York, stood where the St Crux Parish Room now stands on Pavement. It was demolished in 1887, in spite of a sizeable campaign to save it.) The window dates from about 1370 and is the work of a famous glass artist, Richard Caldbeck. It shows scenes from the Passion and contains an unusual shield in the right-hand light of the emblems representing the Passion. On its renovation and installation in All Saints' it took the glaziers almost two years to reassemble the puzzle of pieces they were presented with. The replaced window saw light again in 1957, only to be badly damaged in an act of deliberate destruction thirteen years later.

In York, All Saints' is known colloquially as the 'lantern church'. The original tower was erected early in the fifteenth century and is particularly prominent. The lantern is still illuminated each evening from dusk. In the past there was an obligation on the verger of All Saints' to keep a light in the tower to guide travellers to the town through the royal forest of Galtres, which lay to the north of York. The tower was rebuilt in 1837, and the lenses from the eighteenth-century lantern can be seen mounted on a plaque on the wall of the south aisle.

All Saints' has a horrible door-knocker — there is a story to it. Known as a Doom, the knocker is believed to be twelfth century (and as such is the oldest part of the church). It depicts a beast swallowing a human being. A person pursued by the authorities was granted sanctuary merely by grasping the ring (apparently even if no-one answered the door). Similar Dooms can be found at Adel in West Yorkshire and at St Gregory's Church in Norwich.

Just inside the main door, on the pillars of the west end of the church, is an interesting list of Benefactions, inscribed on wooden plaques ('Charity Boards'). Here are recorded the gifts bequeathed by individuals to the support of the poor of the parish — the most practical role of the church in days past. We learn, for example, of:

Dame Susanna Marshall by her Will dated 1st. day of August 1628 gave to this Parish £5. Yearly for ever ... to 10 Poor Widows in the said Parish a 2d loaf each, every Lord's day.

and of

Mrs. Mary Foster, Wife of John Foster, of this Parish aforesaid by Will dated 22nd. Novr. 1715, gave to the Feoffees of this Parish the sum of 12£. the Interest of which to be distributed in Bread every Sunday in the month to the most needful Poor in this Parish for ever.

and of

Thomas Wilson EsqR. of this Parish Alderman, vested in the year 1812, one hundred pounds Navy five per Cent Annuity, which was afterwards converted into 105 New 3 per Cents ... the Dividend to be laid out about Christmas in every year in Coals for the Poor residing in or belonging to the Parish of All Saints' Pavement.

and of many more.

HOLY TRINITY, ON GOODRAMGATE

For visitors who do not know Holy Trinity Church, it is very easily overlooked, sited off the roads of the town in its own garden in the angle of Goodramgate and Petergate, behind the Minster Song School and York College for Girls. It is reached through a gate off Goodramgate, or by a small alley, Hornpot Lane, which runs north off Petergate. Holy Trinity is first definitely mentioned towards the end of the first quarter of the twelfth century. (Earlier documents mentioning the church in 1082 and 1093 may be forgeries.) It was owned by the Diocese of Durham until 1538 when the Church was dissolved.

The herring-bone patterned stonework in the south wall is all that remains of the original Norman church that stood on this site. The present church dates from the thirteenth century when the nave and choir were built. The rest of the fabric of the church was built in the fourteenth century. The box pews were bought and installed by those who used the church during the seventeenth and eighteenth centuries, and the double level pulpit cost £6 in 1695. The reredos dates from 1721. Originally painted by Thomas Horsley it was restored in 1823. The layout is typical of an English post-Restoration church, and reflects church interior design prior to the influence of the Oxford Movement and the wide revival of Anglo-Catholicism.

On the south side of the church is a small chapel, built onto the church in the fifteenth century and dedicated to St James. It was originally reserved for private worship by the de Howne family (who later became Holme), and was a bequest of Robert de Howne, who died in 1396. Here private Mass would be said for the family by a hired priest, while Mass was said for the rest of the congregation in the main body of the church. To allow the priest in the chapel to observe the moments of consecration at the main altar, and so synchronize his ceremony in the de Howne chapel with that at the high altar, there is a small 'peep-hole' or 'squint' (properly referred to as a 'hagioscope') in the north-east corner of the chapel.

On the west wall of the chapel are the arms of George I, shown with England encompassing Scotland, Ireland, Hanover and France.

The present east window was glazed between 1471 and 1480 and was a gift to the church from its rector, John Walker (who is the figure kneeling down, in the centre light). The five figures are (from the left) St George (and dragon), St John the Baptist (with the Lamb of God and dressed in a camel skin), the Trinity (the Father holding the Corpus Christi with the Holy Ghost above, symbolized as usual by a dove), St John the Evangelist (with chalice and dragon, forced to show its venom when St John made the sign of the cross) and St Christopher (carrying the child Christ). The second lower panel shows the Virgin Mary with Christ and her parents. The centre lower panel is the crowning of the Virgin by the Trinity. The right lower panel is St Ursula with two girls representing the 11,000 virgins (probably one of the most remarkable mistranslations of medieval literature — there were originally only eleven). The window is considered most valuable — certainly there is very little glass of this period in the churches of York. Few windows depicting the Trinity survived the Reformation and the Civil War.

The tower of Holy Trinity is interesting, not only in it being unusually low for its horizontal measurements, but for the small gabled roof that caps it. Such tower roofs, known as 'pack-saddle' roofs, are rare in England (though more common in continental Europe). The present roof of Holy Trinity is comparatively recent but replaces an older pack-saddle. Also of interest is the nineteenth-century 'medieval style' chimney (the associated fireplace having long since been removed).

HOLY TRINITY, ON MICKLEGATE

Holy Trinity Priory was founded by St Oswald in the tenth century and was given by Ralph Pagnell (or Paynel) to the great French Monastery of Marmoutier in 1089. The gift brought with it substantial lands throughout England, including Boothby Pagnell in Lincolnshire and Newport Pagnell in Buckinghamshire. Several churches in the city were owned by the priory of which St Martin-cum-Gregory, All Saints' on North Street and St Cuthbert's on Peasholme Green all still survive. The priory rose to considerable power and wealth, and was empowered to install its own nominees in a number of influential positions (including that of the Bishop of Leeds).

The monastery of Holy Trinity stretched from the city wall in the south to St Martin's Church, bounded by Micklegate and by what is now Bishophill Junior — an area of some seven acres and a sizeable portion of this part of the medieval walled town. The gate of the priory survived until 1855 when it was demolished to make way for Priory Street. The present Holy Trinity Church was the priory chapel and was originally dedicated to Christ. On 4th June, 1137, a huge fire swept through York. (The town, built of tinder, wood, lathe and daub, was too crowded to be safe.) Holy Trinity Priory, then described as being 'in the suburbs' was destroyed, and with it Christ's Church. The present church dates from the rebuilding following the fire.

The rebuilt Holy Trinity was cruciform with a central tower. In a storm on 15th February, 1551, the tower fell, demolishing under it the choir, transepts and the aisles of the nave, and seriously damaging the clerestory and triforium of the nave. (The piers of this tower still support the church.) The nave, though damaged, became the only part of the building to be left in use, the chancel arch and southern side of the nave being walled up. The present chancel was created where the crossing had been. Being an easy source of stone the collapsed parts of the church were used for repairs to Ouse Bridge (in 1564) and to strengthen the city's defences (in 1603).

In the nineteenth century the church was expanded again. The south aisle was added in 1850 and the present chancel and vestry were built in 1886. The west end of the church was started in 1902 and completed three years later. The only stained glass in Holy Trinity (which is in the east and west windows) dates from this latest period and is by C.E. Kemp (who was responsible for much of the late Victorian stained glass in York).

The tower at the north-west corner of Holy Trinity is interesting. It originally belonged to an adjacent church dedicated to St Nicholas, which stood on Micklegate, and the chapel in the tower retains the dedication to the saint. How the church of Holy Trinity Priory came to assume responsibility for the parish of St Nicholas is not completely clear, but it seems that in the early 1450s the tower of St Nicholas' was threatening to fall. In 1453 the parishioners, unable to find the money for the necessary work, approached the priory for help. The priory agreed and annexed St Nicholas' Church, together with its parochial responsibilities. The tower reopened in 1455, a century before the tower of Holy Trinity fell. However, there was more to the story than this as a document dated 1st May, 1455, refers to St Nicholas' as having been appropriated by the priory 'in ancient days'. By 1495 the now redundant Church of St Nicholas had fallen into dereliction.

Interestingly, when all French properties were seized by Act of Parliament towards the end of the Hundred Years' War, Holy Trinity Priory, uniquely, seems to have maintained its independence. The end of the priory came a little over a century later with the Dissolution.

The Church of Holy Trinity was used by the laity as well as the clergy of the priory, and retained pastoral obligations (possibly those assumed from the parish of St Nicholas). The extensive churchyard was used for the burial of lay members of the priory and parish. The churchyard of Holy Trinity contains the only surviving stocks in York, now somewhat rotten.

ST ANDREW'S, ST ANDREWSGATE/SPEN LANE
This is not the St Andrew's Church mentioned in the Domesday Book (that was St Andrew's on Fishergate) but it probably does predate the Conquest, when it was owned by the Dean and Chapter of the Minster. The present hall was built in the 1390s. It had become redundant by 1548 when an attempt was made to unite the parish with that of All Saints' on Peasholme Green (itself redundant by the beginning of the seventeenth century). Because All Saints' itself was falling into disuse the union was never enacted and in 1586 the parish was united with that of St Saviour's instead. (The parish remained an administrative unit for the

secular purposes of local government until the present century.)

That the building survived at all is remarkable — it is the only church to have become redundant in or before Tudor times which still stands in the city today. Over the centuries it has been much altered to the extent that most of the original building has now been lost. The latest restoration was completed only recently when an attractive tiled roof was added. St Andrew's is probably unique amongst the churches of the city in that it was used as a brothel (just off the busy centre of King's Square. While in one end of the building the business of the brothel was being pursued, the other end was being used as a stable. Later, between the 1730s and 1823, the hall housed part of St Peter's School, after which it became, for a while, St Peter's Infant School. Today it is an Evangelical church.

St Cuthbert's, on Peasholme Green

Mentioned in the Domesday Book, St Cuthbert's is a pre-Conquest church which was enlarged in medieval times, as can be seen in the exterior face of the east wall where an entire former gable end is visible (most of which is reused Roman stone). The present building is thought to date from the tenth century, but the first written record of it is dated 18th February, 1371. The suggestions that St Cuthbert's might have been the site of Edwin's original Minster, and of the enthronement there of St Cuthbert as Bishop of Lindisfarne seem improbable.

With the exception of the older part of the east wall, and the modern vestry and porch, the majority of the present church is the result of a rebuilding which took place during the second quarter of the fifteenth century. The tower dates from the beginning of the sixteenth century.

From 1089, St Cuthbert's was owned by Holy Trinity Priory (see Holy Trinity, on Micklegate, p. 64). When the Priory was dissolved, in November 1539, the church passed to the Crown, which retained it until 1868 when it was given to the archbishop.

St Cuthbert's narrowly escaped demolition when four parishes of the area were merged under an Act of Union, passed in 1547. It was saved only when Sir Martyn Bowes (Lord Mayor of London in 1545 and a member of one of the most influential of York families) petitioned the city corporation on behalf of the church. His ancestor, Sir William Bowes, had paid for the building of the church during the first half of the previous century and it was Sir Martyn's own family's parish church (they lived in the house that is today the Black Swan Inn, just a hundred yards from St Cuthbert's). The Corporation finally agreed to preserve the church in 1561, but told Bowes that the parish was very poor and would need generous gifts if it was to continue to exist. In the end the other three adjacent parishes (All Saints', Peasholme Green, St Helen-on-the-Walls and St Mary's, Layerthorpe) were incorporated into St Cuthbert's in 1586.

Restorations in 1830, 1864 and 1911 have preserved the building. (It seems that the slightly alarming lean to the west which the tower has acquired over the years is little to worry about. Similarly the outward lean of the walls. An attempt to return the walls to the perpendicular was made in 1864 and was partially successful.)

Today the building is owned and used by the parish of St Michael-le-Belfry as a pastoral and administrative centre. Part of the inside has been converted into offices by the construction of a building within the building. The conversion has been carried out with taste and tact creating rather attractive though functional offices.

St Denys', on Walmgate

Only two of the six medieval churches which once stood on Walmgate have survived to the present day. The date of the first church on this site is not known, but the finding of two Anglo-Danish tombstones suggests that there was a church here before the Conquest. The earliest document referring to St Denys' is dated 1154.

St Denys' is perhaps the most altered church in the town. First mentioned in the twelfth century, the incumbency of St Denys' was an hereditary position. During the middle of the twelfth century the living of the parish was given by the incumbent priest, one Alexander, to St Leonard's Hospital (see Chapter Five). At the Dissolution of the hospital in 1539 the church passed to the Crown which kept it until 1868 when it was given to the archbishop.

A small building seems to have grown over the years into a cruciform church with a central tower, considerably larger than the present building. Transepts were added at the beginning of the thirteenth century and there was a thirteenth-century chancel which extended to the east of the present east end of the church.

Structurally, the church has had a rather pathetic history. After a long fight for survival, the spire finally went in 1798 following damage by a severe wind two decades earlier. It had been bombarded during the siege of 1644, and struck by lightning in 1730. The removal of the spire was part of a major rebuilding of the west end of the church necessitated by the collapse of the west wall, associated with the digging of a drain nearby (as part of a programme to attempt to reclaim the King's Fishpool — see Chapter One). The old nave was removed and the present nave represents part of what was the old chancel. The arch of the south door dates from the middle of the twelfth century. It was rescued and placed in the south aisle during the emergency work carried out in 1797–8. The present tower was added in 1847, the original tower having been removed in 1802 as a result of ground water threatening to undermine the foundations.

There are a number of interesting windows in St Denys', particularly the windows of the north aisle. Of the ten windows of this church, seven are fourteenth or fifteenth century. The centre light of the first window from the west of the north aisle is the oldest glass in any parish church in the city, dating from the early twelfth century or possibly from the eleventh. The east window of this aisle contains twenty fourteenth-century panels of a Jesse tree. The east window itself is fifteenth century and shows the figure of St Denys himself, the first Bishop of Paris and the patron saint of France.

The parish records of St Denys are complete from 1558, except, it is suspected, for one page. The page which records the burial of the highwayman Dick Turpin in 1739 in the churchyard of St George's has been removed. (St George's stood behind St Denys' on Fishergate. It was absorbed into the parish of St Denys in 1586 and by the eighteenth century the building had become derelict, although the churchyard itself continued to be used for burials, recorded in the registers of St Denys.)

St Helen's, in St Helen's Square

St Helen's, in spite of its urban setting and formal connections (as the official church of the Lord Mayor, whose residence, the Manor House, faces its entrance), is a bright and beautiful little church — one of the most popular in York.

The ground on which it stands has been a place of continuous worship for longer than any other piece of land in York. In early Roman times there was a temple to Diana on this site (a significant and imposing position, opposite the main gate into the walled fortress, which stood on the south-east side of what is now St Helen's Square). When the Roman Emperor Constantius Chlorus died in 306, he was succeeded by his son, Constantine the Great, who was proclaimed Emperor here in York. Whilst not the first Emperor to show Christian sympathies, Constantine was the first to declare Rome a Christian State. St Helen (or Helena) was Constantine's mother and she remains a favourite saint amongst Yorkshire people. (In Yorkshire there are more churches dedicated to St Helen than to any other saint, including St Mary and the apostles).

The present church dates from the thirteenth century and first appears in the records in 1235, but has undergone many changes since then. Like most of the churches in York it started life as a small rectangular Norman church, on the site of the present chancel. There is some surviving Norman stonework in the south wall of the nave. The church was considerably enlarged in the thirteenth century by extension westwards and by the addition of the north aisle. The south aisle was added in the fourteenth century. The octagonal font is twelfth century and may have belonged to an earlier church here. In the fifteenth century both aisles were widened and the west end of the nave was rebuilt with the addition of an octagonal drum tower, which is both a lantern tower and a bell turret.

The first record of the church is dated 1235 and at that time St Helen's was owned by a priory at Moxby in North Yorkshire. It remained the property of the priory until the Dissolution in 1539 when it passed to the Crown. The advowson was transferred to the archbishop in 1868.

The area around Stonegate was a centre for glass painters, stainers and leaders, working mainly on the Minster. St Helen's became the church of the Glass Makers Guild and much of its building and maintenance was endowed by them. Their arms can be seen in the west window of the south aisle (probably the work of one of York's many famous glass artists, Henry Gyles, working during the latter years of the seventeenth century).

Once the lights of St Helen's were filled with the colour of the finest of medieval glass. Most has been lost over the years and the little that remains is now incorporated into the west window, patched up with Victorian filling of no particular merit. The west window depicts St Helen in the third panel from the left, flanked to the left by the Virgin Mary, depicted as the Queen of Heaven, and to the right by Edward the Confessor. The first of the four panels is St William of York (see Chapter Two). The lower parts of the window depict the coronation of the Virgin Mary.

The east window is nineteenth century. The four figures are the evangelists. It is an attractive window, but deep blue predominates and, when a building was erected on Stonegate that came within a few feet of the east window, any hope of the morning sun illuminating the window in any sort of glory, vanished.

Originally, St Helen's stood on Stonegate, which ran down to meet Coney Street and Davygate just in front of where the Mansion House now stands. Between the entrance to St Helen's and the end of Stonegate was St Helen's churchyard, through which ran a narrow footpath joining Davygate and Blake Street. Over the years, burials had raised the ground level of the churchyard several feet above that of the surrounding streets, and indeed above the level of the church itself. Steps ran down from the churchyard to the church door.

In the 1730s the new Assembly Rooms opened and immediately became the fashionable centre of Georgian York. Unfortunately for the carriages that tried to approach the new Rooms along the busy Coney Street and Davygate routes from the south, the raised churchyard presented a barrier to transport. To ask the gentlefolk of Georgian York to walk a hundred yards through muddy streets was unthinkable. With the new Rooms about to be built (and, no doubt, the money that they could raise in mind) in October 1729, the vicar and the church-warden of St Helen's suggested to the corporation that they might like to purchase the churchyard. This the city did in September 1733, for ninety pounds. The ground was subsequently levelled, and St Helen's Square created.

This left the church without anywhere to bury its dead. By way of a replacement churchyard in 1745 St Helen's was given a plot of land a hundred yards to the south, on the west side of Davygate, created the previous year by the demolition of Davy Hall. (In medieval times, Davy Hall had been the only Lardiner's Prison in England, used solely for the imprisonment of persons breaking the forest laws.) Today this is a small, paved, shaded courtyard, lined with memorial stones, opening onto Davygate.

Much renovation of the church was carried out in the early years of the nineteenth century, and again in the 1850s and 1860s. In 1875 it was discovered that the lantern tower was about to collapse. The original tower (presumably dating from the middle of the fifteenth century) was removed and replaced with an exact copy.

That St Helen's has survived at all is remarkable. It has twice been condemned. In 1547 it was proposed that the parish should be united with one of the adjacent parishes — St Martin-le-Grand, St Michael-le-Belfry or St Sampson's. In preparation for this the church was somewhat prematurely sold. The union of the parishes was never enacted but by 1553 demolition work had actually started, St Helen's having been judged redundant by the property developers who had acquired the freehold to the land upon which it stood. A huge protest by the residents of the district and beyond managed to secure a reprieve at the eleventh hour. An Act of Parliament was passed, protecting the church of St Helen's, and authorizing rebuilding.

In 1910 the parish, amid much argument, resentment and animosity, was joined with that of St Martin-le-Grand on Coney Street. It was not long before the disused church fell into disrepair and decay. By 1920 it looked as if all that could be done with the site was to raze St Helen's in order to gainfully resell the land. However, the rector launched an appeal and through dedication, hard work and a local love of the building, money poured in. Building work commenced in 1921. Much of the interior of the modern church dates from this restoration. The church reopened in 1923.

On 29th April, 1942, central York suffered its only major air raid of the Second World War. St Martin-le-Grand was destroyed, gutted by an incendiary bomb. St Helen's assumed the role of parish church for both parishes and in 1954 the two parishes were formally united. Today St Helen's represents a city-centre parish with few residents, yet such is St Helen's popularity with church goers from both York and beyond that it is currently one of the best attended churches in the city.

St John the Evangelist, on Micklegate (Ousebridge)

In 1934 the parish of St John was united with that of Holy Trinity. The church became redundant and fell into decay. It remained in this state until 1955 when it was taken over by York Civic Trust. The Trust restored it and created a building that could be used for purposes other than worship a change of function being made easier by the absence of a structural chancel. The Civic Trust leased the church to the University, and it housed the Department of Architecture until 1968 when the department moved to Micklegate House. Since 1968 the church has been used as York Arts Centre, a small theatre. In 1963 St John's lost its churchyard when Micklegate was widened.

Although much of the exterior appears Victorian, the church itself dates from the twelfth century (the first known mention of St John's is in 1189), and there is twelfth-century stonework still to be seen inside (in what is now the foyer of the theatre, where a Norman window looks out upon a brick wall to the west). The majority of the interior stonework is Perpendicular in style. In 1850 the east end was shortened to enable North Street to be widened, and the wall at this end dates from that time. Inside, the easternmost arches of the east end betray this in their being narrower than the two adjacent pairs of arches.

The ceiling bosses are worth noting. Now tucked away in a storeroom, three of them depict arms of the influential Yorke family. A fourth depicts aggressive- and belligerent-looking sheep supporting the shield of the Company of the Merchants of the Staple of Calais (see Chapter One).

In medieval times the church was usually referred to as 'St John the Evangelist at Ouse Bridge end'. Its close proximity to the river has, on a number of occasions, presented problems. The whole area of the town flanking the Ouse on both banks is susceptible to flooding, particularly during the winter when heavy rains or melting snows in the Yorkshire Dales are forced through the bottle-neck of York. The floor of the church has been raised at least twice (in 1763 and 1819) following particularly severe floods.

The tower of St John's is interesting in that it is the only twelfth-century tower in the city. It was originally outside the church, which encompassed the tower in the fourteenth and fifteenth centuries as the aisles were extended to the west. It once carried a spire but this blew down in 1551. The spire was never replaced but the tower was repaired in brick only to be damaged again during the siege of the city in 1644. It was again repaired and the present wooden belfry dates from this work, completed by 1646. The belfry is thought to be the only surviving building in York erected during the period of Parliamentarian occupation of the city following the siege — the only touch of republicanism in a predominantly Royalist city.

The bells were rehung during the restoration of 1955. Two of the peal of eight were cast by the famous bell-master William Oldfield in 1633, and were first hung in the church when the belfry was built in 1646. Another three had been rescued during the siege of the city by Sir Thomas Fairfax and came from St Nicholas' Hospital (which was situated on the south side of Lawrence Street and was damaged beyond restoration during the siege). They are rung by students from the university each Sunday.

Some of the best of the medieval stained glass of St John's Church can now be seen in the west windows of the St John Chapel in the north transept of the Minster. The rest of the glass from St John's was given to the North Riding Mental Hospital, and the remainder of the fittings to various local churches.

ST LAWRENCE'S, ON LAWRENCE STREET

All that remains today of the medieval Church of St Lawrence is the tower. Sir Thomas Fairfax was married in this church, as was Sir John Vanbrugh to

Henrietta Maria Yarburgh of Heslington Hall. Until St Paul's, Heslington, was built in 1869, the parish of St Lawrence encompassed most of the large area around Heslington village. It was at one time one of the largest parishes in the city, having been united with the adjacent parishes of St Michael-without-Walmgate Bar, St Helen's on Fishergate, All Saints' on Fishergate, St Edward's on Lawrence Street and, following its destruction during the bombardment of Walmgate Bar in 1644, St Nicholas' on Walmgate. In fact, Sir Thomas Fairfax contributed to the destruction of the church he was married in by siting artillery in the churchyard, making it a prime target for the Royalist forces besieged in the city. In addition, he had placed his largest guns on Lamel Hill (in the grounds of the Retreat Hospital at the top of Heslington Road) putting St Lawrence's Church exactly in his line of fire.

The old church had been largely fourteenth-century, with some thirteenth- and twelfth-century stonework surviving until the demolition. St Lawrence's was rebuilt during the second half of the seventeenth century. All but the tower of the Restoration church was taken down during 1881–3 and replaced by the present Victorian building, constructed over the following decade. The architect was J.S. Hall who was brought from Canterbury to perform the task. The result has been described by Sir Nikolaus Pevsner as 'an extremely competent handling of the Early English style' (an opinion not shared by everyone).

The tower of the medieval church, which survived both the bombardment of 1644 and the Victorians, is of particular interest as one of the few remaining pieces of Norman architecture in York.

St Margaret's, on Walmgate

St Margaret's is first mentioned early in the third quarter of the twelfth century when it was given, together with the neighbouring Church of St Mary, to St Peter's Hospital (later St Leonard's, see Chapter Five). The two churches were united some time before 1308. (Of the site of St Mary's, or the extent of its parish, nothing is now known.) The church passed to the Crown at the Dissolution and was given to the archbishop in 1868. In 1586 the Church of St Peter-le-Willows (which stood next to Walmgate Bar, just inside the walls) was united with St Margaret's, and in 1955 the parish of St Margaret's was incorporated into that of St Denys'.

The building, set in one of the largest churchyards in the city, dates from the twelfth-century church but was mostly rebuilt in Victorian times (1851–2). The tower, which is brick, was erected in 1684 to replace an older tower and spire which collapsed twelve years earlier. St Margaret's is actually built on an extensive terrace above what was, for 800 years after the Conquest, the artificial lake of the King's Fishpool. One of the three (authorized) landings on the lake was at St Margaret's Church.

The rather splendid doorway of St Margaret's dates from the middle of the twelfth century. Recessed, and surmounted by a gable, it is carved with dragons, devils and a number of other distinctly un-Christian symbols, including the signs of the Zodiac. This door came from the Hospital of St Nicholas on Lawrence Street, some time during the Republic, following the destruction of the latter during the siege of York in 1644. Currently St Margaret's is being used as a storehouse by the Theatre Royal.

ST MARTIN-CUM-GREGORY, ON MICKLEGATE

St Martin's was owned by the adjacent Holy Trinity Priory, and dates from the time of the building of the priory. In the late eleventh century the priory was given to the Monastery of Marmoutier (see Holy Trinity, on Micklegate, p. 64) hence the dedication to St Martin of Tours. St Martin is a favourite saint in the city of York. A former soldier in the Roman army, where he served under Constantine the Great (who influenced him to no small degree), in 371 he was enthroned as Bishop of Tours, and subsequently founded the Abbey of Marmoutier, just outside the city of Tours. (He is also the patron saint of unreformed drunks and publicans!)

St Martin-cum-Gregory is one of the six surviving York churches mentioned in the Domesday Book. (There has been some debate over the years as to whether the St Martin's Church mentioned in the Book is this church or St Martin-le-Grand on Coney Street. It is now agreed that the Domesday St Martin's is almost certainly this church.) On 4th June, 1137, the original building was destroyed, along with most of the rest of the city, by a huge fire. The rebuilt chancel dates from early in the thirteenth century, but in its present form the building is mostly fourteenth and early fifteenth century. Of the pre-Conquest church only part of the foundations survive. Although considerably altered during a Victorian restoration between 1840 and 1846, the church has retained much of its original character. The vestry dates from this work of the mid-1840s.

St Martin's might not have survived at all — demolition of the building was started in 1548 and the roof had been removed before the work was halted by the Corporation following petitioning by powerful parishioners. It was decided to unite the parish with that of St Gregory (which stood on the north side of Barker Lane, the small lane joining Micklegate and Toft Green and then known as Gregory Lane). Under the Act signed by Edward VI later that year it was St Gregory's that disappeared. St Martin-cum-Gregory is the only one of York's churches to retain the double-barrelled name of a united benefice.

The tower, built in the mid-fifteenth century, looks to be brick, but this is only a façade. The brick facing to the tower was added in 1677. (The Gothic embellishments are Victorian.) Originally the tower carried a wooden spire. It blew down in 1551, was patched up but was finally removed during the Restoration in 1677. On the south wall there is an interesting set of 'charity boards'.

When Henry Tudor's army defeated Richard III, in 1485, Tudor followed his seizure of the kingdom with a 'character assassination' of the former king. All complimentary or neutral references to either the former king or the Neville family (with whom he grew up) were to be erased from the country. The efficiency of Tudor's administration left little material evidence of Richard, even in this, his own city. One place where Richard's arms can be seen in York is in the west window of the south aisle of St Martin-cum-Gregory, of which Richard became patron in 1476. His arms, a white boar with fearsome looking tusks, are in the lower centre of this small window.

In 1745, Charles Edward Stuart gathered an army in Scotland and marched south on England to claim the throne as his birth right. Many people in the north of England gathered behind him and as he marched south his support was such that he was assured of winning, probably without even a fight. By the time the army reached Derby self-doubt had crept in. The 'Bonnie Prince' decided to turn back. Pursued by the English, many of his followers were killed. Those who surrendered to capture in or around York were taken into custody. The problem for the militia was what to do with such a large number of prisoners. St Martin-cum-Gregory was requisitioned as a temporary prison. In the window of the north aisle the prisoners carved their names with a diamond. They remain to be read today.

There is much interesting painted glass in the church, some medieval, some later. The east window of the south aisle contains fourteenth-century glass in the subdued colours typical of much of York's glass. The central light is St Martin himself, portrayed on horseback sharing his cloak with a poor man.

In the north aisle of St Martin's is a memorial window by William Peckitt, to his daughters, both of whom died young. William Peckitt was one of York's best-known glass artists and was responsible for much of the eighteenth-century Minster glass. St Martin's was Peckitt's parish church. The west window of the north aisle is all from Peckitt's workshop. The central panel, portraying an urn, is a memorial to Peckitt, who died in 1795. It was painted and installed by his wife, Mary. William Peckitt himself is buried in the chancel, and another famous York glass artist, Henry Gyles (d.1709) is buried in the churchyard.

From medieval times until 1828, St Martin's churchyard (or, in later years when the churchyard proved too small and overflowed, Micklegate itself) was the site of the wholesale butter market for the whole of Northumbria, which was held on all days except Sundays, the main trading days being Tuesdays, Thursdays and Saturdays, the days on which the domestic food market was held on Pavement. At its height, approaching five million pounds of butter passed through St Martin's churchyard each year (chiefly for export to London).

St Martin-cum-Gregory was united with the adjacent Holy Trinity Church in 1953 and is now deconsecrated. Since restoration of the fabric of the building in 1971 it has housed a variety of occasional secular uses.

ST MARTIN-LE-GRAND, ON CONEY STREET

St Martin-le-Grand was one of the most beautiful and, in its time, one of the most influential churches in York. Records of St Martin's date from the second half of the twelfth century but there was almost certainly a church on this site before the Conquest, and its parish encompasses the Guildhall and the city's centres of urban and fiscal life. (The church contained a pew reserved for the use of the Lord Mayor and his guests.)

The present building dates from the late twelfth century when it consisted of a small hall. It was enlarged during the following two centuries but in the first half of the fifteenth century the whole church was extensively rebuilt, as a result of a bequeathal in the will of the vicar, Robert Semar (dated 7th June, 1443). Semar insisted that the new church must be completed within seven years of the reading of his will. The rebuilding was carried out under the direction of Robert Couper, the mason responsible for the construction of the original Guildhall, who received his last payment for the work six years and two months later.

The one serious air raid that the city centre of York experienced during the Second World War, on the night of 29th April, 1942, destroyed both St Martin-le-Grand and the Guildhall. The Guildhall was rebuilt completely (see Chapter Five) but only the south side of St Martin's was restored (between 1961–8 by York Civic Trust; the architect was George Pace), the south aisle and the tower having escaped damage in the raid. In 1968, the south aisle of St Martin's was reopened as a Chapel of Remembrance, to the memory of those who fell in the wars of 1914–18 and 1939–45. The north side of the church, judged beyond restoration, was paved and turned into a garden dedicated to the memory of those who lost their lives in these two wars.

What was formerly the west window of St Martin's (also donated to the church by Semar in 1437) was removed and buried for safety during the 1939–45 war. Now in the south transept of the church, it is one of the finest fifteenth-century lights in the city. The dedication of the church is to St Martin of Tours (see St Martin-cum-Gregory, p. 73). The window portrays thirteen scenes from his life.

There are a number of splendid panels of painted glass in the south wall, the finest among them depicting St Barbara (fourth window from the west, with tower and palm), St George (third window from the west, with dragon) and the Trinity (second window from the left, with the four evangelists). The Trinity is an unusual subject among the examples of pre-Reformation glass in the city, most images portraying God having been destroyed during the iconoclastic fervour of the Republic. All three lights are fifteenth century and were restored when the church was repaired during the 1960s. During the restoration of these windows, fourteenth-century glass was found among the fifteenth-century windows. Out of this the first window from the east in the south wall was constructed. The east window itself was designed, painted and built by a famous local glass artist, Harry Stammers (who died in 1969). It portrays the towers and spires of the churches of York amidst the air raid of 1942.

Coney Street outside St Martin's Church was the site of the malt market in medieval times, held on Tuesdays, Thursdays and Saturdays — the same days as the food market was held on Pavement.

The parish of St Martin was absorbed into its sister church, St Helen's, in 1954 — an ironic twist of fate, for St Helen's had previously been all but swallowed up by St Martin's in 1910 (see p. 68).

ST MARY'S, BISHOPHILL JUNIOR

The tower of St Mary's is the oldest enclosed building in York, with the exception of the ruined Anglian tower behind the library, and the church contains much of the Norman architecture left in the city. The north wall as far as the chancel, and the wall between the nave and the tower date from the time of the Conquest or very shortly after. Stones found in and around the church confirm that there has been a church on this site at least since the days of Alcuin in the eighth century, and it has even been suggested that the original Minster, built by Edwin, might have been on or close to this site. At the end of the eleventh century the church comprised the tower and a small cell which is now the nave. The north aisle was added in the twelfth century, and the chancel early in the thirteenth century. The south aisle is fourteenth century, as is the chapel in the north-east corner.

Standing on a small moraine above the river Ouse, the church was originally known as St Mary's Bishop's, as it belonged to the Archbishop of York (and later to the Dean and Chapter). It was thus distinguished from the older church, St Mary's Senior. (St Mary's Senior, the road in front of which has now become known as Bishophill Senior, was demolished only recently. Parts of this church were rescued and incorporated into St Clement's on Scarcroft Road and in the Church of the Holy Redeemer on Boroughbridge Road.) Today only the churchyard of St Mary's Senior survives. The road running past St Mary's Bishop's became known as Bishophill Junior — the name it retains to this day.

Of the city's churches, St Mary's is one of the most attractive. It is compact and lacks any pretension (in spite of 'restoration' work carried out by Atkinson and Atkinson during the 1860s, which involved the destruction and rebuilding of much of the south aisle). Unlike most of York's churches, but like the neighbouring churches of St Martin-cum-Gregory, All Saints' on North Street and Holy Trinity, St Mary's has a structurally distinct chancel.

ST MARY'S, ON CASTLEGATE

Shortly after Cnut came to power in 1016 a minster was built on this site. An inscribed stone, recording the dedication, was found during restoration work carried out in 1868 and the church is recorded in the Domesday Book.

A little stonework from the original church survives. It was a small aisleless hall, about twenty-one feet wide. The church was enlarged over the following three centuries but, in the fifteenth century, St Mary's was extensively restored and rebuilt, the final additions being the tower and the westernmost bays of the aisles. Since then it has been little changed and is one of the least altered medieval churches in York.

An unusual feature of St Mary's is its octagonal tower and spire. The spire, like that of All Saints' on North Street, is surprisingly wide for the tower on which it stands and, again like All Saints', may reflect the position of St Mary's next to a friary, in this case the House of the Franciscans, the main gate to which stood opposite St Mary's on the site now occupied by Castlegate House.

For a short while during the reign of Edward II, when the wars with Scotland resulted in the government moving to York for convenience, St Mary's was the home of His Majesty's Exchequer.

The church was combined with St Michael's on Spurriergate in 1885 and the two churches fully united in 1935. By the 1960s, however, St Mary's had fallen into disuse. Today it is being used as a museum of the social and economic history of York.

St Michael and All Angels', on Spurriergate

A church has stood on this site since before the Conquest. It was given to St Mary's Abbey by William II in the first year of his reign, as part of the grant of land which, added to the previous gifts from Count Alan of Richmond and from the archbishop, allowed the founding of the great Benedictine house. By reason of being designated as belonging to the Abbey the church is not mentioned in the Domesday Book. The parish of St Michael has the only surviving pre-Reformation accounts in York, dating from 1518. Along with the rest of the property owned by St Mary's, the church passed to the Crown at the Dissolution of the Abbey in November 1539, and in 1868 was given to the Archbishop. In 1885 it was annexed to St Mary's Church on Castlegate, and the two parishes were fully united in 1935.

The structure of the present church dates from the early eleventh century and was enlarged by the addition of aisles in the twelfth century, and by the extension of these during the fourteenth century. In the fifteenth century the church was remodelled and an aisled church with a clerestory was created.

The demands of traffic using both Spurriergate and Ousegate had, by the early nineteenth century, created pressure for the widening of both streets. The result was an extensive rebuilding of the church carried out during 1821. The clerestory was removed and the church re-roofed. The whole of both the south and east walls were completely rebuilt with the church seven feet shorter in length to the east.

Restoration was carried out in 1867 when much of the north wall was rebuilt. St Michael's is one of the most interesting of the churches of inner York. Almost square in shape, the gracile columns give the building a neo-Classical atmosphere.

The columns are particularly interesting. The quatrefoil piers with waterleaf capitals (not common in churches but beloved by the designers of Cistercian architecture) are a Norman design copied in the fifteenth century. The tower is fifteenth century, but was shortened in 1965 when further restoration work was carried out. It was as part of this work that the majority of the internal fittings of the church were removed.

Much of the stained glass in the south aisle dates from the middle of the fifteenth century and some is amongst the most valued stained glass in the city. It was removed during the Second World War and when it was reinserted in 1948, many mistakes accumulated by ignorant or uncareful maintenance over the centuries were rectified (although some windows remain somewhat jumbled). The east window of the south aisle contains a light depicting the Virgin surrounded with a golden halo and holding a misplaced (bearded!) infant Christ. Known as 'The Woman Clothed with the Sun', the window is very unusual in that it contains 'jewels' — pieces of coloured glass cut with facets and glued to the window. There are similar jewels of glass in the St Cuthbert Window in the south choir transept of the Minster. (The best-known work of this type is that by John Prudde in the Beauchamp Chapel of St Mary's, Warwick, which is contemporary with this window, and it is possible that Prudde's workshop, or a student of Prudde, was responsible for the jewelled lights in St Michael's.) The third panel of the east window of the south aisle depicts 'Lucifer Falling from Heaven' (an extremely rare subject for church glass). The window also depicts eight of the nine orders of angels. In the centre window of the south wall are two panels from a Jesse tree (the ancestral tree of Christ from Jesse, the father of King David).

The clock on the north wall of St Michael's is interesting. Restored in 1896 the workings are now housed in a glass case.

In the days when the food market was held on Pavement, at the east end of All Saints' Church, business was regulated by the ringing of the bells of St Michael's (at eight o'clock each working day), a role the church assumed from St William's Chapel (see Ouse Bridge, Chapter Five). Evensong was heralded by a peal of bells, and under local law trading had then to stop. The practice was discontinued in 1931 but resumed in 1986. Today the bells are rung by a computer.

St Michael-le-Belfry, on Petergate

All the medieval churches in York have architecturally evolved over a long period of time, usually starting as a small chapel, evolving by way of a cruciform church to eventually become a rectangular shape as the corners of the cross were built up. St Michael-le-Belfry, which is wholly Tudor and built in the style of the late Perpendicular period, is not therefore strictly medieval. It differs from earlier York churches in that it was all built at one time (between 1525 and 1536) in the rectangular shape which by then had become the accepted and expected shape for a York church. St Michael-le-Belfry presumably takes its name from its proximity to the south-west tower of the Minster, which houses the Minster's peal of twelve bells. The architect in the sixteenth century was a well-known York master mason, John Foreman, although the west front of the present church dates from Victorian restorations carried out in 1853 and 1884.

The Tudor church was built on the site of an earlier church, mentioned in the Domesday Book and owned by the Minster. It was demolished as a result of neglect by the Dean and Chapter.

It has been argued that the north–west to south–east alignment of St Michael's betrays the antiquity of the site as a place of worship. This is the line of the old Roman *Via Principalis* suggesting that St-Michael-le-Belfry predates the building of the adjacent, and dominating Minster built along the conventional east–west axis. Writing in the eleventh century, the biographer of St John of Beverley, who was Bishop of York 705–18, tells of St John worshipping in a church referred to as that of St Michael the Archangel, usually assumed to have been here. It has even been suggested that St Michael's may stand on the site of Edwin's original Minster, built when the Roman headquarters occupied much of the area of the present Minster.

The reredos was carved by John Etty in the first decade of the eighteenth century, and installed in 1712. Originally the centre panel contained the script of the Ten Commandments. It was replaced in 1926 by the present copy of Velázquez's *Adoration of the Shepherds* (the original of which is in the National Gallery). The gallery, originally carrying the organ, was erected in 1785 although the fine arms supported by lion and unicorn date from the early eighteenth century and the reign of Queen Anne.

Most of the glass in St Michael's dates from the building of the church and is by Anglo-Flemish artists (who also built the windows of the south transept of the Minster, including the famous Rose Window). Good glass of this period is extremely rare, and the windows of St Michael's are very fine. Parts of the east window of the chancel are fourteenth century and depict St Peter and St Paul, the Coronation of the Virgin, the Annunciation, the Nativity, the Crucifixion and the Resurrection. The borders contain monkeys, bells and birds and are similar to windows in the nave of the Minster. The east window of the north aisle also predates the present church. The medieval glass looks to have come from several windows — probably from the church which stood on this site before the present Tudor church.

The lower panels of the second window from the east in the south aisle show the donor of the window, his wife, and what appear to be their thirty-two children (although it has been suggested that they might represent a school, or perhaps a sponsoring body such as a guild).

The windows of the north wall were created when the church was restored during the period 1958–60.

In 1586, St Michael's absorbed the parish of the ancient church of St Wilfrid's which stood on the site now occupied by the Assembly Rooms. St Michael-le-Belfrey is the church in which Guy Fawkes was baptised (on 15th April, 1570). (Fawkes was almost certainly born in a house in Stonegate, the lease for which, made out to his mother, still exists, although Youngs Hotel, opposite St Michael's Church and built over a century after Fawkes' death, is one of several places which claim to have been his birthplace.)

St Olave's, on Marygate

St Olave's Church was founded by Siward, Earl of Northumbria three decades before his death in 1055 (see Chapter One) in memory of his friend, Olaf Haroldsson, to whom the church is dedicated. (Olave is an anglicised form of the Norwegian name Olaf.) King Olaf was killed by his own guard in an uprising in 1030. He was in his mid-thirties and King of Norway, trying to convert the country to Christianity (hence his canonization, which took place only two years later). He and Siward had come to know each other many years before and when Olaf died, Siward had a church built and dedicated it to God and to his friend and opponent. When Siward himself died, his heart, if his instructions were carried out, was cut out of his body and buried under the altar of St Olave's Church. The church stands on the perimeter of the site of *Earlsburh*, Siward's stronghold.

St Olave's became the property of Count Alan of Brittany when William I installed Alan as Earl of Richmond. In 1080 St Olave's was given by the Count to a monk called Stephen who was attached to the Benedictine monasteries at Whitby and Lastingham. A further gift, eight years later, of four acres of land adjacent to the east side of the church (from the archbishop), followed by further gifts from William II in 1089, led to the founding of the Benedictine House dedicated to St Mary, of which St Olave's became the abbey chapel. The abbey occupied the ground today known as the Museum Gardens.

St Olave's became the subject of dispute between St Mary's Abbey and the Dean and Chapter of the Minster over who should pay for its maintenance (one of many sources of animosity between the rival institutions). Like St Nicholas' (dependent on Holy Trinity Priory) and St Michael-le-Belfry (dependent on the Chapter of the Minster), the upkeep of St Olave's was for a long time ignored by the abbey, for reasons of penny-pinching. Internal arguments broke out between the prior and the sacrist of the abbey as to who was responsible. In the end the abbey solved its internal dispute by arguing that, because the church was used by local lay persons, it was a parish church and therefore the responsibility of the Chapter of the Minster. The Dean and Chapter, predictably, disagreed.

The bickering degenerated to such an extent even the Pope himself was drawn into the argument. The Pope intervened in 1404 and ordered that the upkeep of the church should be paid for by the parishioners who lived in the vicinity of St Mary's. It seems a particularly harsh decision against the powerless parishioners in order to placate the powerful Abbey and Minster. St Olave's was not a parish church (the congregation had no rights as to the management of the church or the government of the parish) but merely a chapel of St Mary's Abbey.

St Olave's was eventually given parochial status half a century later (on 24th October, 1466, by Archbishop George Neville) in a compromise agreement made between the Minster and the abbey. The abbey was to provide materials and money for immediate repairs to the church, after which the maintenance and upkeep would become the sole responsibility of the parishioners. All future gifts and legacies would pass to the parish. However, the tithes from lands owned by the church would continue to pass to the sacrist of the abbey. (These were substantial — St Olave's owned farms in Fulford, Askham Bryan, Knapton, Upper Poppleton and Nether Poppleton, as well as property in Clifton and Rawcliffe.) On 3rd March, 1466, the abbey handed over materials for the repair (including twenty large oak tree trunks) together with vestments, a silver chalice, silver plate and ten pounds in gold, at a ceremony held in the Chapel of St Mary-at-the-Gate (see below), and thereby rid itself of financial responsibility for St Olave's.

The Abbey fell at the Dissolution, on the 29th November, 1539, but because it was now a parish church, St Olave's survived. The advowson of the church seems to have passed to the Crown, and from the Crown to the archbishop in 1558. In 1586 the parish of St Giles (after which Gillygate takes its name) was merged into that of St Olave's. In 1573 the living of the parish passed into private hands and various families held the advowson until 1871 when the de Grey family and the archbishop exchanged St Olave's for a country parish. It has remained in the hands of the archbishop since then.

Structurally, St Olave's is something of a puzzle. During the siege of York in 1644, guns are thought to have been placed on the roof of the church, making it a prime target. (There is a slight puzzle concerning this. The contemporary report describes the guns as Parliamentarian — which cannot have been the case.) The church suffered greatly as a result and if there are any remains of Siward's original church (other than the foundations) they are difficult to find today. Through want of the funds to rebuild, it was temporarily patched up during the reign of Charles II but remained in need of restoration for several decades.

St Olave's was eventually almost totally rebuilt on a more modest scale during 1720-1, following an offer of stone for the work to be taken from St Mary's Abbey (an offer which was initially made two decades earlier by Queen Anne). It is from this work that the church takes its present form, with the exceptions of the Victorian Lady Chapel (originally built as a vestry) and the present vestry built in the first decade of the twentieth century. Prior to the rebuilding, the church had a clerestory.

Adjacent to the tower of St Olave's and the gate of St Mary's Abbey there used to stand a small chapel known as St Mary-at-the-Gate, built for the use of visitors to the Abbey. A little of the stonework survives.

The east window of St Olave's is fifteenth-century glass. However, in a city full of fifteenth-century glass of the highest standard perhaps the most interesting of St Olave's stained glass is in the Lady Chapel, where a pair of lights depict the Annunciation of the Virgin, with the Crucifixion in the background and a Holy Ghost represented by a dove above the Archangel Gabriel. It is a fine example of the work of a modern glass artist and is by Harry Stammers.

William Etty, York's most famous artist, is buried in St Olave's churchyard, adjacent to Museum Gardens from where the tomb can be seen.

St Sampson's, on Church Street

This is probably a pre-Conquest site and an early eleventh-century cross was found being used as a structural stone in a house in Newgate, behind the church. Excavation of the site revealed a Norman wall. The earliest known written evidence of a church on this site dates from 1154, when King Stephen gave St Saviour's and the nearby St Bennet's (which stood in Grape Lane and had vanished by the middle of the fourteenth century) to Pontefract Priory. By the end of the first quarter of the thirteenth century it had passed to the archdeacons of Richmond. Early in the fourteenth century it was passed by the king to the archbishop, but in 1383 the church passed back to the Crown. During a visit to York in 1394, Richard II gave the advowson of the church to the College of the Vicars'-Choral (see St William's College, Chapter Five) who retained the church until 1934 when it passed once again to the archbishop.

Plans for the parish to be merged with that of St Helen's in 1549 were never carried through as a result of an Act of Parliament passed to save St Helen's (see St Helen's, p. 68) but in 1886 St Sampson's absorbed the parish of Holy Trinity, King's Square (which was demolished in 1937).

The nave, chancel and aisles of the church were rebuilt between 1444 and 1450 (the result of a bequeathal) and the tower was added in 1485. The present building cannot, however, really be thought of as old. In 1843 there was a fire in the church. It was decided that all that could be done was to rebuild the fabric of the building from scratch. Most of the present St Sampson's dates from this second rebuilding in 1848 (though the door is the fifteenth-century door). Nevertheless, the Victorian rebuilding was true to the original Perpendicular style and the church is by no means nineteenth-century Gothic. The tower is the original fifteenth-century structure (apart from a little repair work following damage during the siege of 1644, and some modern patching).

The windows are mostly early twentieth century, with some Victorian and a little seventeenth-century glass. Today it is used as a social centre, which is very much true to the spirit of use to which the medieval churches were put (between periods of worship) when originally built. It is a rather picturesque little church in the centre of the busiest part of the city.

Part of the east side of Church Street was within the churchyard and still belongs to St Sampson's. The boundary can be seen marked by a brass strip set in the pavement.

ST SAVIOUR'S, ST SAVIOURGATE

Originally known as St Saviour-in-the-Marsh, the church stood on the edge of swampy ground which extended from the Foss to the south. This unpleasant sounding area was, in medieval times, one of the most fashionable parts of the town and St Saviour's was the parish church of many wealthy merchants. The church stands on the site of a pre-Conquest church and Saxon oak coffins have been found beneath the building. It is first mentioned as part of the gifts of lands and advowsons by William II to the newly founded St Mary's Abbey in, or about, 1089. (It is probable that this was a confirmation of a gift of the church to the abbey made by William I, and that its ownership by St Mary's is the reason for St Saviour's not being specifically mentioned in the Domesday Book.)

The entire church was built during the first half of the fifteenth century, the tower and spire being the last part to be started, in 1458. (The spire blew down in 1822.) At the Dissolution, as part of the abbey, the church was plundered and the lead removed from the roof. Within two years the building was reported to be in a state of decay, but was repaired, and in 1586 the church absorbed the adjacent parishes of St John, Hungate, and St Andrew. At some time the living passed from the Crown into private hands. The advowson passed to the archbishop in 1933.

During 1844–5 both aisles were extensively rebuilt and in 1867 the interior was redesigned. The church became redundant in 1954 when the parish was united with that of All Saints' on Pavement, and the fittings were removed the following year when the building was leased to the Corporation. For a while it was used as a storeroom by the Castle Museum, but recently it was taken over by York Archeological Trust who are currently using the building as an exhibition centre.

A Roman dedication stone, found in King's Square and originally part of one of the four gates to the Roman fortress, dating from *c.* 108AD. The complete inscription is believed to have been 'The Emperor Caesar Nerva Trajan Augustus, son of the deified Nerva, Conqueror of Dacia, *pontifex maximus*; in his twelfth year of tribunician power, six times acclaimed *imperator*; five times *consul*; father of his country, built this gate by the agency of the 9th Legion Hispana'.

CHAPTER FOUR

A SHORT GUIDE TO THE CITY'S DEFENCES

There are 108 walled towns in England and Wales. At a little less than three miles in circumference, of which just over two miles are actual stonework (the rest being natural defences in the form of rivers and the site of a former lake) York's city walls are the longest of these. They are also the best preserved. The four main gates (known in the city as 'bars') are unique and are more like castle gate-houses than city gates. The present medieval walls enclose an area of 263 acres (about 106 hectares) of which the site of the original Roman fort, from which the town evolved, accounts for approximately twenty per cent. Built of pale honey-coloured magnesium limestone, brought by river barges from quarries outside Sherburn-in-Elmet and Tadcaster, they make an impressive sight, particularly on a sunny spring morning when the grass-covered earthen ramparts are covered with a splendid sea of daffodils.

York's city walls developed from those surrounding the Roman fort on the east bank of the Ouse. The fort was built in a rectangle aligned north–east to south–west, along the line of the river. Originally a wooden palisade, this was replaced by a stone wall under the the orders of the Emperor Trajan early in the second century AD. The walls were considerably rebuilt and strengthened a hundred years later when the Roman Emperor Severus moved his Court to York, and the following century two successive emperors, Constantius Chlorus and his son Constantine the Great, both of whom were for a while based in York, rebuilt and strengthened the walls yet again. It is from this latest period, at the beginning of the fourth century, that most of the surviving parts of the Roman wall date.

The present medieval wall follows the former perimeter of the Roman fort from its south-west corner in the modern Museum Gardens to a point just past Monk Bar. From here the medieval wall leaves the course of the Roman fortress defences. As a Roman civilian town evolved on the west bank of the Ouse, that too was protected by a town wall, and a stretch of the medieval wall follows the line of this Roman wall between Micklegate Bar and Lendal Bridge (see p. 95). The Roman fort and settlements are described in Chapters One and Two.

With the expansion of York during Anglo-Saxon and Danish times, the area enclosed by the wall was extended on both sides of the Ouse to accommodate the growing urban community, reaching the present circumference of the town's defences some time before the Norman Conquest. The Normans enlarged the ramparts of the walls to a height of twenty-five feet and a thickness at their base of a hundred feet. They also dug a ditch around the outside, ten feet deep and fifty feet wide. By the year 1100, the defences comprised a ditch and rampart surmounted for the most part by a wooden palisade, except where the Roman and Anglo-Saxon stone wall remained. Stone gates were first erected in this wall towards the end of the eleventh century. The oldest post-Conquest stonework is the outer arch of Bootham Bar, built around the year 1100, but the wooden gate-houses at Micklegate Bar and Walmgate Bar were replaced in stone shortly after this. By 1200 all four bars were of stone and had been extended upwards to create a gate-house above the arch.

Perhaps the most unusual feature of York's medieval walls is that they stand on an earthen-work rampart — the only city walls in England to have been built in this way. Along the western and northern stretches of the wall, from Micklegate Bar to past Monk Bar, the wall follows the line of the Roman defences and is built on the Roman rampart, heightened during Anglo-Saxon, Viking, Norman and medieval times. The rampart between Walmgate and Micklegate was most probably erected early in the period of the Norman occupation, shortly after 1070.

The surviving rampart is up to a hundred feet thick and thirty feet high, and in the Middle Ages was surrounded by a ditch or moat. Once sixty feet wide and ten feet deep, most of the ditch is now filled in (although some remains can still be seen along Lord Mayor's Walk). It is thought that the pre-Norman stretches of the ditch were, for the most part, dry. The base of the Norman rampart (that is, from Foss Islands Road to Micklegate Bar) was, however, at the level of the medieval Foss and was water-filled. (The fishing rights to the moat in the Walmgate area were let by the council.) A ditch also ran around the inside of much of the wall. Its purpose seems to have been for drainage of the town and in places, in common with other drainage ditches in the town, was referred to as the King's or Queen's Ditch or Dyke. In the Aldwark area, where it was known as the Werkdyke, the inner moat seems to have been substantial and was created when the Norman rampart was thrown up from the inside as well as from the outside of the wall.

It is not clear when the work of replacing the palisade with a stone wall was begun, but it was most probably during the reign of Henry III, early in the second half of the thirteenth century and shortly after the replacement of the wooden castle keep with the present stone structure known as Clifford's Tower (see p. 101–4).

The building and maintenance of the stone walls was an expensive undertaking. To help with the funding a tax, known as murage, was levied on all animals, vehicles and their cargoes entering and leaving the city. (It was one of the few taxes from which the Dean and Chapter of the Minster were not exempt.) In 1305 the people of York petitioned Edward I, asking him to recover murage to the value of seventy-three pounds which the mayor, one Henry Lespicer, had appropriated. Presumably as a result of the subsequent action taken by Parliament, the walls were strengthened in 1308.

Between 1311 and 1312 the walls were heightened and strengthened still further, following a four-month stay in the city by Edward II. The king was anxious about the possibility of an invasion by a Scots army. In fact, the city has come under attack from besieging armies on a number of occasions since the Conquest, particularly during the fourteenth-century wars with the Scots-Norman barons.

Determined to recover the disastrous losses incurred by his father to Robert Bruce, the fourteen-year-old Edward III set out in the summer of 1327, with his advisers and a large army, to invade Scotland. At Durham they received news that the Scots had launched a counter-invasion and, having crossed the Solway, were making their way down the west coast — a tactic they had used with good effect in 1319 when the besieging of York had led to the defeat of an English army in the Battle of the White (see Chapter One). Fearful for the city, and particularly for his mother, brother and sisters who were staying in York awaiting Edward's return, the young king wrote to the City Corporation from Durham, on 15th July, 1327, instructing the mayor and bailiffs to engage all available labour to strengthen the walls, 'on the forfeiture of everything you can forfeit to us, immediately at sight of these presents, without excuse or delay'.

It is known that even after this work the wooden palisade in the Walmgate area had still not been replaced in stone. This was eventually started in 1345. (The contract for this work, drawn up between the Corporation and a master mason, Thomas de Staunton, still exists.)

The final result of the building programmes of Henry III, his son, grandson and great-grandson, are the medieval stone walls which encircle York today, completed by the middle of the fourteenth century. Today the height of the wall above the top of the rampart varies, and in many places the height inside is less than that of the outer face. In general the walls stand to a height of about thirteen feet above the rampart and are approximately six feet thick.

The greatest siege the city's defences have had to face came in the late spring and early summer of 1644. Combined Parliamentarian forces 30,000 men strong encircled the city, during which time the walls and bars (particularly Walmgate Bar) were badly damaged by cannon fire. The physical defences held out (although York surrendered on not ungenerous terms after three months). The repairs effected to the walls after the battering they received in 1644 can be seen in a number of places. The cost was born, in part, from assets seized by Parliament from Royalist estates.

The medieval walls do not completely encircle the town, and never did. There is no wall or rampart along what is today Foss Islands Road, where a marsh and shallow lake (from which the road takes its name) provided a natural defence. The lake, known as the King's Fishpool, was created in the late 1060s or early 1070s as a consequence of the Foss being dammed to flood a moat around the castle. (See York Castle, p. 100.)

The second gap in the walls is between Fishergate on the east side of the Foss, and Baile Hill on the west side of the Ouse. The triangle of land between the confluence of the two rivers provided the ideal site for the medieval castle. The castle in part provided the defences for this approach to the town. A tower and a twenty yard stretch of the wall to the west of the castle were demolished in 1826.

There are two other short stretches where the medieval wall has been lost. A hundred foot stretch between the Museum Gardens Lodge and the start of the Roman portion of the walls in the City Library garden had disappeared before 1575, and a hundred yard stretch of wall adjacent to Bootham Bar was demolished in the early 1830s to make way for St Leonard's Place (see p. 128).

It is only by good luck that the walls still stand at all. In the late eighteenth century, when they had become redundant for defensive purposes and were viewed as nothing more than a nuisance to travellers, there were several moves to pull down long stretches. Doubts were raised as to whether the Corporation had the authority to order this and so, in 1798, a committee was set up to investigate the legal ramblings. They reported that the city had no right to demolish the walls. As a result the Corporation petitioned Parliament in the May of 1800 for an Act enabling the destruction of the medieval defences. The request was vetoed in Parliament (possibly by the intervention of George III himself) and another Act was passed specifically protecting the ancient defences of the town. The Corporation chose to ignore the law and started to demolish the walls.

The walls survived due to the farsightedness of one person — Archbishop Markham, by then an elderly man. At the time he was seen by many as a selfish conservative who could not accept progress and who had no consideration for the views of the majority. The archbishop found a legal loophole and sued the Corporation for the revenue which could have been collected at Skeldergate Postern during the Lammastide Fair (held at the beginning of each August to celebrate the start of the harvest season). Postern towers existed at seven strategic points around the walls. (Four have survived.) Posterns were minor gates into the walled city (literally, back doors) which were blocked by earth and rubble during times of siege, rather than being manned as were the bars. Skeldergate Postern, together with its tower, known as the Crane Tower, had been demolished by the Corporation in February 1807, and the case came before Durham Assizes that July. Markham won. The city walls seemed to have found an immovable champion when, the following year, at the age of eighty-eight, Archbishop Markham died.

Two other postern towers, at Layerthorpe and Castlegate, and the barbicans of Bootham, Monk and Micklegate Bars, were all knocked down in the early

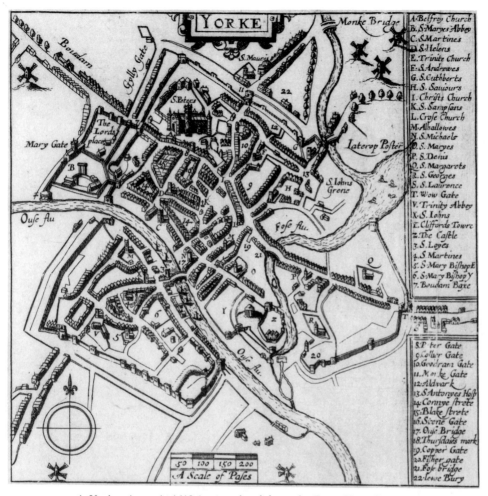

Legend columns on the map:

A. Belfrey Church
B. S. Maryes Abbey
C. S. Martines
D. S. Helens
E. Trinite Church
F. S. Andrewes
G. S. Cuthberts
H. S. Saviours
I. Christs Church
K. S. Sampsons
L. Crose Church
M. Alhallowes
N. S. Michaels
O. S. Maryes
P. S. Denis
Q. S. Margarets
R. S. Georges
S. S. Laurence
T. Wow Gate
V. Trinity Abbey
X. S. Iohns
Y. Cliffords Towre
1. The Castle
2. S. Loyes
3. S. Martines
4. S. Mary BishopE
5. S. Mary Bishop Y
6. Boudam Bare

8. Peter Gate
9. Collier Gate
10. Goodram Gate
11. Monke gate
12. Aldvark
13. S. Antonyes Hosp
14. Cornye strete
15. Blake strete
16. Sverie Gate
17. Ouse Bridge
18. Thursdaies mark
19. Copper Gate
20. Fisher gate
21. Fose bridge
22. Iewe Bury

YORKE

Monke Bridge
Boudam
Iolly Gate
S. Maurie
S. Peters
The Lords place
Mary Gate
Laterop Poster
S. Iohns Grene
Ouse flu
Fose flu
Ouse flu

50 100 150 200
A Scale of Pases

1 York as it was in 1618 (surveyed and drawn by Franz Hogenberg).

2 Walmgate Bar, as seen from inside the city walls *c.* 1841 (by Francis Bedford). The little house has survived to this day.

3a *Above:* The Roman Multangular Tower, King's Manor and Bootham Bar, seen from what are now the Museum Gardens (by Joseph Halfpenny, 1807).

3b *Below:* Clifford's Tower (by Francis Place). Note the asymmetric shape of the *motte* as a result of erosion caused by repeated flooding of the River Ouse.

4 Bootham Bar as it appeared in 1827 (by J. Redaway). The barbican itself, the structure in front of the gate, was demolished in 1832.

5a *Above:* Micklegate Bar in 1782 (by T. Hearne). The barbican leading to the gate collapsed in 1810 and was subsequently removed.

5b *Below:* Castlegate Postern Tower, part of the castle fortifications, stood to the west of the castle until 1826.

Ancient Entrance to Minster.

7 *Above:* The opening page of the St Matthew Gospel in the York Gospel Book (*c.*980), one of the treasures of York Minster.

6a *Opposite, top:* The west front of the Minster at the end of the seventeenth century (by Francis Place).

6b *Opposite, below:* The old gate into the Minster close, which stood on Goodramgate adjacent to St William's College. It was demolished in the nineteenth century.

8 The Shambles. Note the cuts of meat hanging outside the shops. The Shambles was formerly a street of butchers.

9 First Water Lane (now known as Cumberland Street) in the early nineteenth century (by Henry Cave).

10a *Above:* Pavement in the early nineteenth century showing the market cross (demolished in the 1830s) and St Crux church (demolished in the 1890s).

10b *Below:* The city and its walls, as they appeared at the end of the seventeenth century (by Francis Place).

11a *Above:* North Street Tower (the Barker Tower), Lendal Tower and St Mary's Abbey Water Tower in the late seventeenth century (by W. Lodge).

11b *Below:* Pavement market and the then newly created Parliament Street, *c.* 1836 (by W. Walton), (*cf* plate 10a, drawn two decades earlier).

12a Holy Trinity Church, Goodramgate, *c*. 1840 (by F. Bedford).

12b Holy Trinity Church (also known as Christ's Church) stood in what is now King's Square (by E. Brown). It was demolished within living memory (in 1937).

13 All Saints' Church, North Street, *c.* 1840 (by F. Bedford).

14a King's Manor as it was at the beginning of the nineteenth century (an engraving by T. Sutherland from a drawing by H. Cave).

14b The doorway out of King's Manor courtyard (by J. Halfpenny). The arms above the door are those of Thomas Wentworth, Earl of Strafford (chapter one).

15 The market cross which stood in St Sampson's Square (formerly the site of the hardware market) until the 1830s.

16a *Above:* The pavilion built in the grounds of Bootham Hospital to house the Yorkshire Fine Art and Industrial Exhibition. (See Exhibition Square, chapter six.)

16b *Below:* The old railway station during its heyday (1861).

nineteenth century, together with the hundred yard stretch of the wall between the Museum Gardens and Bootham Bar, already mentioned. The stone gate at Bootham Bar only survived because the Corporation found itself short of money when the barbican was being demolished. The barbicans, from which the bars take their name, were short fortified corridors attached to the outside of the city gates, allowing those inside to trap hostile attackers between outer and inner doors. Only the barbican of Walmgate Bar survives today. As with Monk Bar and Micklegate Bar, the name Bootham Bar, now a misnomer, remains in use, today referring to the gateway alone.

The battle between the Corporation and the preservationists became increasingly embittered. The Corporation started paying itinerant labourers to damage the walls in the dark of the night, in order to have an excuse to demolish particular sections. On the other side a journalist and architectural historian, William Hargrove, took the place of Archbishop Markham in rallying the public to protect the medieval wall.

In the end, the efforts of Markham and Hargrove protected the walls long enough for times to start changing. With the growth of romanticism, public opinion began to sway towards the preservation of things past. Protests were heard throughout Britain. The influential York artist, William Etty, took up the cause. Sir Walter Scott declared that he was going to walk to York from Edinburgh in an effort to save Micklegate Bar (although this proved unnecessary). Yet it should be remembered that the upkeep of the walls remains costly. In former times this was paid for by murage. Today it is the tax-payers of the city who fund the maintenance of the walls.

A WALK AROUND YORK'S MEDIEVAL WALLS

A logical place to start a brief description of a circumnavigation of the defensive walls of York is the Red Tower, where the wall starts on Foss Islands Road. This small red-brick building marks the position of the shore of the former lake known as the King's Fishpool. In spite of its small size and comparatively frail appearance, it was a defensive post, and has loopholes for looking out and shooting through. The walls of the tower are four feet thick.

Following the defeat of Richard III in 1485, the threat of uprisings against Henry VII had been ever-present in Richard's homelands of north Yorkshire. Such a revolt came towards the end of April 1489, when the people of the Yorkshire Dales (enraged by the imposition of a tax to finance a foreign war) were organized into effective revolt by Sir John Egremont, a former servant of Richard's. The men of Richmondshire marched on York and besieged the city. Early in May, Walmgate and Fishergate Bars were burnt and badly damaged. Following the uprising, the king ordered that York's defences be strengthened against further possible rebellion. The Red Tower, constructed in 1490, was part of the restoration of the town's walls that followed.

The foundations and lower portions of the tower are of limestone ashlars. These cannot be seen today, the tower standing five feet shorter than when built as a result of the ground around silting up — the tower originally stood in the waters of the King's Fishpool. The flat roof of the tower, which once carried a parapet and cannon, was replaced by the pitched roof when the building was restored in 1858.

The Red Tower is the only brick building in the walls. (The clay pits where bricks were made were on the banks of the former lake, very close to the tower.) The building of the Red Tower in brick, rather than stone, provoked much animosity amongst the town's stone masons, culminating in the murder of John Patrik, one of the 'tilers' who had laid the bricks of the tower (bricks at that time being known as 'wall tiles').

From the Red Tower, the wall runs southward to the first of the four main gates into the city — Walmgate Bar. Walmgate Bar is the only one of the city's four bars to have retained its barbican intact. The gate bears the coat of arms of Henry V, but some stonework actually dates from the twelfth century and the majority of the bar was built during the fourteenth century. The bar was badly damaged by fire in the rebellion of 1489 but, unlike Fishergate Bar, was repaired.

In the course of the siege of York in 1644, Republican artillery was positioned outside Walmgate Bar, on Lamel Hill (in the grounds of the present Retreat Hospital to the south-east). In the exchange that followed, Walmgate Bar was severely damaged. Repairs were carried out intermittently throughout the next three years. (There is larger, better cut stonework at the top of the bar.) In 1831 the Estates Committee recommended that Walmgate Bar be demolished. However, changing attitudes to the city's defences saved the gate and in 1840 the Corporation extensively restored it (see North Street Postern, p. 95). The wooden doors of Walmgate Bar are thought to be the original doors installed in the fourteenth century. The outer, barbican doors were made of iron.

During the siege, Walmgate Bar was undermined with the intention of blowing it up with gunpowder. The plot was discovered, but the mine below remained and eventually slowly subsided — look for the slight sag in the stonework of the barbican itself.

Attached to the inner face of Walmgate Bar is an unusual little two-storey building with a balcony roof, supported above the level of the gate by stone pillars with Doric capitals. It is late Tudor and although its original purpose is today a mystery, two other bars had similar rooms attached. It was the birthplace of the locally known nineteenth-century artist and historian John Browne.

Continuing around the wall the next structure is a much more modest gate known as Fishergate Bar. The gate was once much larger, and may have had a barbican like that at Walmgate Bar (although it can never have been as large). The wall was sealed here following damage by fire to the original gate at this point, during the short siege in 1489. (Some of the fire damage inflicted in 1489 is still visible in the central arch.) The towers that flanked the walled-up gateway were subsequently put to a variety of uses (including a brothel at the end of the fifteenth century, a prison for recusants a century later, and a quarantine cell for possible plague victims at the beginning of the seventeenth century). Over the years the side towers were plundered for their stone (for example, to repair the old Castle Mills Bridge, nearby) and by the eighteenth century had fallen into such severe disrepair that they had to be removed. The gateway was reopened in 1826 and restored in 1961.

The last buildings on this portion of the walls are Fishergate Postern and its tower, marking the point at which the wall again met the lake. Fishergate Postern once contained a portcullis. Fishergate Postern Tower was built between 1504–7, but replaced an earlier tower at this point.

After Fishergate Postern the wall stops, continuing 400 yards to the west, across both the Foss and the Ouse. This gap, between the two rivers, is the site of the former castle (see p. 101). In medieval times, the wall continued at the west side of the curtain wall of the castle with a tower and postern (similar to Fishergate Postern) known as Castlegate Postern. This, together with an adjacent stretch of wall, was demolished in May 1826, to allow for expansion of the prison (see p. 108).

Today, the wall resumes to the west of what is now Tower Street, considerably reduced in height as a result of the surrounding ground being raised to lessen the frequency of flooding. The ledge along the parapet, on the inside of the wall along this stretch, is much narrower than elsewhere (where comfortable walkways exist). In fact, this would have been the width of the medieval ledge around all the walls, and those manning the defences would have stood on a wooden gallery of which this ledge was but the inner support. The wider walk around the rest of the wall was probably built at the end of the fifteenth century.

Where the wall meets the Ouse there is a tower known variously as Davy Tower, the Sugar House and Friargate Postern Tower. On the opposite bank of the Ouse the walls used to resume at a tower known as the Crane Tower (see p. 92). The two towers together guarded the entrance to the town by water. From the fourteenth to the sixteenth century, a heavy chain used to be stretched across the Ouse between the two towers to prevent boats from passing until a toll had been paid to the town, upon which the chain would be lowered to the river-bed allowing passage. A similar chain controlled water traffic entering and leaving the town from and to the north, and was sited close to the Victorian Lendal Bridge (see p. 115). By 1553 the practice had become obsolete and the chains were sold.

The Davy Tower probably takes its name from a tenant in the late thirteenth century, one John Davy. The Davy family held the powerful position of hereditary Lardiners (see Davygate, Chapter Six) and one of the family had been responsible for overseeing the rebuilding of the castle during the reign of Henry II, in the second half of the twelfth century.

The name Sugar House is seventeenth century and euphemistically refers to a public convenience. This was actually a wooden building erected adjacent to the Davy Tower. It was demolished in 1731 and replaced by a stone gateway with iron gates, known either as Friargate Postern or the Iron Gate. Friargate Postern refers to its position close to the site of the former Franciscan Friary and at the end of Friargate. The gateway was demolished c.1840. Davy Tower itself found service for a while as a brothel. Today it is a private house. The brick upper part was added in 1750 to serve as a summer-house.

The wall is joined again across the Ouse at a small tower which was built in 1878, when a short stretch of wall between here and the river was removed to allow access to the new Skeldergate Bridge. A postern tower, known as the Crane Tower (possibly from the nearby Crane Farm) or Skeldergate Postern Tower, stood on the river here until 1807 when it was demolished with much resulting controversy.

Baile Hill, the artificial mound where the walls resume, was the site of a Norman castle (probably the first to be built in York) erected on the orders of William I during the years immediately following the Conquest. Prior to that it had been the site of a Roman cemetery. Like its twin mound on which Clifford's Tower now stands, Baile Hill was originally surmounted by a wooden stockade, some of the remains of which were uncovered during excavations carried out in 1968-9. Earlier excavations had failed to find traces of the Norman keep, due to the mound having been heightened in 1644 to carry a gun or guns during the siege of York. The remains of a ditch around Baile Hill can still be made out in places.

The old French word *baile*, or its anglicized form 'bailey', strictly means nothing more than a palisade, but usually implies the outer curtain wall of a castle. This would often, as here, (but not always, as with Clifford's Tower) enclose the keep, built on a raised mound, a *motte*, here known as Baile Hill. The bailey would also enclose the other buildings of the castle (see York Castle, p. 100). The whole complex of this site is known locally as 'the Old Baile' to distinguish it from the other castle across the Ouse, of which Clifford's Tower was the keep. The Old Baile seems to have become redundant as part of the city's defences some time shortly after 1070. Baile Hill has been covered with trees since 1722. In 1802 the York and Ainsty Gaol was built beside Baile Hill, within the Old Baile. It was demolished in 1880 to make way for the houses which presently stand along the north-west side of the site.

South of Baile Hill the wall turns north-west at a corner tower. Known as the Bitchdaughter Tower, for reasons which have remained obscure, it was once a royal prison and a significant building. The upper rooms of the tower were dismantled and stone from the tower was then used to repair Ouse Bridge, following its collapse in 1565. The lower room of the tower contains a fireplace, with which it was fitted in 1645 when the tower was restored, following the siege of York, to act as a guardhouse. In the nineteenth century the room saw useful service once again — but only as a stable for cattle.

The walls continue to the north-east passing over the next gate, Victoria Bar. This was opened in 1838 and was created with money raised by the Lord Mayor, George Hudson (who had a number of holes made in the walls at various places, see p. 123). When Victoria Bar was being built, the remains of a small postern gate were found. The gate had been known to have existed from medieval records, where it is referred to as the *Lounlith* meaning the 'Hidden Gate' (as opposed to the *Micklelith*, or the 'Great Gate', 400 yards away and now known as Micklegate Bar). The *Lounlith* predated the medieval stone wall and presumably referred to an opening in the earthen rampart.

Fifty yards past Victoria Bar is another circular tower known as the Sadler Tower. Like the Bitchdaughter Tower, this too has an under-room fitted with a fireplace. In the wall close to this tower is an example of a stone shattered by a cannon ball, probably in 1644.

The stretch of the walls from just after Victoria Bar to Micklegate Bar was once the southern boundary of Holy Trinity Priory. The Priory enclosed an area of about seven acres — a significant proportion of the walled town south of the river. The square church tower a hundred yards or so inside the walls is Saxon and belongs to the Church of St Mary on Bishophill Junior. It is the oldest building in York still in use.

The next major structure is Micklegate Bar. The lower parts of the bar date from early in the twelfth century (note the semi-circular Romanesque arch) and are of earlier construction than the rest of the medieval walls. (Three Roman stone coffins have been reused in the building of Micklegate Bar.)

The barbican, similar to that still standing at Walmgate Bar, partially collapsed in 1810 and was removed completely in 1826. The doors which led out onto the battlements of the barbican can be seen on the outside of the gate-house. The gates were removed in 1827 as they had fallen into disuse — since 1797 it had been impossible to lock the doors as a result of the keeper's children having lost the keys while playing with them.

The three small statues on the top of the bar are of medieval knights. They are by R. Ridley and date only from 1950 when they replaced earlier similar but eroded figures. The three higher Arms on the outside of the bar are those of King Edward III (middle) and two Arms of the city. The lower Arms commemorate restoration of the bar in 1737 and are those of the Lord Mayor at the time, Sir John Lister-Kaye.

Arches to each side of the main gate of Micklegate Bar were created by the City Corporation in 1753, to try to relieve the pressure on the gate from ever-increasing traffic, particularly from coaches. The work was entrusted to John Carr, for which he charged the city £230. The side arch on the south-east side is that created by Carr. Carr's single arch on the north side was enlarged, creating the two side arches of today, in 1863.

Since Roman times, this has been the entrance to the city from the south and London. (The Roman gate actually stood a few yards to the north-west of the present medieval gate.) Originally the road from this gate ran in a straight line, approximately following what are today Toft Green and Tanner's Row, to a Roman bridge over the Ouse, about a hundred yards downstream from Lendal Bridge. Some time following the withdrawal of the Romans this bridge was lost and was later replaced by a bridge where Ouse Bridge stands today. As a result the main road through this part of the town, Micklegate itself, does not run in a straight line, as the main street in Roman times did, but curves from the Bar to Ouse Bridge, adding to the attraction of this part of York.

The upper parts of Micklegate Bar are on three floors, the top one of which was used as a prison for nobles. A gruesome piece of York's past is that, because it was the most important and the busiest of the four bars, the heads or other parts of executed traitors (that is usually to say, the losers during times of civil unrest) used to be put on spikes on the top of Micklegate Bar and left until they rotted away (or were stolen by sympathizers, to be buried with honour). The practice continued to as late as 1754.

A little way past Micklegate Bar the wall turns to the north-east at another corner tower known as Toft Tower (the area inside the walls at this point being Toft Green). In this area the medieval walls follow the line of the Roman *Colonia* wall and Toft Tower is probably built on the foundations of an earlier Roman corner tower. Toft Tower itself was badly damaged during the siege of 1644, and its repair is reflected in it being of a different stone from that of the rest of the walls. (Pennine gritstone rather than Tadcaster limestone.)

York's first railway station was opened on 29th May, 1839. This was initially a temporary building just outside the wall at the west angle, but a permanent building was soon ready and opened the following year. Now long disused, this is the building just inside the west corner of the walls, a hundred yards past Micklegate Bar.

The following section of the walls, just past the west angle, was completely rebuilt in the 1830s, when large arched openings in the wall at this point were created to allow trains access to the new station. The first two arches date from this rebuilding. The second two from 1874 when they were knocked through to allow road access to the station. By the 1870s the demands on the station had become more than it was capable of handling and limited space and access prevented further expansion. The new station which replaced it (and which still thrives today) stands just outside the west angle of the walls, together with the dominating Royal Station Hotel built at the same time.

Outside the walls along this section is a burial ground. It contains the remains of some of those who perished during a cholera epidemic in 1832. The pressure for graves was solved by using the defensive ditch outside the rampart to contain the bodies.

Continuing north-east, the walls meet the Ouse again at Lendal Bridge (itself opened in 1863). In 1603 there was an outbreak of plague (see Burton Stone Lane, Chapter Six). When, during that same year this section of the wall collapsed, it was guarded to prevent anyone from entering the city and bringing with them the disease, until repairs could be effected with stone taken from the ruined Holy Trinity Priory.

The gate in the city wall where it meets the river is known as North Street Postern. It was built in 1840 by the Great North of England Railway Company and replaced an older postern. The original postern was nothing more than a small door, created by the Dominican friars (whose House was on Toft Green) around 1298. Even after it had been heightened in 1577 (at cost of £1. 8s. 6d.) following a request from Henry Hastings, Earl of Huntingdon and Lord President of the Council of the North (to allow him to pass through on his 'great horse') the gate was still only four feet nine inches high. The company created the new arch to allow access to their coal-yard by road. For the right to do so the Corporation charged the company £500 and used the money to restore Walmgate Bar.

The circular tower on the quayside, adjacent to North Street Postern, is known as the Barker Tower. The name derives from the tanning industry which dominated the area between the tower and All Saints' Church. Tanners were frequently referred to as 'barkers' from their use of tree bark as a source of the preservative, tannin. (The Barker Tower is sometimes also referred to as North Street Postern Tower.) The tower originally had a flat roof and a parapet to carry a gun. The merlons still survive below the seventeenth-century conical tiled roof, while the 'embrasures' have been turned into true windows (two of them enlarged for the purpose). For a time, from 1879, the tower was used as a mortuary. It was restored in 1930 and again in 1970.

From at least medieval times, a ferry operated here from the Barker Tower to the quay opposite (known as St Leonard's Landing, from which Lendal takes its name) and the tower was, for many years, occupied by the ferryman and his family. The ferry closed in 1863 with the opening of Lendal Bridge.

The tower on the opposite bank of the river (the north bank) is Lendal Tower, or St Leonard's Tower. A little less than a hundred yards up Museum Street from the tower stood the great main gate into the former St Leonard's Hospital, looking out over the Ouse (see Chapter Five). Between them, Lendal Tower and the Barker Tower originally guarded the approach to the city by water from the north, by means of a heavy chain as at the Crane Tower (see p. 91). Adjacent to Lendal Tower was a small postern similar to the old gate next to North Street Tower.

Lendal Tower has been much altered and, apart from on the side facing the river, little medieval stonework survives. From 1631, the tower housed a pumping house for the town's water supply, originally pumped by horses turning a wheel inside the tower. A new upper floor was added in 1677 to give height to a cistern, and at the end of the seventeenth century the tower carried on its top the sails of a wind pump. In the 1750s a 4.7 horsepower steam engine was installed. This was replaced by one of four times that power in the 1780s. In 1846 the New York Waterworks Company was founded and the pumping operation was moved to Acomb. The extra storey was demolished and in 1932 the tower was converted into offices for the company, in which use it remains today.

The city wall proper continues from Lendal Tower alongside Museum Street and then turns north-west, at part of the ruins of the medieval St Leonard's Hospital. (The hospital itself is described in Chapter Five.) From this corner to the Multangular Tower (about a hundred and thirty feet) the walls are those of the Roman fortress. With the Multangular Tower they are one of the most complete pieces of Roman masonry in Britain, standing (apart from lacking the original parapet) to the original height of seventeen feet. (In the early fourth century when it was built, the wall would have appeared somewhat higher, but the debris of the centuries have raised the ground level on either side of its base.)

The lower part of the Multangular Tower is Roman, dating from the time of the Emperor Constantine who was declared Emperor in York in AD 306. The upper part, of larger blocks, is fourteenth century. It was given the name 'Multangular' in 1683 by Martin Lister, physician, zoologist and amateur historian, and one of York's many famous men of the period. Lister was the first person of modern times to realize that the tower was of Roman construction. Prior to being cleared in 1831 by the Yorkshire Philosophical Society (who had then recently acquired the tower and the surrounding grounds from the Crown) the Multangular Tower had accumulated debris to the extent that the ground level was at the level of the medieval windows. The Multangular Tower marked the west corner of the front of the Roman fort.

In the City Library garden, next to the Multangular Tower, can be seen the foundations of a large Roman bread oven, once part of the fortress's bake-house and presumably sited against the walls so as to be well away from buildings to which it might pose a fire hazard.

Just inside the walls to the north of the Multangular Tower is a small ruined tower known as the Anglian Tower. It was built during the period of Anglo-Saxon rule in the city (possibly during the reign of Edwin), probably to repair a breach in the Roman wall. It is built of limestone, but not the hard, Tadcaster limestone used by the builders of the medieval wall (and the Romans before them) but a softer stone brought from the Yorkshire Wolds, to the north-east of the town.

The Anglian Tower is the only non-ecclesiastical Anglo-Saxon building known in Britain and it was accidentally discovered in 1839 by workmen digging a tunnel through the ramparts. In 1969 this whole stretch of the wall was excavated, revealing not only the tower but the Roman, Anglo-Saxon and Danish ramparts and walls. Just past the Anglian Tower, the archaeologists left untouched parts of the rampart from each successive period in the wall's history — Roman, Anglo-Saxon, Viking, Norman, medieval — providing visible evidence of how the height of the earth bank grew with the passing centuries.

There was a tragic incident now associated with the excavation of this tower. On the 2nd July, 1970, an investigative trench dug into the rampart collapsed, killing Jeffrey Radley, the senior archaeologist involved. The tower carries a small plaque in his memory.

Shortly after the Anglian Tower there is a hundred yard stretch of the city wall missing. This was demolished (along with an interval tower and the barbican of Bootham Bar, below) during the 1830s, when St Leonard's Place was created.

The medieval wall continues again on the opposite side of Exhibition Square at Bootham Bar. Bootham Bar, on the site of the *Porta Principalis Dextra*, the north-western gateway of the Roman fort, is the only one of the modern city's gates to stand on the site of what was one of the main Roman entrances to the city. The present gate-house contains eleventh-century stonework, but mostly dates from the thirteenth and fourteenth centuries. It has been partly rebuilt on a number of occasions, most extensively in 1645 following its damage during the siege of the previous year. The most recent renovation was carried out between 1968–70.

The barbican of the gate, removed in 1832, was replaced by buttresses. Interestingly, unlike at the other three bars, there are no doors in the first-floor room of the gate to allow access to the parapets of a barbican, and it has been suggested that the gate-house may have been built first and the barbican added at a later date. The wooden portcullis can be seen inside the bar, although it is no longer functional.

The Arms on the outside of the bar are those of the Royal House of Stuart, and two Arms of the city. The three small statues looking out from the top of the gate were added in 1894, replacing earlier figures which had suffered badly from corrosion. The outer two are figures of a mason and a knight. The central figure is Nicholas Langton, a famous fourteenth-century figure and Lord Mayor of the town. In 1326 Langton successfully claimed before a Court of the King's Council that the archbishop, rather than the City Corporation, was responsible for the maintenance of the part of the walls around the Old Baile, on the grounds of historical precedence.

The few yards of wall to the south of Bootham Bar, including the steps up to the bar on the outside of the city wall, were built in 1834 following the demolition of the original wall and the barbican.

Thirty yards north-east of Bootham Bar the wall turns through ninety degrees and runs to the south-east. The corner tower at this point marks the corner of the former Roman fort. This tower has variously been known as the Bawing Tower (in the fourteenth century, meaning 'bowing' or 'bending'), the Frost Tower (in the fifteenth century) and the Robin Hood Tower (from the middle of the seventeenth century to the present day). The origins of the latter name is a mystery, but the name Frost Tower is thought to be after William Frost who was Lord Mayor of York five times at the beginning of the fifteenth century. The present tower was built in 1888 to replace the medieval tower which had fallen down by the beginning of the eighteenth century.

The attractive section of the walls after Bootham Bar gives perhaps the best view from anywhere in York of the Minster and its associated buildings such as the Deanery, the Minster Library and the Treasurer's House. The scale and style of the Minster Chapter House is especially striking from here, as is the central lantern tower of the Minster which, particularly from this angle, gives the impression of having been built to a design originally intended to carry a spire (see Chapter Two). From the north-west corner of the wall (behind the Minster Deanery) the present medieval wall stands on Roman foundations — easily distinguished by the different style of stonework. At this point one is standing on the Roman wall almost at its full height (not including its parapet) with medieval stonework added on top of this.

Outside this stretch of the city wall one can see a ditch — all that remains of the ditch which once encircled the town (see p. 92).

The old Roman north-east gate into the town, the *Porta Decumana*, was actually to the north-west of the present Monk Bar, behind the Treasurer's House and about a hundred and twenty yards before the bar is reached. On the other side of Lord Mayor's Walk, the road outside the walls at this point, a narrow paved pathway runs between two blocks of buildings. Known as Groves Lane, this is all that remains of the main Roman approach to the fort from Malton and the coastal towns beyond — the *Via Decumana*. The site of the Roman gate into the fort can be imagined if Groves Lane were continued in a straight line across Lord Mayor's Walk and the moat, to meet the wall, as indeed it used to. Inside the walls this line continues as Chapter House Street, along the side of the Treasurer's House. (This is the point on the wall that was in the centre of this side of the rectangular Roman fort.) The site of the gateway was most probably moved to allow the public street to avoid the Minster Liberty. As at Micklegate, Goodramgate reflects the alignment of the town as it was when the gate stood a hundred yards to the north-east of the present bar. A tower is recorded as still standing in the wall at this point as late as the end of the seventeenth century.

The next major structure to be encountered in this tour of the walls is Monk Bar itself. It is the highest and the largest of the town's gates — four storeys high and large enough to be the only one of the city's bars to need a vaulted interior. Indeed, the design of Monk Bar is that of a castle in miniature, such that the occupants would be able to defend themselves whether attacked from outside the walls or from within the city, by missile, battering or fire.

The first three storeys are fourteenth century and were built to replace an earlier medieval gate on the site of the Roman gate. The top storey was added a century later. Like Micklegate Bar, Monk Bar was used in Tudor times as a prison (from 1583 for imprisoning recusants). Later it was used as an exclusive gaol for Freemen of the City found guilty of transgression of the law.

The barbican was partly removed in 1815 and finally demolished in 1825 to make way for a footpath. Like those of Micklegate Bar, the doors which gave access to the battlements of the barbican can be seen on the outside of the gate. All four of the city's bars retain their portcullises, but the one in Monk Bar is the only one which still works. The arms on the bar are those of the Royal House of Plantagenet and of the city. Notice the seventeenth-century statues on the parapet — clutching boulders, ready to be hurled down on any hostile party attempting to gain access to the town. The purpose of the small balcony on the inside of the gate-house is a mystery, but was used in the seventeenth century for the reading of public proclamations.

Just past Monk Bar, on the inside of the walls before the medieval, timber-framed Merchant Taylors' Hall (see Chapter Five) is reached, are the foundations of what was a Roman tower. (Small towers were built into the Roman fortress walls at regular intervals.) A few yards on are further remains — this time of the foundations of what was the tower at the north-east corner of the Roman fort, now known as Aldwark Tower. From here the original Roman fortress defences turned at a right angle and ran south-west, between St Andrewgate and Goodramgate, through King's Square, to a second multangular tower (probably identical to the surviving tower in the Museum Gardens) which stood at the south-east corner of the Roman fort, close to the junction of Feasegate and Market Street. The two multangular towers, together with the huge gritstone gate halfway between them (on the site of St Helen's Square) must have formed an impressive main front to the Roman fort when approached from the main road to York from the south.

Outside the walls, adjacent to the interval tower, is a small brick dome. The dome covers a brick-lined pit sunk into the earthen rampart, about twenty feet deep, dug at the beginning of the nineteenth century. It is an ice house. When the Ouse froze during the winter (which in the less mild days of previous centuries happened extensively every year) ice was collected and stored in this building. Thus insulated by the earth and the heavy cold air which lay in the pit, the ice remained, thawing only very slowly, to be used by the fishmongers of the town during the hot summer months.

A little past the two Roman towers is the Merchant Taylors' Hall (see Chapter Five) and a little past the hall stood the Church of St Helen-on-the-Walls. One of the oldest sites of religious worship in the city, the church had been built on the site of a pre-Christian Roman temple. In AD 306 the Emperor Constantius Chlorus died in the city and his cremation is said to have taken place here. (His ashes were returned to Rome.) St Helen or Helena, to whom the later Christian church was dedicated, was his wife. In 1586 the parish of St Helen-on-the-Wall was amalgamated with the adjacent parish of St Cuthbert and the medieval church was demolished soon after.

The semi-circular interval tower just past the Merchant Taylors' Hall is known

99

as Harlothill Tower. Harlot Hill referred to the earthen rampart outside the wall at this point, and is recorded as Herlot Hill as early as 1340. (Here the rampart is at its widest anywhere on the walls.) In the fourteenth century *herlot* implied 'beggar'. However, by the eighteenth century the word and the area had acquired the modern connotation. By the eighteenth century the name of the street outside the walls at this point was by then itself being colloquially referred to as Harlot Hill rather than by its official name of Barker Hill. (Today it is St Maurice's Road, named after a church demolished during the nineteenth century.) The narrow lane which continues the line of St Andrewgate outside the city wall, behind Sainsbury's Supermarket and the Yorkshire Water offices, to meet the Foss close to Monk Bridge, was euphemistically known as Love Lane.

Our circumnavigation of the town's ancient defences ends when the Foss is reached; a small tower, known as Layerthorpe Tower, marks the point at which the walls once again met the lake of the King's Fishpool. The tower, supported by corbels and an arch, is of unique design and may reflect hasty repair. Originally there was a large postern tower just past this point, similar to Fishergate Postern, with a gate into the city. Known as Layerthorpe Postern (or occasionally as Peasholme Green Postern) it was demolished in 1829 when it proved necessary to rebuild Layerthorpe Bridge, the latter having been allowed to fall into a state of dangerous disrepair. From drawings and etchings of the gateway, it can be seen to have been a unique and interesting building, and formed the western part of the old Layerthorpe Bridge.

YORK CASTLE

The first known post-Roman fortification in the town which could loosely be described as a 'castle' was the stronghold of the Viking earls of Northumbria. This stood in what is now the Yorkshire Museum Gardens and was known as the Earlsburh. A *burh*, or borough, was a fortified enclosure, designed to protect people and animals alike.

In the tenth century there was a palace of some sort in the square which today remembers the royal residence in its name — King's Square. It is thought that this building was the gate-house of the Roman fort, still standing in Viking times. The relationship between the earls' *burh* and the palace in King's Square is unclear — it is possible that they were used concomitantly. In 937, Athelstan, king of the West Saxons, dismantled a 'castle' in York. The earls may have moved to the Earlsborough site following the destruction of the gate-house, or vice versa. The former seems the more probable as Earlsborough was certainly the seat of the eleventh-century Earls of Northumbria, and here the best known of these, Earl Siward, founded St Olave's Church. In the late eleventh century the church became the seed of the Benedictine Abbey of St Mary, which subsequently occupied the site of Earlsborough (see St Olave's Church, Chapter Three and St Mary's Abbey, Chapters Three and Five).

The predecessor of the surviving medieval castle was built by William I in 1068. It was of *motte* and *baile* construction (that is, a stockade keep on top of an earthen mound, and a strong curtain wall, or bailey). This was destroyed during Anglo-Danish-Scots insurrection which brought William back to the town the following year, and a second castle of the same type was erected to support the first castle, which was repaired (see Chapter One). Both mounds survive today. One, on the east bank of the Ouse, carries Clifford's Tower. The other, on the west bank of the Ouse almost opposite Clifford's Tower, is today known as Baile Hill and is described above.

It is unclear which mound carried the first of the Norman castles, although Baile Hill is the site thought by many to be the more probable in that it bears the name of 'Old Baile' (and has since before the beginning of the thirteenth century when *vetus ballium* — literally, 'the old fort' — first occurs in surviving records). This could merely reflect the fact that it had long been ruined, but the interpretation of 'Old Baile' as meaning the first castle is supported by the site of Clifford's Tower being referred to in medieval times as the *Newarke*, or new fortification. It is said that the second *motte* and keep were erected in eight days. If this stood on the site of Clifford's Tower, it would suggest that the initial *motte* was much smaller than its present form.

Baile Hill fell into disuse almost immediately, presumably on the building and consolidation of a complex of buildings around the east keep, which created a single substantial fortress. The remainder of this chapter is devoted to the eastern site, which developed into the medieval stone castle.

For the building of the eastern *motte*, a position was chosen on a clay spur between the Ouse and the Foss, a little upstream from their confluence, giving natural defence by water on two sides of this triangular area. At some point (perhaps not in the earliest days of this castle) a decision was taken to site the keep outside the bailey. In addition, both keep and bailey were to be surrounded by moats. In order to raise the level of the Foss to flood the moat, a dam was built across the river, immediately to the south of the castle site. The result was disastrous for the Anglo-Danish town. The Vale of York is mostly very flat and the cost of raising the Foss by twenty feet was the ruthless flooding of one entire shire (one of the four administrative districts of the town, equivalent to the later 'wards'). Much productive land and many valuable buildings were lost.

The lake created, about a hundred and twenty acres in area, became known as the King's Fishpool. It added to the city's defences, but not to the civilian town. Rights of fishing were exclusively those of the king (and later the Carmelite Friars). The shallow lake and marsh remained until drained in the middle of the nineteenth century.

The original castle was of wood. The keep of this was destroyed by fire in March 1190 (see Chapter One). It was rebuilt soon after, but again in wood. The motivation to have the castle rebuilt in stone came in the form of the oscillating tensions between Henry III and his brother-in-law, Alexander II of Scotland. The two countries came close to war in 1237, and armed conflict was only averted by the intervention of the Pope. The terms of the resulting Treaty of York (signed at a meeting of the two kings in the city) were broken by Alexander in 1244. Henry, furious, ordered an army of invasion to be assembled at Newcastle and himself rushed to the north, passing through the city. Again a settlement was agreed upon before armed hostilities broke out (this time through the intervention of Archbishop Walter de Gray).

The event, however, brought to Henry's mind the possible vulnerability of the town. From the start the castle in York was a royal castle, owned by the king and garrisoned by troops directly responsible to him. (The majority of English medieval castles were owned, maintained and garrisoned by feudal knights and earls.) The king must have been aware of the state of York's defences — this was his third visit to the town since his succession to the throne. Henry ordered that work on a new stone castle was to begin immediately.

A great deal of building was carried out over the following decades. The result was a large moated limestone castle. A curtain wall with substantial towers and two large gate-houses, sited close to the north and south corners, enclosed an area of approximately three acres. Within the wall Henry had built a large hall, a large kitchen, a prison, a smaller hall and the numerous stables, barracks, stores, and other buildings needed by a self-contained military community. Just outside the curtain wall, beside the dam on the Foss, a large castle chapel was built. Although demolished in 1856, its former site retains the name St George's Field, from the dedication of the chapel.

The keep, now known as Clifford's Tower, was built outside the castle wall, on a *motte* about forty-eight feet high, two hundred and thirty feet in diameter at its base and a hundred and ten feet across the top plateau. (Originally it was even wider at both the top and the bottom, erosion during the frequent floodings of the rivers having taken its toll.) The clover-leaf design of the keep is unusual, although the keep at Pontefract was of similar design, and quatrefoil keeps exist at Amblény in Aisne, and Étampes in the Essone regions of northern France. Only York and Étampes are quatrefoil internally as well as externally. The master mason was probably Henry de Reyns (who was responsible for much of Westminster Abbey). Henry de Reyns and a master carpenter, Simon, were in York by the spring of 1245 to advise on the work.

The tower stands thirty-three and a half feet high, with walls nine and a half feet thick. It is seventy-nine feet across on the diagonal (sixty feet internally), and sixty-two feet across the sides (forty-three feet internally). Originally the tower had two floors and a flat roof. Corbelled turrets occupy three of the intersections of the 'clover leaves', the fourth being covered by a gate-house with a chapel above. The *motte* was surrounded by its own moat which adjoined that of the rest of the castle, and the keep and bailey were connected by a bridge.

Taking the price of bread then and now as an indication of true 'buying power', the work on the castle cost the equivalent of a little less than a million pounds at today's prices. (Remarkably little, by modern standards, although this was almost ten times the cost of rebuilding the tower in wood following its destruction in 1190.)

The origin of the name of 'Clifford's Tower' has been forgotten. It was suggested in the eighteenth century that the Clifford family were the Constables of the Castle by hereditary right. This is a mistake arising from a misinterpretation of a seventeenth-century writer, who suggested merely that members of the family had held the post. The earliest member of the family known to have been sheriff of Yorkshire (whose office included custody of the castle) was Henry Clifford, sheriff in 1522, and the name applied to the tower is recorded first in 1596. Prior to that the keep is referred to simply as the King's Tower or the Great Tower.

The gate-house carries the Arms of a later Henry Clifford, Earl of Cumberland, who garrisoned the castle for Charles I in 1642 (below the Arms of Charles I himself). They were added when the gate-house was repaired later in the seventeenth century, following severe damage during the siege of 1644. (It has also been suggested that the tower might take its name from Sir Roger Clifford, hanged in chains from the tower in 1322, following the Battle of Boroughbridge. Given the discrepancy of nearly three hundred years between the event and the name coming into use, this seems much less likely.)

From time to time during the Scots wars of the fourteenth century, the castle housed the Exchequer, the Royal Courts of Justice and the Treasury (although the kings themselves usually preferred to stay in the House of the Franciscan Friars, which stood adjacent to the west side of the castle). A Royal Mint was also housed here until 1546, when it moved to a site in part of the former St Leonard's Hospital.

The fabric of the castle began to decline from the end of the fifteenth century. Richard III had started to dismantle parts of the fortress as a preliminary to rebuilding. His defeat in 1485 brought the work to a stop and by 1535 the castle was described as being in ruins. It was repaired on a number of occasions during the following decades, but during the last decade of the century, the gaoler, one Robert Redhead, engaged himself in the dismantling of the buildings in order to sell the stone for his own profit. In an effort not to be noticed until as late as possible, he stripped Clifford's Tower from the inside and it was not until he started to remove the battlements that the Corporation seriously attempted to curb his avaricious enthusiasm. The town petitioned the Lord Chancellor, who took steps to save the tower.

Clifford's Tower was badly damaged in the siege of 1644 and repaired in 1652, only to be gutted by fire on 23rd April, 1684, the fortieth anniversary of the start of the siege. It was being used by the militia at the time as a store for gunpowder. The powder was rescued from the fire — saving what still stands of the tower.

103

There was little love lost between the army and the town and at the time arson was suspected, high spirits being the result of the St George's Day celebrations of that night. The tower escaped plans for its demolition in the nineteenth century and in 1902 the tower was excavated and underpinned with concrete.

The castle site came to be known as the Eye of the Ridings (or the Eye of Yorkshire), perhaps for political as well as geographic reasons. Until the nineteenth century this was where Parliamentary elections were held and declared for all three Ridings, as well as for the city itself. Prior to 1928 the car park to the east of Clifford's Tower was the site of York Prison, the castle having found continuous use in this capacity since its foundation.

Apart from Clifford's Tower, all that survives today of this once substantial medieval castle complex is a 350-foot stretch of curtain wall, behind the Debtors' Prison on the south-east side of the site, twenty-five feet high and including two towers. (The former Debtors' Prison, the former Women's Prison and the Assize Courts, which now occupy the eastern part of the former castle, are covered separately under the Crown Court in Chapter Five).

THE SECULAR AND SEMI-SECULAR BUILDINGS OF YORK

York is peppered with buildings of historical and architectural interest, many of them medieval. (The term 'medieval' is used here to describe the period between 1066 and 1485.) The oldest houses in the town make up the terrace on Goodramgate known as Lady's Row and are described below. With the exceptions of the city's defences and two walls of a ruined Norman house behind number 48 Stonegate, no non-ecclesiastical buildings in York predate Lady's Row, built in the early fourteenth century.

There is not enough space here to list even the majority of the fine buildings to be found in the city. Brief descriptions of many of these can be found in Volumes III, IV and V of *The City of York*, compiled by The Royal Commission on Historical Monuments and published by Her Majesty's Stationery Office. Walking around York it may be helpful to know that it was not permissible to build jettied buildings (that is, buildings with projecting upper floors) after 1644, and that prior to 1644 the use of brick was permitted only for the construction of public buildings.

ASSEMBLY ROOMS (BLAKE STREET)

The Assembly Rooms were designed by Richard Boyle, the third Earl of Burlington and a skilled and talented amateur architect. The Rooms were intended to fill the need for a suitable hall in which to hold the regular balls and concerts which by the second quarter of the eighteenth century were taking place more than once a week in the city. King's Manor, which had played this role for want of a more suitable building, lacked a large enough hall and was proving inadequate for the more sizeable social events.

Money was raised by selling shares in the building and there was no shortage of eager subscribers. Building was started with the laying of the foundation stone on 1st March, 1731, and the Rooms were first used for a ball during the meeting of York Races held the August of the following year, although they were not finally completed until 1735.

Throughout the eighteenth century the Assembly Rooms were the centre of fashionable life in York, dinners, dances and parties being held there to which the socialites of York would expect to be invited. The Rooms also served as a regular meeting place for the gentlemen of the town, and illegal gambling also took place.

Architecturally the Assembly Rooms are perhaps most interesting for the influence they show of the work of the Roman architect Vitruvius as revived by Palladio (whose work Burlington had studied when visiting Italy). They have been described as the first neo-Classical buildings in Northern Europe. Burlington decorated the Rotunda with a mural of himself portrayed as Constantine the Great. A portico extending into Blake Street was added early in the nineteenth century but removed in the late 1940s. The Assembly Rooms influenced architectural design throughout Britain over the decades that followed and Burlington became one of England's most influential eighteenth-century architects (perhaps best known for his reworking of Burlington Arcade in Piccadilly, London, originally the work of the first earl, his great-grandfather).

Following 1945 the Corporation took over the Rooms and completely restored them. They were reopened with a Georgian costume ball in 1951 (as part of the Festival of Britain) attended by the descendants of some of the original subscribers.

BLUE BRIDGE (NEW WALK)

Following the success of York's first Georgian promenade, Lord Mayor's Walk, a broad, tree-lined riverside walk from the confluence of the Foss and Ouse southwards, opened in 1732 and to this day retains the name New Walk. The New Walk was also a social success, but was a little too far from the centre of the city to be easily reached. In 1738 this was rectified by the creation of a footbridge over the Foss, joining New Walk to St George's Field (the area between the Ouse and the Castle).

The timbers of the first bridge were painted blue, and the name and colour have stuck with the bridge to this day. The present Blue Bridge is actually the sixth to have crossed the Foss at this point. It was built in 1930 and opens to allow access to the Foss staiths upstream.

Further along New Walk, at the bottom of Hartoft Street, is a strange domed building of ashlars. It is a well house. The 'Lady Well' (or 'Pikeing Well'), produced waters of reputedly miraculous properties. Mindful of the success of Bath and various other spas in attracting wealthy visitors, in 1756 the Corporation had John Carr build the well-head and an adjacent grotto (now long gone).

BOOTHAM PARK HOSPITAL (OFF BOOTHAM)

The original brick and stone building of eleven bays which now forms the front of the extensively enlarged hospital was completed in 1777, again the work of John Carr. At the time it was only the fifth lunatic asylum in England (the others being in Newcastle-upon-Tyne, Manchester and two in London). It was instigated by Archbishop Drummond who, with twenty-four gentlemen of the city, put up the two and a half thousand pounds required. (The Corporation, who believed that the mentally ill were in need of financial rather than medical assistance, only donated a hundred guineas.) When it opened the fifty-four patients or their families paid eight shillings a week — a not insignificant amount, which resulted in the poor being excluded.

There were far more patients hoping to receive treatment than the hospital was able to admit. By 1813 the fifty-four residents for which the building had been designed had risen to 160. The obvious demand for such an institution, which the opening of the hospital had highlighted, led to a number of private mental hospitals opening in the area during the years that followed. One of these, the Friends' Retreat on Heslington Road which opened in 1815, continues to thrive today. It was not, however, until 1899 that the city admitted that there was a need for a mental hospital and in 1906 York City Asylum, now Naburn Hospital, opened. Naburn Hospital was united with Bootham Park 1952.

CASTLE MILLS
See *Raindale Mill*

CASTLE MILLS BRIDGE (FISHERGATE)
The first recorded Castle Mills Bridge, which was wooden, was built in 1583. Prior to that bridge being built it is probable that the Foss dam, which had existed since the 1070s, provided a road across the river at this point. The Tudor bridge was destroyed during the siege of York in 1644 and was replaced the following year. In 1733 this in turn was replaced by an arched stone bridge, which was washed away in floods during the winter of 1746 and again replaced.

In 1793 the Foss Navigation Company built a new bridge consisting of a single semi-circular stone arch. (Semi-circular bridges were unusual by the eighteenth century — for a given weight of stone they are particularly weak.) It was widened in 1800 and extensively restored in 1836–7, but by 1848 was pronounced unsafe by the architect G.T. Andrews (who built many of the buildings of York constructed between 1830 and 1850). It was repaired by 1851, but a century later the demands of heavy motor traffic had proved too much for the old bridge and it was replaced by the present bridge in 1955.

CASTLE MUSEUM
See *Crown Court*

CITY ART GALLERY
The building which now houses the City Art Gallery was purpose-built for the city's second Exhibition of Fine Art and Industry, held in 1879. The building, designed by E. Taylor (with W. Atkinson as honorary consultant architect), opened in May of that year. (See Exhibition Square, Chapter Five.) Three years

after the Exhibition, John Burton of Poppleton gave a collection of paintings (then valued at £75,000) to the city. His gift formed the basis of a permanent collection and in 1890 the Corporation bought the building from the Yorkshire Fine Art and Industrial Institution.

CROWN COURT AND CASTLE MUSEUM (YORK CASTLE)

The southern part of the former castle site is now occupied by three buildings, set on three sides of a quadrangle. The buildings on the south-east and north-east sides of this quadrangle were, respectively, prisons for male and female debtors. Today they are occupied by the Castle Museum. The third building, on the south-west side of the quadrangle, houses the two Crown Court rooms.

The Debtors' Prison was built in limestone between 1701 and 1705, over half a century before either of the other two. There is a persistent local belief, unsupported by contemporary documented evidence, that the Debtors' Prison was designed by Sir John Vanbrugh. This is possible — the fluted pillar above the entrance is typical of Vanbrugh's style and he was in Yorkshire in the first few years of the 1700s supervising the building of Castle Howard. However, the design of the Debtors' Prison is rather heavy and lacks Vanbrugh's sensitivity. More probably the prison is the work of a local artist, William Wakefield (who lived in Huby and was later concerned with repairs to the castle itself). In its time it was considered to be the finest prison building in the world. An interesting feature of the exterior of the Debtors' Prison is the central bell tower and its single-hand clock, made by John Terry of York in 1716.

The Assize Courts were designed by John Carr and built during the 1770s. They were later extended by the addition of the wings by Peter Atkinson (the elder) in 1812.

The prison for female debtors was also designed by Carr in association with Richard Raisin and William Shepherd to match the Courts opposite. Constructed immediately after the Courts, with an almost identical façade, Peter Atkinson again added the wings in 1803. Both buildings are of fine grained sandstone (some taken from ruined parts of the castle).

Male and female criminals (rather than debtors) shared segregated parts of a separate offenders' prison. There had been a prison for criminals in the castle from the time the castle was first built. The last of these, a graceless brick building, was erected in 1826 and stood to the north-east of Clifford's Tower. It became redundant in 1929 and was demolished in 1935. Today the site is a car park.

The whole of the castle site was acquired by the City Corporation in 1934 (for £8,000). The Debtors' Prison was converted into the Castle Museum, which opened in 1938, and was extended by taking over the Women's Prison building in 1952. The gallery linking the two halves of the museum opened in 1969. The Castle Museum is famous for its reconstructed Victorian shopping street,

Kirkgate, and is one of the best-known and most visited museums in Britain. The Crown Courts remain in daily use.

DEBTORS' PRISON
See *Crown Court*

FOSS BRIDGE (ON FOSSGATE)
There have been at least three bridges at this point since the first record of a Foss Bridge early in the twelfth century. Like the old Ouse Bridge, it carried houses and shops. The wooden bridge built as a replacement in the fifteenth century, when the Foss was much wider, had three arches and carried forty-two houses (nineteen on the south side and twenty-three on the north). The rents from the buildings on Foss Bridge and Ouse Bridge was paid to the City Corporation, who used the money to maintain and repair the bridges.

A chapel dedicated to St Anne was built on the north-east end of the bridge in the first quarter of the fifteenth century. The chapel was paid for from the assets of the Guild of the Holy Trinity which broke up through internal argument in 1418. It remained in use until 1555, after which it was not demolished but remained disused and gradually decayed over the next century and a half — at one point stone from the chapel was taken to repair not just Foss Bridge, but Ouse Bridge as well.

The present gritstone bridge, which opened in 1812, was designed by Peter Atkinson the younger. An Act of Parliament was needed to allow the demolition and replacement of the fifteenth-century Foss Bridge and the old Ouse Bridge (see p. 119).

The old bridge was the site of the sea-fish market (the lower part of Fossgate used to be knows as Fish Shambles). For centuries the market was held outside, but in 1724 the bridge was roofed to provide a covered market-place. The fish market was combined with the markets in Pavement and St Sampson's Square towards the end of the eighteenth century. Foss Bridge was also the site of the metals market. Trade in raw metals (particularly lead from the mines of the Yorkshire Dales) was an important source of revenue for York and for some of the monasteries of North Yorkshire (particularly Jervaulx Abbey).

Dorothy Wilson's Hospital at the east end of Foss Bridge was founded by the will of Dorothy Wilson who died in 1717 as a residence for ten poor women, preference being given to retired domestic servants. The hospital is supported by the income from lands around Yorkshire owned by the founder. It was rebuilt in 1812 and converted to small self-contained flats in 1958. (Her will also included the establishment of the Green Coat Boys' School for twenty poor boys, which was built behind the hospital, and a companion school for girls, which was held in the Merchant Adventurers' Hall across the Foss.)

GRAY'S COURT
See *Treasurer's House*

GUILDHALL (ST HELEN'S SQUARE)
In 1938 it was discovered that the Guildhall had been badly attacked over the previous centuries by death-watch beetle, and was in urgent need of repair. The £12,000 pounds required was raised and work started the following year. On 29th April, 1942, the restoration of the Guildhall was within a month of being completed. That night central York experienced the only serious air raid it suffered during the Second World War. Incendiary bombs fell along the north bank of the Ouse destroying, amongst other things, the Church of St Martin-le-Grand and the Guildhall. The vaulted riverside room known as the Inner Chamber was the only part of the medieval Guildhall that survived the fire that followed the bombing. (There is a persistent belief in the town that the object of the attack was the destruction of the Minster, although this has been conclusively shown not to have been the case.)

In 1956 it was decided that the Guildhall should be rebuilt, keeping as far as was possible to the original design. Work started in 1958, and the rebuilt Guildhall was opened on the 21st June, 1960, by Her Royal Highness, Queen Elizabeth the Queen Mother. The oak pillars were cut from single tree-trunks and are unusual in that they are octagonal in cross-section.

A 'Common Hall' in York is recorded as early as 1256, but there was probably a hall here much earlier. The ground was rented from Durham Cathedral Priory and may have been part of a gift of land in the city given to St Cuthbert on his consecration as Bishop of Lindisfarne in 685. The thirteenth-century hall was owned by the Guild of St Christopher and St George, who had allowed the Corporation to use it. Destroyed in 1942, the hall had been built in the fifteenth century. Work began on the gate-house (demolished in 1726) in 1446, and on the Guildhall proper three years later, under the direction of master mason Robert Couper. The main fabric was finished by 1454 but, as is the way with such things, the interior took longer than the actual building and it was the next decade before the Guildhall was completed.

It seems that the Corporation originally intended to pay for the building of a new hall themselves, but found they were short of funds. They appealed for help to the Guild of St Christopher and St George, who agreed to pay half the costs of the new building. In return, the Corporation gave the Guild an adjacent plot of land on which to build a chapel (today the site of the Mansion House) and certain rights of use of the new hall on specified days each year. (The Corporation were so short of money that halfway through the construction of the new building they passed a motion agreeing that council members late for meetings should be fined and the fines given to the construction fund.)

The Guildhall, as well as being used by the Corporation for official business and ceremonies, was used by the town for a variety of purposes, including the sittings of the Courts of Assizes and the public performance of plays. Every Monday the medieval Court of Common Pleas met in the Guildhall, presided over by the mayor or the sheriff, to hear disputes over contracts, wills, etc. Actual council meetings (the mayor and the twenty-four elected councillors) were usually held in the Tollbooth on Ouse Bridge (see p. 119) until 1808 when plans for the demolition of the bridge meant the council had to find a new meeting place. A purpose-built chamber was added to the Guildhall, designed by Peter Atkinson (who went straight from working on the chamber to working on the new Ouse Bridge).

During the Civil War the Inner Chamber of the Guildhall was pressed into service as an arms store. Queen Henrietta Maria brought supplies of arms to the city before the battle of Marston Moor, and some were stored here. The room was over-filled, the floor collapsed and the chamber was badly damaged and unusable for at least eighteen months.

The old Guildhall was partially glazed at the time it was built, and over the years the shutters on the remaining windows were replaced by glass. The first recorded painted glass in the Guildhall was the work of Henry Gyles and was inserted in 1684. This, together with later glass, was lost when the hall was bombed in 1942. However, a splendid contribution to the architecture of the city is the new west window. Designed by Harry Harvey, the window depicts the history of York.

The first of the five lights shows, from the top to the bottom, the Minster, the Merchant Adventurers' Hall and Micklegate, Bootham, Monk and Walmgate Bars. The second light shows the city's history — the Romans at the top, followed by the Vikings, then the Parliamentarian and Royalist armies, and finally the west window of the original Guildhall in the fire which destroyed it. The third light shows the city's Arms, the Lord Mayor and his Corporation, and a religious mystery play. The fourth light is dedicated to the commercial history of the city showing sheep being traded, a medieval merchant ship, an early train and the old Ouse Bridge, demolished in 1810. The last light shows the cultural history of York with the baptism of King Edwin at the top, Alcuin teaching scholars in the Minster School and a Georgian lady and gentleman.

The tracery depicts historical persons who have had an impact on the city's history and culture — the Emperor Constantine; kings Athelstan and Edward III (with his queen, Philippa); Sir Thomas Fairfax; Archbishop Walter de Gray; John Thornton, Richard Boyle and William Etty, and, somewhat quirkily, Robinson Crusoe (who, in Defoe's novel, was born in the city). The coats of arms in the top left and right corners are those of the Guilds of Glaziers and Merchant Adventurers.

The rather unattractive Victorian Gothic council buildings were built around the Guildhall in 1888–9. The architect was E.G. Mawbey.

KING'S MANOR (OFF EXHIBITION SQUARE)

King's Manor was, until the Dissolution of the church, the palace of the abbot of the adjacent St Mary's Abbey (see p. 129). Subsequently it became Crown property (from which King's Manor takes its regal name) and was made the seat of the Council of the North.

The Council of the North was created by Richard III who, having grown up in the Yorkshire Dales, realized that government from London was inadequate for the old Northumbria, whose inhabitants were not only fiercely independent but also very different in character and temperament from the peoples of the south. The Council was originally based at Sheriff Hutton, but was moved to King's Manor at the time of the Dissolution. As such it was the legal centre of the north of England and once again brought to York the importance and status of a provincial capital. The first Lord President of the Council to take up residence in King's Manor was Robert Holgate (later to become the first Protestant Archbishop of York).

In 1541, Henry VIII visited York with Catherine Howard and stayed in the Manor, as did James I during his slow meander south to take up the English throne, following the death of his cousin Elizabeth (who herself never saw fit to visit York). Twenty years later James' son, Charles I, visited York and also stayed in King's Manor.

The Council of the North was abolished by Parliament in 1641 and its last Lord President, Thomas, Viscount Wentworth, subsequently Earl of Strafford, was executed. Having failed to obtain in open court a verdict of guilty on any of the charges laid against Wentworth, the 'Long Parliament', determined to ensure the downfall of those who wielded the power behind the king, passed a special act to ensure his execution.

During the siege of York in 1644 the Manor served as the Royalist headquarters and command centre. On the 16th June, Parliamentarian forces under the command of the Earl of Manchester mined St Mary's Tower (see p. 129) and 300 republican troops poured into the city and besieged King's Manor. The siege which followed was one of the major events during the battle for control of the city. The invading troops were all captured, but not before much damage had been suffered by the building.

Since the Civil War, King's Manor has been leased as commercial buildings and private accommodation. (The artist Francis Place lived here for a time in the late seventeenth century.) Subsequently it has been used by four different schools. A boarding school for young ladies occupied part of the Manor in the early eighteenth century. Later, the Manor National School for Boys opened in the building in January 1813, and this was joined by its companion school for girls and infants in 1844. The girls school closed in the 1880s and the boys were force to move out in 1922 as a result of the building being condemned as uninhabitable. The Yorkshire School for the Blind was founded in another part of the building in 1834 in memory of William Wilberforce, the member of Parliament for Yorkshire who up to his death in 1833 campaigned relentlessly to bring about the abolition of, firstly, the trade in slaves and subsequently slavery itself. This school eventually came to occupy the whole Manor, before moving to Dringhouses on the outskirts of York, in the mid-1950s.

By the middle of the twentieth century, King's Manor had fallen into a dilapidated condition. It was eventually acquired by the City Corporation in 1958, for £30,000. Since 1963 it has been leased to the University of York. For a while it was the main administrative centre of the university but since the restoration of Heslington Hall (the present home of the main body of the university) King's Manor has been used primarily by graduate students and academics engaged in historical and architectural research.

King's Manor is a structural collage of bits and pieces added during different periods. Very little remains of the first palace, built during the 1270s, apart from a few ashlars incorporated into later walls. Originally the present front was the back and the palace faced St Mary's Abbey, with an open courtyard enclosed by wings on the north and south sides. The original courtyard is now fully enclosed and a second courtyard was created to the west during the reign of Henry VIII. Much of the brickwork dates from c. 1480 when the palace was extensively rebuilt and enlarged, as does the terracotta fenestration. The Manor is an example of the early use of brick as a structural material in the city (see the Merchant Adventurers' Hall, p. 116). The windows, however, are the earliest known use in Britain of terracotta as a building material.

The Council Chamber, the most important and impressive room in the Manor, dates from 1580 when Henry Hastings, Earl of Huntingdon, was Lord President. In memory of him it is known as the Huntingdon Room and an interesting frieze above the fireplace shows his Arms together with those of the Dudleys (his wife's family).

The wing at the north end of what is now the front was hurriedly purpose-built in 1562 as suitable apartments for two queens to meet and reconcile their differences. However, Elizabeth I and Mary, Queen of Scotland were overtaken by the politics of those around them and the meeting never took place. The rear part of this wing was added in 1620, presumably in even more of a hurry — the foundations are poor and the building has developed an alarming lean to the west.

King's Manor continued to be subject to alternating periods of disrepair and renovation until the present century. Thomas Wentworth and his predecessor as Lord President, Lord Sheffield, were responsible for several extensions to the Manor. At about 10 a.m. on the last day of October 1628, seven chimneys fell in a gale, killing Edward Osborne, the vice-president of the Council. Wentworth immediately ordered £1,000 to be spent on renovation and repairs — a huge sum in the seventeenth century. It was Wentworth who had the Royal Arms placed over the present main entrance in honour of Charles I, at a time when the king's relationship with his Parliament was rapidly deteriorating. (Wentworth's own Arms can be seen above the west doorway of the original courtyard.)

At the far end of the Manor is a modern building built on a fine vaulted cellar. The cellar was built as a vittels store in about 1620 (not, as is frequently stated, as a necessity merely to hold the food and wine needed for the ten-day visit of Henry VIII in 1541). The modern upper part, by Bernard Fielden, is now occupied by the university's Department of Medieval Studies. The appearance is somewhat spoilt by external concrete staircases, but is well proportioned, while the interior is pleasant and spacious.

KNAVESMIRE (TADCASTER ROAD)

The Knavesmire, where York's race meetings are held, is actually part of the common land known as Micklegate Stray, extending from the Ouse in the east to Acomb in the west (across what is now known as Hob Moor and was formerly known as York Moor). Race meetings have been held here on an occasional basis since at least 1530, and regularly since 1708. In 1755, money for a grandstand was raised by the Marquis of Rockingham, and designs invited. The contract was awarded to a thirty-two-year-old stone mason who had recently arrived in the city — John Carr. (Carr is the most innovative and imaginative of the architects to have worked in the city over the last 400 years, with the possible exception of John Vanbrugh.) The grandstand opened two years later. Originally of two storeys, it stood beside the track proper until 1925 when the lower storey alone was moved to its present site in the Paddock.

Prior to the mid-sixteenth century the Knavesmire was known as Knaresmire, deriving from the Scandinavian personal name Knorr. It was being referred to as the Knavesmire by 1625. The city's 'Tyburn' gallows, which in turn took their name from London's Tyburn, stood in the north-west corner of the Knavesmire, opposite the end of Pulleyn Drive, until executions were transferred to the castle in 1802. They were the site of the demise of Dick Turpin in 1739, and many others. Prior to their erection in 1379, the city used the gallows belonging to St Mary's Abbey on Burton Stone Lane (see p. 129).

LADY ANN MIDDLETON'S HOTEL (ON SKELDERGATE)

The hotel actually occupies three houses and takes its name from a hospice for the widows of twenty Freemen of the City founded in 1659 by Ann Middleton, the wife of Peter Middleton, a sheriff of York. The seventeenth-century building was demolished in the 1820s and the present Skeldergate House, by Peter Atkinson (the younger), erected in its place and completed by 1829. The two lesser buildings of the hotel are now known as Cromwell House and Chaplin House. Cromwell House is a converted nineteenth-century saw mill. Chaplin House was built c.1700 and recently named in remembrance of Sir Charlie Chaplin, who frequently visited the house, then the home of the artist Hans Hess.

LAYERTHORPE BRIDGE (LAYERTHORPE)

There has been a bridge over the Foss on this site at least since 1309, and there is some evidence to suggest that there may have been a bridge here as early as the late tenth century. In 1309 it was referred to as Leirfordbrigend, suggesting that prior to the bridge there was a ford at this point. The central arch of the triple-span medieval bridge was destroyed during the siege of 1644, and some planks were put across the gap as a temporary measure in April 1646. These remained the means of crossing the Foss at this point for the next decade. The present bridge was erected as a replacement for the one which was finally built in 1656. In 1828 it had been 'repaired' by the Foss Navigation Company who attempted the work with such ineptitude that the bridge had to be demolished.

The present attractive thirty-five foot single-span stone arch replacement was built by Peter Atkinson (the younger) in 1829, and paid for by the sweet manufacturers H. Craven and Sons. However, to see the bridge properly, one really needs a boat. In building the bridge, Atkinson demolished Layerthorpe Postern, one of the fortified medieval gates into the city (see Chapter Four). Layerthorpe Bridge was one of the three landings on the artificial medieval lake of the King's Fishpool (the other two were at St Margaret's Church on Walmgate and at the Carmelite Friary on Hungate).

LENDAL BRIDGE (MUSEUM STREET)

The coming of the railway to York in the mid-nineteenth century brought a increase in volume of freight carried by road to and from the north-west part of the town. In consequence, the pressure on the one river crossing, Ouse Bridge, grew to the point that Micklegate became a serious hindrance to the commercial life of the city. The only solution was to build another bridge to relieve the traffic. The bridge was first discussed in 1838 when the first railway station opened, but the Yorkshire and North Eastern Railway Company and York City Corporation both insisted that the other should pay, and so nothing was done until Parliament passed the Lendal Bridge and York Improvement Act in 1860, authorizing the Corporation to borrow up to £35,000 for the purpose. This attractive single-span iron bridge was opened in 1863, having taken two years to complete — twice as long as had been envisaged.

The site eventually chosen, after much debate, was the point at which the city wall crossed the river upstream. There had been a ferry at this point, between St Leonard's Landing on the east bank and the Barker Tower on the west, since at least medieval times. A lattice-girder design by William Dredge was finally accepted by the Corporation and the bridge was started in 1861. The work was progressing ahead of schedule when tragedy struck. The half completed bridge collapsed into the Ouse taking with it the lives of five men. Thomas Page (who designed Westminster Bridge) was called in and it was he who designed the present bridge and oversaw its construction. The final cost was £35,500. Tolls were taken on the bridge to help repay the loan and were not abolished until 1898.

The bridge is decorated with the two coats of arms of the city. One represents the crossed keys which were given by Christ to St Peter (to whom the Minster is dedicated). The other is the red cross of St George on a white background, with five lions (see p. 146).

MANSION HOUSE (ON ST HELEN'S SQUARE)

York's Mansion House is the oldest of England's three (the other two being Doncaster and the City of London, which it predates by a decade). It is the official residence of the Lord Mayor during his year of office and stands on the southwest side of St Helen's Square. The building of a Mansion House as the official residence of the Lord Mayor was first discussed during 1723. It was thought desirable to have an official town residence to discourage mayors from their not uncommon 'retirement to the country during their term of office', and, indeed, after its completion the Lord Mayor was expected to hold an open house on two days every week.

The site chosen was that occupied by what had been the Chapel of the Guild of St Christopher (the Guildhall Chapel). By the 1720s the building had become the Cross Keys, an apparently rather dirty little public house. This was demolished and construction was started in the winter of 1725. The Corporation attempted to meet the cost by soliciting donations, through current income and loans. It soon ran far over budget and caused the Corporation financial worries for many years after its completion.

Architecturally it is a conservative building and there is some dispute as to who the architect was. It has been believed by many in York that the house was designed by Richard Boyle, Earl of Burlington (who was responsible for the Assembly Rooms close by, started shortly after the completion of the Mansion House). Latterly however it has been pointed out that Boyle's buildings are more strongly Classical in design, and there are other compelling reasons for believing that Burlington is almost certainly not the architect. A more likely candidate is William Etty (grandfather of William Etty the painter). Whoever was responsible for the Mansion House it is a fine building, dominating, in a subdued way, its corner of the town.

MERCHANT ADVENTURERS' HALL (PICCADILLY/FOSSGATE)

The undercroft of the Merchant Adventurers' Hall is the oldest brick building in York. It was originally built by the Guild of Our Lord and the Blessed Virgin, and has been described as almost a national monument to the fourteenth-century cult of the Virgin, which was particularly strong in York (see Lady's Row, p. 145). The land was given by Sir William Percy on 6th December, 1356, and the Guild itself formally came into being when it received its Royal Charter of Incorporation on 20th March, 1357. Building started the following year. Records of the

116

purchase in 1358 of 20,000 bricks for six pounds from the Carmelite Friars, and of a hundred oak trees for twenty-one pounds from the estate at Thorpe Underwood, still exist. The hall was dedicated to St Mary the Virgin, and each year a feast was held on 15th August, the Feast of the Assumption.

The Guild of Our Lord and the Blessed Virgin accepted freemen of all occupations, not necessarily resident in York. Indeed, donations towards the cost of building the hall came from as far as Newcastle and London. By the beginning of the fifteenth century however, the Mercers in particular had begun to associate themselves with the hall. The Guild of Merchant Adventurers was formed by an amalgamation of the Guild of Mercers and the Guild of Our Lord and the Blessed Virgin. The Guild of Mercers was the original merchant guild in the city, and was formed by the merchants associated with the Company of the Staple (see Chapter One). Throughout the Middle Ages, the Guild of Mercers (and later the Guild of Merchant Adventurers) controlled the export and import of a number of goods, but most importantly, wool and woollen cloth. The power of the Guild was considerable. As late as the nineteenth century one could not open a shop in York without their permission.

Originally a single great hall comprised the upper floor. A large fireplace was installed in 1420 'to make the hall more commodious for eating' and the hall was subdivided in 1571. The undercroft was used as a hospital for the elderly, and the foundation of a hospital had been the primary reason for the formation of the Guild of Our Lord and the Blessed Virgin. There was a chapel on the site before the hall was built, but this was demolished and the present chapel constructed in 1411. At the end of the seventeenth century the chapel was acquired for worship by French Protestants living in or visiting the city.

In 1571 the interior of the hall was refurbished. The walls were panelled and plastered, and ceilings with attics above were fitted. During the twentieth century the hall has been extensively renovated and repaired. The plaster was stripped from the walls in 1893, and the ceilings removed in 1910 and during the 1920s. The replacement of rotting timbers continued until the 1950s.

MERCHANT TAYLORS' HALL (ALDWARK)

The Guild of Taylors in York received its Royal Charter of Incorporation from Charles II on 26th April, 1662. Its origins are, however, much older and the guild is mentioned as early as 1386 when 128 Master Taylors are recorded as members of the guild. The Taylors were the second most numerous body of Freemen in the city in the fourteenth century (second only to the Weavers). As with the Merchant Adventurers, the Merchant Taylors were very closely associated with a religious order, the Fraternity of St John the Baptist, which had been in existence for at least seventy years by the time of its formal incorporation by Henry VI in 1453. The fraternity maintained an altar in the Minster, and this, their hall, was also known as St John the Baptist's Hall until the seventeenth century. The guild continued after the fraternity was abolished at the Dissolution in 1539, absorbing, in 1551, the Guild of Drapers and by 1585 that of the Dyers.

The hall itself is first mentioned in a city charter dated 2nd December, 1415, and seems to have been built around 1400. A single-storey building consisting of what is now the Great Hall, the Merchant Taylors' Hall is a somewhat more modest building than the other three surviving guildhalls in the city. The smaller room projecting from the south side of the Great Hall (now known as the Little Hall) was added later in the fifteenth century as a council chamber.

Originally half-timbered, the brickwork dates from c.1672 and from 1715, at which date the roof was tiled. The Arms above the fireplace in the main hall are those of the Drapers' Company of London, and those over the fireplace in the Little Hall of the York Company of Merchant Taylors. The south window of the Little Hall was painted by a famous York glass artist, Henry Gyles. It carries the date 1679, but the portrait of Queen Anne was added on her accession in 1702 and cost the guild ten shillings.

The buildings to the east of the hall are Almshouses, built in 1729 to replace a *Maison Dieu*, a hospital for sick persons unable to afford to pay for treatment. The Almshouses were demolished at the beginning of the century.

The hall has been leased for various functions since it was built. There is evidence of it being used as a theatre towards the end of the sixteenth century, and from 1715 until 1739 Thomas Keregan's theatre company often performed in the hall. (The company was later to become the Theatre Royal — see p. 128.) From 1813 to 1823, the hall was the home of the National School for Girls, and from 1877 to 1889 the home of the Aldwark Wastrel Unsectarian School for children of all ages.

MONK BRIDGE (HEWORTH GREEN)
The present bridge was built in 1794 by Peter Atkinson (the elder). There are surviving records of a bridge on this site since at least medieval times (the earliest mention is in 1390) and the site was used as a crossing of the Foss by the Romans. (The modern Heworth Green follows the line of the old Roman road to Malton.) The medieval bridge was of three arches and by the sixteenth century the bridge had five arches. It was destroyed during the siege of 1644, but restored soon afterwards. In the 1790s the Crown prosecuted the City Corporation over the state of the bridge built during the period of Republican rule. The result of this legal action was the present bridge, the cost of which was shared between the Corporation and the Foss Navigation Company. Monk Bridge was repaired, partly rebuilt and widened between 1924 and 1926.

OBSERVATORY
The Yorkshire Philosophical Society's small astronomical Observatory in the botanical gardens was proposed as a result of the founding of the British Society

for the Advancement of Science in 1831. The octagonal building was actually erected in 1833 to house a gift of several fine instruments given to the Society at the same foundation meeting, by one Dr Pearson. The lead roof of the building was also a gift from Dr Pearson. It had been designed for him by John Smeaton (the water-wheel engineer who built the Victorian Eddystone lighthouse) as a roof for the summer-house in Pearson's garden, in which role it served in Leicestershire for many years before being brought to York.

At one time the Observatory was home to the largest refracting telescope in Europe, which was made for the Society by the company of Thomas Cooke (who also made the 'Father Time' clock of St Martin-le-Grand on Coney Street, and the famous meridian transit telescope in the Royal Greenwich Observatory).

OUSE BRIDGE (OUSEGATE)

The earliest bridge over the Ouse in York (indeed, the first bridge upstream from the sea) was sited outside the main gate of the Roman fort, approximately where the Guildhall now stands. During Anglo-Saxon times this bridge was lost, presumably in a flood. For a while York did not have a bridge at all and must have existed as virtually two separate towns. There was almost certainly a river crossing at York before the arrival of the legions, and following the loss of the Roman bridge the people of the town must have reverted to crossing the river by ford or ferry, most probably at the site of the present Ouse Bridge.

The replacement for the lost Roman bridge, the first bridge on the site of the present Ouse Bridge, is believed to have been built during the time of the Vikings, probably in the ninth, or possibly in the early tenth century. The bridge at this point remained the only bridge over the Ouse in the town until the middle of the nineteenth century.

Since Viking times, there have been at least four bridges here. The story of the collapse of Ouse Bridge under the weight of the crowds that turned out to welcome the return of Archbishop William Fitzherbert (later St William of York) in the spring of 1154 (and the associated miracle) is told in Chapter Two. Whether the story is true or not it is quite probable that a wooden Ouse Bridge collapsed at about this time. A chapel built on the north side of the bridge at the west end, during the second half of the twelfth century, was dedicated to St William in the 1220s. The chapel, owned by the Corporation, was of stone (a little of it survives in the Yorkshire Museum) and, assuming that a stone building would not have been built on a wooden bridge, the bridge itself must have been of stone by the end of the twelfth century (a date supported by the architectural style of the medieval bridge) and the chapel may have been built at the same time as a new stone bridge.

The chapel was enlarged following a battle between the followers of John Comyn, a Scots-Norman knight, and the men of the city, which took place on the bridge in 1267 (see Chapter One), and paid for by payments made in compensation. By the mid-fifteenth century the chapel tower, surmounted by a steeple, held a clock and a bell. The clock became the official town clock by which York regulated its business, and the working day started and ended in the city with the ringing of the town bell for a quarter of an hour when the clock on St William's Chapel indicated 5 a.m. and 8 p.m. each day. (Later this function was taken over by St Michael's Church on the corner of Ousegate and Spurriergate, fifty yards from the bridge.)

Following the Dissolution, the Corporation stopped paying for the chapel and services had ceased by the 1580s. The building was put to various secular uses including those of a school, a house of correction, a civic records office, a sheriffs' court and, in the seventeenth century, a trading exchange. It was demolished early in the nineteenth century (see p. 122).

Next to the chapel the medieval bridge carried the City Corporation Building, housing the Records Office and Exchequer, with the Council Chamber itself on the upper floor above these. Here the Privy Council met (the elected officers of the city, comprising the Lord Mayor, sheriff and twenty-four councillors). Larger public meetings, elections, etc, were held in the Guildhall itself. It seems probable that this building was also erected at the same time as the stone bridge, in which case the adjoining St William's Chapel was most probably built for civic religious assembly and worship.

Adjacent to the chapel and the Council Chamber were the municipal prisons, of which there were two by the beginning of the fifteenth century — a Sheriff's Prison used for criminals and the Mayor's Prison used mainly for civil offenders. They were nicknamed the 'kidcotes'. Each was divided into two to segregate the sexes (at least by later Tudor times), and in two again — an upper level and a lower level. On the upper levels prisoners were allowed to beg for food from people using the bridge. The kidcotes were terrible places, particularly the lower levels which were used for particularly severe punishment. These were below the level of the bridge pavement and were without windows. Contemporary accounts leave us with a picture of dark, damp and very cold stone-walled rooms, with prisoners not infrequently succumbing to disease, damp, hypothermia and malnutrition.

On the south side of the bridge at the west end, opposite the chapel, was the Tollbooth where fees were collected from vehicles using the bridge. The amounts varied from time to time but were dependent on the nature of the load being carried. The money raised was used to maintain both Ouse and Foss Bridges, both of which were in frequent need of repair. In addition, the Tollbooth served as the city treasury office and was also the place where the Mayor's court often met in medieval times. The function of the court seems to have been to resolve civil disputes. Close to the Tollbooth on this side of the bridge there was a *Maison Dieu*, funded in part by a grant from the city.

Just as the sea-fish market was held on Foss Bridge, so the fresh fish market was held at Ouse Bridge, the landing staith being at the east end of the bridge, below the north side. (The staith, known as the Fishlanding, no longer exists.) Prior to the sixteenth century the wool market was also probably held on the bridge, where the Merchant Adventurers' Company rented a hall for the purpose in the same building as the Council Chamber.

Carrying so many of the town's important civic buildings, Ouse Bridge became the centre of local government and the focus of the city in medieval times. By the mid-sixteenth century the bridge was completely lined with shops and other tenements — in 1563 twenty-one such premises were recorded as standing on the north side of the bridge and twenty-six on the south. The medieval stone bridge had six arches, of which only the centre two were suitable for navigation and the outer two were dry. The second arch on each side, known as the King's and Queen's Bows, being the arches on the same corresponding sides of the river as King's and Queen's Staiths, were hired out by the Corporation for the setting of fish traps (probably illegally).

During the winter of 1564–5 disaster struck when, following a sudden thaw, ice piled up against the central pier and brought about the partial collapse of the bridge. The two central arches were swept away, destroying twelve houses and killing a number of people. For a little less than two years York was again without a bridge while repairs were carried out, and the Corporation set up a ferry, free to citizens of York and charging others a return fare of 1d. for a rider and horse and ½d. for a person on foot. The foundation stone for the replacement for the two central vaults was laid in March 1565.

York, however, was going through bad times and it proved impossible to raise the money to repair the bridge, less than half of the estimated cost being forthcoming. It appears that the expensive difficulty was the creation of foundations for the central pier. In July 1565, the Lord Mayor of York wrote for help to Sir Martyn Bowes, the Lord Mayor of London. Bowes, who came from a powerful York family, offered to lend York London's master bridge builder, Thomas Harper, to act as consultant, paid for by the City of London. Although Harper and his assistant spent less than a month in the town, their advice left York with plans for a splendid single arch to replace the two lost, alleviating the need for a new central pier.

Construction was started the following spring. On its completion the single central arch of eighty-one feet was one of the longest spans in Europe. However, the limitations of the strength of the new arch, unsupported by a central pier, meant that this portion of the bridge would never again carry buildings, and on reopening the bridge carried only seventeen tenements (approximately a third of the number with which it had been lined before the collapse).

The new bridge was built, in large part, with stone taken from various buildings no longer in use — the Bitchdaughter Tower in the city walls (by Tudor times redundant for defensive purposes), Holy Trinity Priory, St Mary's Abbey and St George's Chapel outside the castle (all ruined at the Dissolution a quarter of a century before) and the remains of St Anne's Chapel on Foss Bridge. The repaired bridge lasted until the second decade of the nineteenth century when it was demolished, under the provisions of an Act of Parliament passed to allow the construction of a wider bridge.

The present triple-span bridge, built of Pennine gritstone, was designed by Peter Atkinson (the younger). Money was raised by public subscription, and an Act of Parliament passed to enable the work to go ahead. The first stone was laid on 10th December, 1810, but the bridge was not completed until a decade later. The original plan was for a bridge with five arches. A second Act of Parliament had to be passed when Atkinson changed his mind to enable the County Council to help with the escalating cost.

As this was the only crossing over the Ouse, the new bridge was constructed in halves, split longitudinally. This allowed one side of the old bridge to remain in use while the first half of the new bridge was being constructed. This came into use on 1st January, 1818. The remaining part of the old bridge was then demolished and the new bridge completed.

With the demolition of the medieval and Tudor bridge the city also lost the St William Chapel, the Council Chamber, the Tollbooth and the other buildings which had survived into the nineteenth century. The Records Office had been moved to the Guildhall in 1738, and the majority of the non-public buildings which had stood here were removed during the late eighteenth century to reduce the load on the bridge. The Council continued to meet on Ouse Bridge until 1808, when its impending demolition meant they were forced to move. A new, purpose-built chamber was constructed as an annex to the Guildhall (see p. 110). The clock from the St William Chapel on the bridge was rescued and is now in Scunthorpe Museum.

The buildings on both approaches to the bridge were also demolished at this time to allow better access to the new, wider bridge. At the same time, King's and Queen's Staiths, adjacent to the north and south ends of the bridge respectively, were also rebuilt. The new King's Staith was rebuilt in gritstone, which has greater resistance to corrosion by water than the magnesium limestone of the previous river walls, but is more expensive to obtain in York. Queen's Staith, formerly the more important but by the nineteenth century the quieter staith, was rebuilt in limestone. The river walls of the north bank upstream of Ouse Bridge, behind Coney Street, are the original medieval limestone walls.

There is supposed to have been a tunnel running from the east end of Ouse Bridge to the Minster — the purpose, reason and use long forgotten.

PICCADILLY BRIDGE (PICCADILLY)
This bridge is included for the sake of completion. Of no architectural merit, it was built as part of the development of the area between the Foss and Pavement started in 1909. The medieval houses which stood here were cleared, and

Piccadilly was created to connect Pavement with Fishergate. (The area between the bridge and Fishergate was then undeveloped, recently drained marshland.) The bridge opened in 1913.

RAILWAY STATIONS (THE WEST ANGLE OF THE CITY WALLS)

The first railway station to be built in York still stands immediately inside the north-western corner of the walls where it was built on the site of the medieval Dominican Friary. Following the Dissolution the land passed into private hands and became the biggest market garden in northern England, before being acquired by the newly formed York and North Midland Railway Company in 1839. The building of the station and its associated goods yards and warehouses led to York becoming an important railway centre, which it remains to this day.

Built to a design drawn up jointly by George Andrews and George Stephenson, the station was opened on 4th January, 1841. In fact the first train from York ran on 29th May, 1839, from a temporary station erected just outside the city wall (where Queen Street runs today). The event was declared a public holiday and was accompanied by much pageantry. Large crowds turned out to cheer and the Minster bells rang out over the town throughout the ceremony. Andrews (who also designed St John's College and St Leonard's Place) specialized in railway stations at a time when the railway was still a novelty. As well as the original station in York he designed the stations at Hull, Market Weighton and Pocklington.

York was the first station to have an associated station hotel (also designed by Andrews). This still survives — it is the brick building at the eastern corner of the old station, and was opened a decade after the station, by which time it was clear that a station hotel could pay its way. Today the area around the old station and hotel continues to be used by British Rail as its north-eastern headquarters.

The building of a station in York owed not a little to George Hudson, the Lord Mayor of the town, who became known as the 'Railway King'. In order to allow trains into and out of the walls, Hudson had his Corporation approve the demolition of this portion of the city walls, and their rebuilding with arched entrances. Initially there was only one such arch, created in 1839. However, as the business conducted by the railway grew, so in 1845 a second archway to the south of the first was created to serve the expanding station (see also Chapter Four).

As rail traffic to and from the town continued to expand, it was realized that in order to expand the station would need more space than was then available, and the decision was taken to build a new railway station just outside the medieval walls, to the west of the original station. Completed in 1877 to a design by Thomas Prosser, and opened with festivities similar to those of thirty-six years before, it is a striking building inside, with a through engine shed 800 feet long, built on a gentle sweeping curve. The Royal Station Hotel, situated to the right of the present station, was completed the following year.

123

RAINDALE MILL (CASTLE MUSEUM)

Behind the Castle Museum, outside the surviving part of the castle bailey, standing on the banks of the Foss, is a small flour mill. There have been flour mills associated with this area since before the Conquest and they became the largest mills in York in the twelfth and thirteenth centuries. In the 1070s, when the King's Fishpool was created by damming the Foss to flood a moat around the castle, two recently built mills are recorded as having been destroyed. After the building of the castle the 'castle mills' belonged to the Crown and were powered by wheels driven by water diverted through a ditch (no trace of which survives). The dam at this point was used as the Foss crossing (the predecessor of the later Castle Mills Bridge) and the millrace and river together created an island, known as the Otter Holmes, now part of St George's Field.

In the twelfth century the mills were given to the Knights Templar, along with the adjacent chapel, after which St George's Field takes its name. Edward II had them valued in 1308 and, short of money to fight the Scots, sequestrated them three years later (the year before the Order of the Templars was formally suppressed). The mills were given to St Leonard's Hospital in 1452, and returned to the Crown yet again on the Dissolution of the Hospital in November 1539. They were leased by the Crown, first into private hands, then to the Corporation, but were sold in July 1600.

In 1603 the mills were bought by Sir Thomas Hesketh, who intended to found a hospital for retired workers on his estates at the nearby village of Heslington and fund its upkeep with the income from the mills. He died before he could realize his ambition, but it was carried out in his name in 1630.

In 1643, during the Civil War the mills were used to grind gunpowder — for which they were not designed. They blew up, but were repaired, only to be inadvertently destroyed again three years later, this time by the Corporation while repairing the Foss dam. Repaired again in 1650, they remained in the possession of the Hesketh and Yarburgh families of Heslington, and in 1778 Henry Yarburgh had steam engines installed in the mills to allow them to continue to work even in dry weather. In 1793 the mills were compulsorily purchased by the Foss Navigation Company.

The Foss Navigation Company had itself fallen into disrepair and neglected its duties. In 1853 the Corporation assumed responsibility for the company. (The reason the Corporation took over the company's duties was that its failure to manage the Foss had created a health hazard to the inhabitants of Layerthorpe.) The Corporation found the mills in a state of dilapidation beyond economic repair. They sold off the equipment in 1855 and finally demolished the mills the following year.

The present mill is run by the Castle Museum. It was brought here in 1965 from the village of Raindale, near Pickering in North Yorkshire, and now mills grain for the interest of visitors to the museum.

ST ANTHONY'S HALL (BORTHWICK INSTITUTE, ON PEASHOLME GREEN)

The original building (now the south-west end of the hall) was started in 1446 when Henry VI granted a Charter for the founding of a Guild of St Martin. Prior to this the guild had been known as St Anthony's and recently it had grown considerably in numbers as a result of having accepted many of the members of a guild which had broken up in disarray in 1418 (the Guild of Holy Trinity; see also Foss Bridge, p. 109) and of having been united with another guild (the Paternoster Guild) in the early 1440s. The new guild, swollen in both members and assets, decided to build itself a suitable hall.

St Anthony's Hall was constructed over the following decade, and may have been almost completed when the chapel was dedicated in 1453. It takes its name from a hospital dedicated to St Anthony of Viennois which probably belonged to the Guild of St Anthony, and predated the present hall on this site. In spite of the erection of a chantry to St Anthony being forbidden, the name continued to be used. The main hall is on the first floor. The south-west end of the ground floor (the bottom left-hand window on Peasholme Green) was a chapel, and the rest of the ground floor a hospital. The fireplaces and chimneys were added at various times during the seventeenth century.

The guild continued after the Dissolution and from 1554 the Hall was used by those surviving craft guilds of the city that did not possess their own building. The age of the guilds had, however, passed and for the next seventy years the main function seems to have been to hold a dinner for the citizens of the city once every three years. The Guild of St Martin was eventually disbanded in 1627.

The Corporation, in the meantime, were putting the hall to practical use. The economic policies pursued by the Tudor administrations, together with a trend in farming from arable to livestock, resulted in mass unemployment. The Corporation, ahead of its time in comparison with elsewhere, set up, in 1567, a cloth-making workshop in the hall to be staffed by the destitute — one of the first 'workhouses'. In addition, in 1586 parts of the hall were converted to act as a short-stay prison, chiefly for vagrants unable to find work (and who had illegally left the parish of their registration). The hall was used as a prison until 1814.

During the siege of York, in July 1644, St Anthony's Hall was pressed into service as both an armoury and a hospital for the wounded. In 1705 the Bluecoat School was founded in the building, which it eventually came to occupy completely. St Anthony's Hall remained the home of the school until 1946. Part of the hall was used in the early eighteenth century as a theatre and, for a short while from 1708, the wool market was held here.

Inside the main hall (which is open to the public during normal working hours) the roofing beams are noteworthy — the first three span the building and were designed to support a ceiling. The remaining, later beams reflect a change in fashion towards open attics.

The building has been extensively added to and altered over the centuries, and

125

was extensively restored during 1952–3, since when it has been the home of the Borthwick Institute of Historical Research (part of the University of York) which specializes in research into legal and administrative aspects of ecclesiastical history.

St John's College (Lord Mayor's Walk)

St John's College is actually two buildings (with later annexes and extensions) opened in 1845 and 1846 as Diocesan training colleges for schoolmasters and schoolmistresses. They are of Tudor style, in Victorian brick and were designed by G.T. Andrews.

St Leonard's Hospital

The great medieval hospital dedicated to St Leonard occupied a site of a little over four acres, inside the city wall on the west side of the town. Although there was probably a hospital run by the Minster prior to the tenth century, the immediate predecessor of the medieval hospital was a gift to the city from Athelstan during his stay in York in AD 937 (see Chapter One). The king entrusted the hospital to a Celtic monastic order known as the Culdees, who had come to York from Scotland (where the order had originated two centuries earlier) and who were pledged to poverty and philanthropy. Athelstan's hospital was associated with the Minster and, like the Minster, was dedicated to St Peter. Where this predecessor of the medieval hospital was situated is not clear but it was most likely close to the west end of the cathedral.

The original hospital burnt down when the town was destroyed by fire during the siege of 1069. The site of the medieval hospital which replaced it extended south-west from the tenth-century site, and was given by William II when he founded a new hospital church in 1089. This too was destroyed (along with the Minster, St Mary's Abbey, Holy Trinity Priory and thirty-nine of the town's forty-five parish churches) when a huge fire swept through much of the city on the 4th and 5th June, 1137. The fire came just as extensive expansion and modernisation of the hospital was nearing completion. King Stephen endowed grants to allow immediate rescue and reconstruction to begin, and the new hospital church was dedicated to St Leonard in a ceremony presided over by Stephen himself. It seems to have been at this re-dedication that the hospital became autonomous and independent of the Minster. (The hospital itself retained the name of the Minster's dedication to St Peter until the thirteenth century.)

The remains of the buildings of the hospital can be found throughout this area of the town (all dating from the rebuilding after the great fire) but little of any particular structure has survived. The Red House, on the corner of St Leonard's Place and Duncombe Place, stands on the site of a former gate-house of the hospital and incorporates stonework from the original building. This can be seen

126

today in the wall facing St Leonard's Place. (The Red House, designed by Sir W. Robinson, was the home of Dr John Burton, who appears in Lawrence Sterne's *Tristram Shandy* as the character Dr Slop.)

The best-preserved parts of the complex of buildings are in the garden of the Central Public Library on Museum Street, where there is a groin-vaulted crypt of four bays, spanning three aisles (a miniature version of the undercroft of Fountain's Abbey near Ripon, with which it is contemporary, and possibly built by the same masons). Built during the first half of the thirteenth century, the crypt supported a chapel, a little of which survives. The original Theatre Royal made use of surviving vaulting of the medieval hospital, and this vaulting was used by Styan in his design for the present theatre (see p. 133). Today's Victorian Theatre Royal is supported in part by twelfth-century masonry.

St Leonard's was more like a monastery than a modern 'hospital', and residents were expected to adhere to the codes of the Austin Friars (whose House was situated nearby, between Lendal and the river). During the 600 years of its existence St Leonard's provided not only the guest house (the *hospitum*, from which hospitals take their name) but almshouses, a monastic school, a nursery for children and an infirmary of over 200 beds.

By the time of its demise, when the Dissolution reached York in the autumn of 1539, St Leonard's was one of the largest hospitals in the country. The hospital site itself occupied all the land between the city wall and what is now Museum Street and Duncombe Place, and from the Multangular Tower to within a hundred yards of the Minster. In addition, the hospital owned much other property in and around York.

As with the Minster itself and St Mary's Abbey (see p. 129), the land enclosed by St Leonard's comprised a 'liberty' — the hospital made and enforced its own law (over and above those of the king) within hospital property. The Mayor, sheriffs or Corporation had no jurisdiction within hospital property, and the hospital even had its own gallows (which stood, together with a small chapel, outside the city, on Green Dykes Lane, close to the modern university).

A record of the staff included the master, 13 brethren, 4 secular priests, 8 sisters, 30 choristers, 2 schoolmasters, 6 servitors (who probably were responsible for overseeing the daily running and upkeep of the hospital) and 206 beadsmen (whose duties would have been those of secular servants, in addition to their liturgical commitments). Together with visitors and the sick being cared for, the institution must have been a significant community.

Following the Dissolution, the hospital grounds seem to have been disused for several years. In 1546, the Royal Mint was moved to the site now occupied by York Central Public Library and the City Treasury, where it remained for seven years. The area became known as Mint Yard. The Mint was again sited here in 1629, but in 1642 was moved to St William's College.

St Leonard's Place and the Theatre Royal

St Leonard's Place, the 150 yards between the north end of Blake Street and Bootham Bar, takes its name from the great hospital dedicated to St Leonard which, for several centuries, occupied this area (see p. 126). St Leonard's Place itself was created between 1835 and 1842 as 'genteel private residences' and was designed by P.F. Robinson and G.T. Andrews. The west side is taken up by a stuccoed crescent in Regency style (now used as offices by the City Council). The crescent is unusual in that the uniform front hides nine houses whose interior designs all differ, being to the individual tastes of the first owners. In building the crescent Andrews and Robinson made extensive use of cast iron for major structural components. The apparently stone columns, for example, are iron.

Opposite the crescent, on the east side of St Leonard's Place, is the Theatre Royal. The theatre company was founded by Thomas Keregan and its continuous history can be traced to a group of players who performed in the Merchant Taylors' Hall from 1715. The company moved to a courtyard on the south side of the Minster in 1734, and to its present site ten years later. Having proven itself a success, the theatre was substantially rebuilt twenty years after the move, under the direction of its ambitious and adventurous manager, Joseph Baker. In 1769, George III granted Tate Wilkinson, Baker's successor, the respectability of a Royal Patent (at a cost of £500) and the players of York became York Theatre Royal.

Until St Leonard's Place was created, the main entrance to the Theatre Royal was on Lop Lane (now Duncombe Place). In the 1830s, when the crescent was built, a new front was added (designed by John Harper) as much to force the older building to conform to the appearance of its new neighbours as to improve the theatre itself. Part of the arcade of this front was rescued when the present theatre was built, and can be seen in front of number 73 Fulford Road.

The Theatre Royal building as it stands today, was erected in 1879 to a design by George Styan (who, appears to have felt little sympathy towards the style of his surroundings). The glass café and foyer were opened in 1968.

Between the Theatre Royal and Bootham Bar are De Grey House and the De Grey Rooms, both built to designs by G.T. Andrews. De Grey House, next to the theatre, is contemporary with the rest of St Leonard's Place. The De Grey Rooms were commissioned six years later by Earl de Grey and his fellow officers of the Yorkshire Hussars, to act as their mess and to be used for public functions for which the Assembly Rooms were considered unsuitably spacious. The City Art Gallery, opposite, was completed in 1879 to house the second of York's Fine Art and Industrial Exhibitions. (See also under Exhibition Square, Chapter Six).

St Mary's Abbey (the Museum Gardens)

Prior to the site being given to the Benedictine Order, the land later occupied by St Mary's Abbey was the stronghold of the Danish earls who governed from

York. Known as *Earlsburh*, it may have been the 'castle' destroyed by Athelstan in 937, during his stay in York following his victory over a Norse army at Brunanburh.

The great Abbey of St Mary stood in what are now the Yorkshire Museum Gardens. The Abbey grew from the donation in 1080 by Count Alan of Brittany and Earl of Richmond, of St Olave's Church on Marygate, to the Benedictine Abbey of St Hilda at Whitby (see St Olave's Church, Chapter Three). Only ruins survive of what was once a considerable collection of buildings, with the exceptions of much of the defensive wall and of the Abbot's Palace, the building now known as King's Manor (see p. 112). In all, St Mary's Abbey covered a site of some thirteen acres, which comprised a 'liberty' in which the abbey had absolute jurisdiction, and was answerable only to the Pope and the Crown.

The size of the abbey can perhaps be imagined from the dimensions of its church, which was about two-thirds the length of the present Minster (and equal in size to the twelfth-century Minster with which it was contemporary). The north wall of the nave still stands against its boundary with St Olave's churchyard. The original abbey was very badly damaged in the great fire of 1137 (see St Leonard's Hospital, p. 126), and in the aftermath was almost completely rebuilt. The church of which the extensive ruins survive today was the third abbey church, started in 1270.

A little less than a hundred yards to the south of the abbey church (between the church and the river) is a large hall, two storeys high and six bays long, with a lower storey of limestone ashlars and a timber-framed upper hall. The lower part was built in the fourteenth century as the workshop of the abbey's tailors (the abbey *sartrinao*). The upper part was added in the fifteenth century and the building subsequently became the guest house of the monastery. By the twentieth century it was ruined, two bays having collapsed completely. It was completely restored and opened in 1930.

The walls around St Mary's can easily be mistaken for part of the city walls. In fact, St Mary's was situated just outside the walled city and had its own defences. The surviving walls are the most extensive of any abbey walls still standing in Britain. The walls are early fourteenth century and are 855 feet in length, extending from the river to the corner of Marygate and Bootham, and along Bootham to Exhibition Square.

An interesting feature of the walls around St Mary's is that the merlons retain the grooves which supported pivoted wooden shutters. The shutters closed the embrasures of the battlements against arrows during times of siege, opened briefly to allow an archer to fire, then rapidly closed. Reconstructions of some of these shutters have been restored to the walls of St Mary's along Marygate. Apart from St Mary's, only Alnwick Castle in Northumberland also retains some of its shutter grooves.

The ruined tower on the banks of the Ouse, at the bottom of Marygate and known as the Water Tower, was built some time shortly after 1318. The arch beside it was created during the eighteenth century to allow access to the riverside promenade for the gentlemen and ladies who lived in the wealthy Bootham area of the town.

Halfway along Marygate is the abbey gate-house, next to St Olave's Church. It is a large hall (forty feet long) and stands on what was a Roman road approaching the city from the north-west, suggesting continuous use for significantly more than a millennium. The gate-house predates the present walls by 200 years. Between the gate-house and St Olave's are the ruins of a small chapel dedicated to St Mary, built a little later for the use of visitors to the Abbey.

The circular, two-storey tower on the corner of Marygate and Bootham is known as St Mary's Tower and dates from the mid-1330s. Its design is unusual, being circular on the outside (thirty-four feet in diameter) but octagonal inside. During 1644, one of the Parliamentarian armies besieging the city undermined St Mary's Tower, blowing it up with gunpowder at about noon on 16th June. It was Trinity Sunday and most of the Royalists defending the city were in the Minster attending Matins.

As Parliamentarian soldiers, under the command of the Earl of Manchester, poured into the grounds of the abbey, Royalists left the city by the gate by Lendal Tower and made their way along the river and up Marygate, cutting off the retreat of the invaders, by now besieging King's Manor (the Royalist headquarters). About three hundred of Manchester's troops were captured, only to be freed again when York surrendered on the 16th July.

When the tower was repaired the builders made what must have been an embarrassing error — the two sides of the repaired breach in the wall did not meet, giving the Bootham side of the tower a unique appearance.

The stretch of wall from Marygate to Exhibition Square was erected in 1266 and further heightened in 1318. The wall originally extended as far as the barbican at Bootham Bar (see Chapter Four). However, at the end of the fifteenth century it was decided to create another gate into the abbey, to allow better access to the abbot's palace (now known as King's Manor, see p. 112). An archway was made and a square Postern Tower built. The tower is now known as Queen Margaret's Tower, after an erroneous belief that the gateway was created for the visit to York of Princess Margaret, daughter of Henry VII, on her way to Scotland to marry James IV (an alliance which led to the Union of Crowns). In fact, the gate was six years old when the princess arrived for her two-day visit. Queen Margaret's Tower is also unusual, the exterior being built of ashlars but the interior lined with brick (see p. 90). The open junction of St Leonard's Place and Bootham was created by the demolition of Bootham barbican in 1832 and the demolition of the Bird in Hand public house in the 1870s (see under Exhibition Square in Chapter Six).

Most of the rest of the extensive buildings of the Abbey have long since disappeared, stone being taken for other purposes (such as the repair of Ouse Bridge in 1566 and of St Olave's Church in the 1720s). Much of the site of the abbey was given to the Yorkshire Philosophical Society and now comprises the site of the Yorkshire Museum and the botanical gardens of the Yorkshire Philosophical Society (see p. 138). The City Art Gallery and Exhibition Square were also part of the abbey grounds (see Exhibition Square in Chapter Six).

The Abbey became very wealthy and very powerful, and great rivalry for status and seniority existed between St Mary's and the Minster. Clashes between the Abbot and the Sacrist of St Mary's, and the Archbishop and the Dean and Chapter of the Minster were frequent, often public, often unbecoming and not infrequently characterized by triviality and petulance. The property of the Abbey comprised a Liberty (see St Leonard's Hospital, p. 126) and the Abbey maintained a gallows which stood outside the town, a little to the west of the modern District Hospital. St Mary's owned land throughout the north-east of England, and much property in the city, including a windmill in Clifton, and a windmill and three water-mills on the Foss, a little above Monk Bridge.

At the time of its demise, St Mary's was the third largest abbey in the country. It came to the end of its history of over four centuries at the Dissolution — the king's men accepted the Abbey on the 29th November, 1539. All its property passed to the Crown.

St Peter's School (Bootham)

The original building, designed by John Harper and completed in 1838, is now the nucleus of the complex of buildings which make up the current home of England's oldest public school. It was built as a small private school and acquired by the Dean and Chapter in 1844 to house St Peter's School, which was then rapidly outgrowing its former home in what is now the Minster Song School on Deangate.

St William's College (East End of the Minster)

Not infrequently, the Minster chantry priests (see p. 58) found themselves without a demanding amount of work on their hands, having little to do apart from say Mass once, perhaps twice a day. Being comfortably paid young men they came to attract a reputation in the town for being more trouble than they might be worth. To be fair to the Dean and Chapter, it should be pointed out that these priests were not usually the appointed vicars-choral of the Minster, but were privately employed and consequently, to a large extent, outside the jurisdiction of the Minster authorities. However, there was little affection lost between the men of the Minster Liberty and the town, and violent clashes were certainly not rare, to the point of the occasional murder.

The Dean and Chapter of the Minster decided that these young priests needed somewhere to live where they might attract less trouble and attention (while still, of course, attracting sponsorship to the Minster itself). Consequently, St William's College was founded, established under the terms of a licence granted by Henry VI in 1455. St William himself had nothing to do with the college. (He had lived over three centuries earlier and his story is told in Chapter Two.)

Until its extension to house the troublesome priests, the building had been a home for Minster canons. Nothing of the original structure remains. The present building was started in 1465 when Edward IV gave the college a gift of a quarry to supply the stone required for a building which was large enough to house the chantry priests. Subsequently, St William's College became home to twenty-three priests and a provost to oversee them.

Following the Dissolution, the college was given into private hands and was thereafter sold a number of times. Much of the original building has been replaced over the intervening centuries, and most of the interior of the present building dates from the seventeenth century. During the eighteenth century it was owned by the Earl of Carlisle, who lived here until Castle Howard was built. In 1900 it was bought by Frank Green (see the Treasurer's House, p. 133) who had the college extensively restored (by Temple Moore, also responsible for the restoration of the Treasurer's House and Gray's Court — see p. 133). Green subsequently sold the building back to the Church for use by the Convocation of York, asking only what he had paid for the unrenovated building.

The front of the building (along College Street) is, however, part of the original mid-fifteenth-century structure (with the exception of the windows which were replaced by Moore). Seated above the door leading from College Street to the courtyard of the college is the figure of St William himself. Inside the courtyard, unusual carved wooden brackets support the first-floor jetties, with figures representing the twelve months of the year.

The dormitory, chapel and hall of the college were on the opposite side of Goodramgate, and much of these buildings also survive in Bedern and Bartle Garth. There was an enclosed gallery to cross Goodramgate at first-floor level. The remains of this can still be seen protruding above the door of number 30 Goodramgate.

Following the abolition of the Council of the North by the 'Long Parliament' in 1641 (see King's Manor, p. 112) Charles I set up his administration in the city. For a time during this brief period in 1642, St William's College housed the Royal Mint and printing press, producing the pamphlets which proclaimed Charles' Divine right to absolute authority.

SCARBOROUGH BRIDGE (EARLSBOROUGH TERRACE)
This is the railway bridge (and footpath) and the most northerly of York's bridges over the Ouse. Until it was opened in 1845, Ouse Bridge had been the only bridge over the river in the town. (See Ouse Bridge, p. 119.) The consultant engineer was no lesser person than George Stephenson, and the bridge took only twelve weeks

to erect (although it had to be somewhat rebuilt and strengthened within two years of opening, following the collapse of a bridge of the same design at Chester). It was repaired and strengthened again in 1874 at which time the footpath was moved from the centre to the downstream side of the railway track.

SKELDERGATE BRIDGE (BISHOPSGATE STREET)

This is the most recent of the bridges over the Ouse to be built within the inner city. By the last quarter of the nineteenth century the need for a relief route for traffic travelling around the south of the town could no longer be ignored. A bridge was needed to take the load of much of the southern traffic off Ouse Bridge, just as Lendal Bridge had taken the traffic moving around the north of the town. Thomas Page (who designed Lendal Bridge) was awarded the contract, this time in partnership with his son.

The design chosen was for a two-piered, three section, iron bridge, with a large central span and two shorter spans between the piers and the banks. Again, the site chosen was where the city walls crossed the Ouse. The bridge opened in 1881.

There was a complication arising from the siting of this bridge which the builders of the previous bridges had not encountered. At the end of the nineteenth century, King's and Queen's Staiths were still busy trading goods carried up the river in sail-rigged boats. While the staiths were downstream of the other three bridges, they were upstream of the proposed new bridge.

Skeldergate Bridge was therefore built to open and allow masted vessels through. It was not, however, the central section of the bridge which was raised, but the section joining the east bank, which is somewhat narrower but wide enough and deep enough to allow deep-keeled vessels to pass through. The small tower at the north-western corner of the bridge housed the engine which raised this section. The tall ships plying trade to the York staiths are long gone, and with them the mechanism to raise the bridge. Skeldergate Bridge now remains firmly closed to all but small craft.

THEATRE ROYAL
See *St Leonard's Place*

TREASURER'S HOUSE AND GRAY'S COURT (CHAPTER HOUSE STREET)

In a city of interesting houses, the history of the Treasurer's House is possibly the most interesting of all. The building is now divided into two parts. Facing the Minster, the winged hall is known as the Treasurer's House (together with the additions fronting onto Chapter House Street) while the part of the building which forms the north end of the courtyard (reached through a gate at the north-east end of Chapter House Street) is now called Gray's Court.

The posts of Treasurer, Chancellor, Precentor and Dean were created by the first Norman Archbishop, Thomas of Bayeux. Thomas arrived in January 1071, and found the Church in a state of chaos following three years of intermittent war in York, culminating in the destruction of the city (including the Minster) by fire, in 1069 (see Chapter One). It was Archbishop Thomas who, as part of a reorganization of all aspects of Church government, ordered the construction of houses befitting the positions held by the senior officers of the Minster. For himself, the archbishop built a splendid palace which stood in what is now the modern Deanery gardens. A little of this palace remains, incorporated into the Minster Library (itself formerly the chapel of the palace).

The responsibilities of the Treasurer comprised the management and security of the Minster treasures, including such things as the valuable ceremonial copes. However, his duties and powers did not stop here. The Treasurer was responsible for the upkeep and repair of the fabric of the building and had jurisdiction over the whole of the Minster with the exception of the choir. (Within the choir, the Dean took precedence, even in matters of security.) The Treasurer was even responsible for maintaining an adequate supply of candles for the altars of the church (for should the church run out of candles, the Dean and Chapter would not receive the donations which accompanied the lighting of a candle). The position was well rewarded. The Treasurer received the highest income of any of the officers of the Minster, including the Dean himself. Paradoxically, he was also politically the least powerful of the four high officials. Perhaps the best-known Treasurer of York is William Fitzherbert, Treasurer during the first half of the twelfth century. He later became Archbishop and, later still, St William of York (see Chapter Two).

The architectural history of the Treasurer's House is somewhat complex. A major Roman road runs under the house, twelve feet below the modern street level. In 1898 a Roman pillar was found in the basement, believed to be on its original site. It has been suggested that perhaps the column was part of a colonnade which lined the approach of the road, the *Via Decumana* to the gate of the *Principia*. An alternative, if less probable suggestion, is that the column was part of a Roman Imperial Palace. Recently, a second Roman pillar was found beneath Chapter House Street.

During the 1960s a plumber was having his lunch in one of the cellars of the house when, in his own words, he 'saw a Roman legion march through one of the walls of the cellar and out by another'. The strangest thing was that he said they appeared to be walking on their knees. A few years later the Roman road was discovered — eighteen inches below the present cellar floor, at about the depth that the soldiers' feet would have been if their knees had been at the current floor level.

The history of the site through Anglo-Saxon and Viking times is not known and the earliest record of a building here comes from the late eleventh century when a house was built for the first Treasurer of the Minster, one Ralph, who took up residence in about the year 1100.

Little is known of Treasurer Ralph's house, and it was presumably destroyed along with the Minster on 4th June, 1137, when almost the whole of York burnt down. There is part of a twelfth-century wall at the back of Gray's Court and some stonework of similar age in the lower part of the Treasurer's House (which may be from elsewhere and reused) presumably dating from the reconstruction of the house after the fire. The oldest building of which we know any detail was built by a Treasurer called John le Roman in the late thirteenth century. A gable of this house is incorporated into the present Gray's Court, and some more of the building survives in the form of two doorways in the cellars of the Treasurer's House. Most of the present fabric of the buildings dates from the seventeenth and eighteenth centuries.

The house was the residence of the Treasurers of the Minster until the Reformation. In 1539, Henry VIII's men arrived in York to relieve the churches and monasteries of their wealth. The last Treasurer, William Clyffe, stayed on for a further seven years until the reign of Edward VI. In 1546 he decided he had had enough and resigned to the king with a famous statement, announcing that 'abrepto omni thesauro, desuit thesaurarii munus' — 'there being no treasure left, there would seem to be no need for a Treasurer', and so he departed. Edward formally abolished the posts of Treasurer and Sub-Treasurer on 26th May, 1547. Today the Dean is responsible for the duties which were formerly those of the Treasurer and his staff.

The king subsequently gave the house to the Protector of Somerset, who sold it to the first Protestant Archbishop of York, Archbishop Holgate. Holgate, one of the wealthiest men in England, was removed from office when Catholicism was restored on the accession of Queen Mary in 1553. On being removed to the Tower of London (where he was lucky to escape the fate of his fellow prisoners, Bishops Latimer and Ridley, and Archbishop Cranmer) he sold the house to his Roman Catholic successor, Nicholas Heath, for 200 marks. On the seizure of the Crown by Elizabeth, and the return to a Protestant Church, Heath himself was removed from office. Following Holgate's example, he sold the house to his Protestant successor, Thomas Young.

Archbishop Young proceeded to demolish the central part of the house to sell the lead to raise money for a mansion for his son George (in the building of which he used the stone from the house). For this act of avaricious vandalism he received little local praise. The general feeling in York can be summed up by Sir John Harrington's comment that he 'wished the lead had been melted and poured down Young's throat'. Ironically, while escorting the lead to London in the role of a security guard, an employee of Young's absconded with the metal.

On the archbishop's death, the house passed to the same George Young. In 1603 he entertained the future James I, on his way south to claim the throne of England on the death of his cousin Elizabeth. Young must have made a good impression as, on the 23rd July, he was knighted by the new king at Whitehall

Palace. James I was to visit the Treasurer's House again, in 1617, on which occasion he knighted eight Yorkshire men in the house.

The majority of the present structure of the Treasurer's House was built by the Young family in the second half of the sixteenth and first half of the seventeenth centuries. In 1629, the house passed to Thomas Young, great-grandson of Archbishop Young. It was Thomas Young who created the ashlar front, complete with the Dutch gables, probably during the 1630s. Dr Rupert Hillyard has suggested that if the dating is correct, these must be amongst the earliest Dutch gables in England. An example of the original pointed gables which they replaced can be seen in Gray's Court.

Young altered the structure of the wings considerably, extending both by a second gable. In so doing he created a front of rather heavy proportions. The pattern of fenestration dates from the work of Thomas Young, bilateral symmetry being abandoned. The Venetian-style first-floor windows of the north wing date from a century later. The original positions of the first-floor windows in the south wing are betrayed by the strange segmental pediments which are now between the two outer pairs of lights.

Young sold the house in 1648 to Sir William Belt, a Royalist. With the rise of the republic, it passed from him to Thomas, Lord Fairfax of Denton, the great Parliamentarian general. Fairfax later built a house to his own design in Bishophill and sold the Treasurer's House to George Aislabie, ancestor of the present Marquis of Ripon. Aislabie was tragically killed in a needless duel with his daughter's fiancé, and the house passed to his son John, the Member of Parliament for Ripon.

John Aislabie entertained the Duke of York (who six years later succeeded to the throne as James II) in the house in 1679. The party was not a success. The dignitaries of York offended James by not being servile enough (or, at least, were judged by the turbulent and unpredictable James not to have shown suitable respect). York suffered by having privileges removed for many years. In the reign of Anne, Aislabie rose in political circles and in the first years of the reign of George I became Chancellor of the Exchequer. Later, he created Studley Royal, two miles from Ripon (the town which he had represented in Parliament for a quarter of a century) which includes in its grounds the ruins of the great Fountains Abbey.

In 1698, Robert Squire bought the house from Aislabie, and substantially repaired and redecorated the building. His daughter inherited the building and, in 1721, having split it into two, Jane Squire sold it to Matthew Robinson. On later resale the smaller of the two parts was bought by the traveller, scholar, Member of Parliament and surveyor of Troy, John Bacon Sawrey Morritt. The Morritt family lived in the house until 1813.

Meanwhile, the larger part was bought by a canon of the Minster, who sold it in 1742 to his Precentor, Jacques Sterne. Amongst those entertained in the house by Sterne was the Duke of Cumberland, who stayed here during his journey south following his defeat of Prince Charles' army at Culloden. Sterne was the uncle of Lawrence Sterne, and local tradition has *Tristram Shandy* written in the house. Sterne extended the house, adding a drawing room at the end of the gallery and a dining room at the east end. This part of the house was split again when Sterne ran into financial problems. Sterne died in 1757 and the part he had retained was bought by the Gray family in 1788, and occupied by them until 1948. Today this is the part of the building known as Gray's Court.

In the 1780s John Goodricke, the astronomer, acquired a room in the house, in which he worked (although there is no evidence that Goodricke ever lived in the building). Goodricke discovered a star he named Algol, belonging to a class of stars known as Cepheids, whose brightness varies with time. Such stars have turned out to be of great interest as they allow astronomers to estimate the distance to far off galaxies, once a Cepheid has been identified in the galaxy. Consequently, Goodricke contributed significantly to the branch of natural philosophy which today we call cosmology. His achievements are all the more remarkable as he was deaf and dumb, and died at the untimely age of twenty-three.

During the nineteenth century various parts of the building had a number of owners and various alterations were made. By 1850 the building was divided into five. In 1898 the three parts of the building now known as the Treasurer's House were acquired by Frank Green. Green came from a wealthy West Riding industrial family, and the freedom that wealth gave him allowed him to indulge his passions for period authenticity (or what he believed to be authenticity).

Frank Green was one of the first serious antique collectors in the country in that he tried to furnish the rooms of his house with contemporary pieces, rather than collections of miscellaneously mixed antiquities. It was he who first furnished the Treasurer's House much as it is today. He reunited the three parts of the house which he had bought so that it was as close to the original form as he knew. For this he engaged the post-Victorian purist architect Temple Moore (who carried out a number of projects around York, including the restoration of St William's College adjacent to the Treasurer's House and also owned by Green). The mullioned and transomed windows of the centre and south wings of the house were put in by Temple Moore in about 1900. The annexed buildings along Chapter House Street also date from this period.

On completion of his work for Green, in 1900, Temple Moore was engaged by Edwin Gray to restore Gray's Court, which Moore started at about the turn of the century. The present windows of Gray's Court were also installed by Moore.

In 1930, having ascertained that no members of his family were interested in the building, Frank Green gave the Treasurer's House, together with the majority of its contents (comprising his life's collection of antique furnishings and fittings) to the National Trust. Today it is a museum of his collection and of the history of the house. Gray's Court now houses the Department of History of the College of Ripon and York St John. The pollarded trees which fill the courtyard of Gray's Court are London Plane — a maple hybrid unusual outside the capital. (The plane is the largest of Britain's trees and if not pollarded they would soon have swamped the Court.)

YORKSHIRE MUSEUM

In the Museum Gardens, facing the Ouse where King's Manor once looked out, is the Yorkshire Museum. It was built in the late 1820s to a design by William Wilkins (the younger) as the home of the Yorkshire Philosophical Society, on a part of the land which had been St Mary's Abbey. A small site was leased from the Crown in 1827 and this was added to over the following decades by purchases and leasing until the Society had jurisdiction over almost all of the former grounds of the Abbey and the ruins of part of St Leonard's Hospital. The museum opened in 1830. The adjoining Tempest Anderson Hall, built in the same style and opened in 1913, is thought to be the country's earliest building constructed using concrete and shuttering. It was paid for personally by Dr Anderson, the President of the Society, and named in his memory on his death the following year.

The Museum Gardens are the botanical gardens of the Yorkshire Philosophical Society. Amongst other things, the gardens contain at least one tree of every species native to Britain.

STONEGATE, PETERGATE AND THE SHAMBLES

In addition to those outstanding buildings of the city which demand attention in their own right, York has three streets containing many buildings each of which in isolation would not be particularly remarkable but which together represent some of the best preserved and most evocative medieval domestic architecture surviving anywhere.

STONEGATE

Like Chapter House Street, Petergate and Coney Street, Stonegate closely follows the line of one of the major Roman roads of the city and has been in constant use for nearly two thousand years. Stonegate was the Roman *Via Praetoria* (see Chapter One). No Roman building survives on the street, which is largely medieval and has been described as being as picturesque as any street in England.

Until the nineteenth century, one of the entrances to the former Minster Liberty (see Petergate, p. 139) was at the north end of Minster Gates. Minster Gates itself has been reserved for persons on foot and blocked by posts, or *stulpes*, since at least medieval times. Ceremonies in the Minster attended by the Corporation involved large and formal processions from the Guildhall along Stonegate and through this gate into the cathedral close.

On the south-west corner of Minster Gates is a small statue of the Roman goddess Minerva. Perhaps better known by her Greek name of Athena, she was the goddess of wisdom and one of the most popular deities of the Greeks and of the Romans (who named the city now known as Bath after her). As goddess of wisdom (symbolized by an accompanying owl) she became associated with books, and was adopted by printers as their own. Many printers and publishers had their workshops in this area. The statue carries the name of John Wolstenholme, and the date 1801. Wolstenholme was a publisher who lived in, and sold his books from, this house.

Further down Stonegate, on the corner of Coffee Yard at a height of about seven feet, a small red devil is chained. 'Devils' were the small errand boys employed by the printers and who, the printers claimed, must, out of mischievousness and when the printer's back was turned, be responsible for the typesetting errors found after printing. The devil thus became the symbol of the Printers' Guild.

The significance of the proximity of medieval printers and publishers with the Minster is obvious and, indeed, much of the property in Stonegate was owned by the Dean and Chapter. The street also contained the workshops of many of York's numerous glass artists. Their guild adopted St Helen's Church which, until the eighteenth century, was on the corner of the street in its own churchyard. Also on Stonegate was the foundry of a famous bell-founder, Richard Tunnoc, who rose to become Lord Mayor (see also The Bell-founder's Window, Chapter Two).

The sign advertising 'Ye Olde Starre Inne', a painted beam crossing the street and known as a 'gallows sign', is a remnant of what used to be a common form of advertising. Today few remain and this is the only one in York. The Olde Starre was an inn as early as the reign of Henry VIII, which would make it the oldest established inn in York (though not the oldest building in the city being used as a public house — that honour goes to part of the Red Lion on Merchantgate).

PETERGATE

Petergate mostly follows the line of the Roman road within the fort, running from the south-east gate, which was on the site of the present King's Square, to the opposite gate which stood on the site of Bootham Bar. Like Stonegate, Petergate has, presumably, been in constant use since the fort was laid out in the first century AD. The street is divided into two parts, High and Low Petergate, to the north-west and south-east of the crossing with Stonegate, respectively.

Until the nineteenth century a row of timber-framed houses and other buildings ran along the north side of Petergate from the city wall at Bootham Bar, and formed part of a curtain enclosing the Minster Liberty (within which the Corporation or sheriffs had no civil or criminal jurisdiction). This entirely enclosed area was known as the Minster Close or Minster Liberty, access to which was by one of five gates. St Peter's Gate stood in High Petergate at the end of Duncombe Place. The gate for pedestrians at Minster Gates has already been mentioned (see Stonegate, p. 138) and a third gate stood on Low Petergate, at the site of the old Deanery. This was closed at the beginning of the fourteenth century (see below). The remaining gates were on Goodramgate, opposite the end of Bedern, and in Ogleforth. Deangate did not then exist. It was created in 1903 to relieve the traffic in Petergate.

The houses of Precentor's Court, which are back to back with part of High Petergate, were thus completely within the Minster Close. The fan-shaped building that comprises numbers 26–36 High Petergate and 1 Precentor's Court is more recent than the rest of this side of High Petergate. Built by J.P. Pritchett in 1838, it stands on the site of the former Peter Prison. The prison belonged to the Dean and Chapter, who imprisoned persons transgressing within the grounds and property in the possession of the Minster (which meant chiefly in-debt tenants). The archbishops had their own prison a few yards away, adjacent to the north wall of the Minster, in which were imprisoned aberrant clergy (see below.) In the early 1820s, the City Council petitioned Parliament for permission to demolish the Peter Prison, the adjacent St Peter's Gate and the old Deanery which was further down Petergate, opposite the end of Grape Lane. Parliament agreed and passed an enabling Act in 1825 — part of the nineteenth century obsession with 'improvement' by replacement.

There was a prison in High Petergate from at least 1575. Number 10 High Petergate, now the Hole in the Wall public house, claims the honour of being the site of part of the original prison. Most of the present Hole in the Wall is eighteenth-century brick, but the underlying fabric of the building is a much older timber-framed structure. Some sixteenth-century stonework survives to this day, and a small window in this, on the east side of the bar, is said to be the 'hole' from which the public house now takes its name. Before it was glazed and its outlook blocked by Precentor's Court, it opened onto the Minster Close. Benevolent clergy are said to have passed food to the prisoners through this window.

However, the story is more complex. In the late eighteenth century there was a public house called the Hole in the Wall a little over a hundred yards away, close to the north wall of the Minster. This was housed in the remains of a building which had been a Chapel of St Mary and the Holy Angels, also known as St Sepulchre's. The crypt of this chapel had been the Archbishop's Prison and when it was demolished, in 1816, a cavity was found in one of the walls — some say this 'hole' was the remains of a door, others that it was a cell for immuring prisoners. It seems plausible that ascribing the site of a prison to the present Hole in the Wall public house is the result of a confusion between the Archbishop's Prison, with the hole in its wall, and perhaps also with the Peter Prison a few dozen yards away.

Number 26 High Petergate is today part of the York Arms Hotel. The bar of number 26 now extends behind number 28 and recently the floor of this part of the house collapsed, revealing the dungeon of the old Peter Prison, complete with shackling rings still attached to the wall.

The York Arms Hotel started as a coffee-house in number 24 High Petergate, an early eighteenth-century building. It was one of the earliest coffee-houses in the city and is believed to be the only eighteenth-century coffee-house to have survived to this day, living on by becoming, in 1821, a public house. (The first coffee-house in the town is thought to have stood on the corner of Coffee Yard and Grape Lane.) The present York Arms Hotel is the result of an amalgamation of this original house with number 26, built in 1838, and later still, with part of number 28 High Petergate.

There is a rumour of a tunnel running under the north side of High Petergate. The rumour may be nothing more than that, but it has been suggested that it connected St Mary's Abbey (immediately outside Bootham Bar) with the Minster Close. As such a tunnel need have been little longer than fifty yards, the story is not implausible. If this is correct, its purpose is now obscure. Another possibility is that, like several other stories of tunnels in the town, it was or is a surviving Roman culvert, similar to those found intact and still functioning under Swinegate and under the Minster (see Chapter Two).

Further down High Petergate, the eighteenth-century Young's Hotel (number 25) is one of several sites in this area which claim to be the birthplace of sixteenth-century Guy Fawkes. It is more probable that he was born in a building in Stonegate, where it is known his mother rented a house. Perhaps the association claimed by the hotel comes from the entry in the register of the Church of St Michael-le-Belfrey, on the opposite side of Petergate, recording Fawkes' baptism on 15th April, 1570.

In medieval times, the south-east end of Low Petergate was associated with the businesses of cloth merchants, and also with glove makers and horn workers. The north-west part of Low Petergate acquired a poor reputation for being the haunt of thieves and prostitutes, a place to avoid if after dark and unaccompanied. Grape Lane, a street of little more than fifty yards, running south from Low Petergate, was described by Francis Drake, a historian of York writing in the early 1730s, as follows:

> Grape Lane ... whose name tending not a little to obscenity, as it is wrote very plain in some ancient writings, I shall not pretend to etymologize. We well know our ancestors used to call a spade a spade, but custom has prevailed upon their descendants to be more modest in expression, whatever they are in action ... this place was of old a licenced brothel, though so near the cathedral church as to be exactly opposite the great gates of the deanery. Many of these places have been formerly so licenced in other cities, etc. of England, particularly the bishop of Winchester's mews in Southwark, which were kept open on that occasion till the time of Henry VIII, who, abhorring such lewdness, got an act of parliament to put them down.

Etymologizing a little for Drake, *grape* is derived from the Old English *grapian*, the root of the modern words 'grab' and 'grope'. In the fourteenth century the street was known as Grapcunt Lane. The old Deanery at the end of Grape Lane was demolished in 1830, when a new Deanery was built in Dean's Park (itself replaced in 1940). As mentioned above, one of the five gates into the Minster Close was sited here. It was closed around 1300 because of the reputation the area had by then acquired.

The brothel itself was owned, perhaps surprisingly, by St Benet's Church, which stood at the south end of Grape Lane. The house, actually a row of houses known as Benet's Rents, was adjacent to the church. The earliest reference to St Benet's is in 1154 when it was used by the vicars-choral of the Minster. By 1338 St Benet's was very poor and in much need of repair — perhaps explaining a lack of over-fastidiousness in its choice of tenants. It has even been suggested that it was the Black Death, which arrived in England in 1349, which put financial pressure on the Church so that it was prepared to let its properties to the highest bidder, regardless of other considerations. (The Black Death meant many extra priests had to be taken on by the churches to say the Masses required.) By 1547 St Benet's had been demolished. Today Low Petergate is a respectable street of shops.

The American Indian, above the window of number 76 Low Petergate, has his own interesting story. The Indian was once a common symbol of tobacconists (and is still widely used as such in the United States of America). It is believed to be the last survivor in Britain. Until it was stolen in the autumn of 1987 he had a smoke-breathing horse.

THE SHAMBLES

The Shambles was a market street, known for its butchers' stalls, and in medieval times the majority of the town's butchers had their premises in the street. As late as the nineteenth century a third of the town's butchers' shops were still sited here. A *shambel* is a bench and originally meat would have been sold here from market stalls. Later, when permanent buildings had replaced temporary stalls, *shambles*, by association with the mess and smell which accumulated on a warm summer's day, came to be used synonymously with the mess itself.

Prior to the fourteenth century the butchers had mainly traded close by in St Saviourgate and St Andrewgate. Then The Shambles had contained the hay market and was known as Haymongergate. Hay was necessary for feeding animals awaiting slaughter, as it was illegal to graze cattle within a radius of six miles of the city centre. (Live cattle were stabled nearby in Feasegate.)

It is the only York street mentioned in the Domesday Book of 1086, at which time it was still an open area used as a market-place. Most of the buildings are medieval and, although no actual medieval shop fronts have survived in The Shambles (or anywhere else in York) six shops retain the wide wooden sills from the days when customers were served from their open windows. The maximum permissible width of these bench-sills was strictly governed by a local law, necessary to prevent blockage of the narrow streets of the town.

In the thirteenth century the custody of the city prison was entrusted to the Butchers' Guild. The town pillory stood at the Pavement end of The Shambles, and here also persons found guilty of treason were executed by beheading. The Butchers' Guild was wealthy and powerful, and built itself a guildhall on Little Shambles. (Little Shambles, today only a few yards long, used to connect The Shambles to Peter Lane.) Known as the Gail Hall (Lane Hall) it was a two-gabled building of significant size — perhaps as big as the Merchant Adventurers' Hall itself. It was demolished early in the nineteenth century.

The attractions of the street to modern eyes cannot be denied. Tourist guides advertise The Shambles as 'the famous medieval street where one can reach out and shake hands with a person in the house opposite'. In fact, unless one has particularly simian arms, this is only true of one particular pair of windows (the uppermost windows of numbers 9 and 42).

A Selection of the Lesser Buildings of Inner York

There are many fine houses in the city, particularly eighteenth-century town houses — too many to describe with justice. However, this chapter would be incomplete without mentioning some of the finest.

Fairfax House, on Castlegate, is perhaps the best example of a period-furnished Georgian town house in England. It was designed by John Carr for a fee of fifty guineas. Carr designed some of the best houses in York, and elsewhere in Yorkshire. (Perhaps his best known building is Harewood House near Leeds.) His client for Fairfax House was the last Viscount Fairfax of Emley. The building was finished in 1762, having taken nearly seven years to complete. It served as a private residence for various owners, until the twentieth century when it became, for a while, a cinema (together with the house next door). Recently restored by York Civic Trust, Fairfax House is now open to the public as a museum of Georgian interior design, housing the Noel Terry collection of Georgian furniture.

Castlegate House is opposite Fairfax House and outwardly perhaps the more interesting of the two. Like Fairfax House, it is of five bays and also designed by John Carr, as the official residence of Peter Johnston, then the Recorder of York. A slightly later, and perhaps more mature work than Fairfax House, Castlegate House was completed in 1763, when its grounds extended to Tower Street and Clifford Street. This was most of the area formerly occupied by the Franciscan Friars. From 1831 until 1857 Castlegate House housed the Mount School.

Peasholme House, on the corner of Peasholme Green and St Saviour's Place, clearly owes much to John Carr's designs, although it was built by a local carpenter, Robert Heworth. This splendid building was allowed to fall into decay in the late nineteenth century, when it was used as a store by a furniture company. The house was restored by York Civic Trust in 1975.

The Judge's Lodgings on Lendal was built by Clifton Wintringham c.1720. The house is unusual for its large height to width ratio, presumably necessitated by the size of the building needed and the ground area available. (The house is built on what was the graveyard of St Wilfrid's Church, which had been a gift to the city from Edward IV in 1461.) The house became the official residence of the Assize judge in 1806. Previously this had been the less ostentatious house behind number 30 Coney Street, still known as Judge's Court.

The area south of the river contains few outstanding public buildings, but many interesting houses of the eighteenth and nineteenth centuries. Micklegate House, opposite Holy Trinity Church, is the largest town house in York. A Georgian building of seven bays, it is another of John Carr's designs and was built for the Bourchier family of Beningbrough as their town residence. It was completed in 1753, predating both Fairfax House and Castlegate House by almost a decade. Today the house is occupied by the University of York and is home to the Department of Architecture. Numbers 53 and 54 Micklegate are also by Carr. The latter, known as Garforth House after the family who commissioned it, is a splendid building, not unlike Fairfax House (which it predates).

A number of interesting smaller buildings survive in the city from the sixteenth and seventeenth centuries. The major part of the structure of Sir Thomas Herbert's house on Pavement (now owned by York Civic Trust and leased as a shop) dates from the sixteenth century, although the front is seventeenth century. An example of a typical large medieval town house, built without foundations (notice the sag in the main beam supporting the first floor) it is well worth a look. Charles Herbert bought this plot of land from the Merchant Adventurers' Guild in 1557. Charles was the great-grandfather of Sir Thomas Herbert, a close friend and adviser of Charles I. Following the king's execution, Sir Thomas Herbert retired to a house in High Petergate, which also stands to this day.

Next door to Sir Thomas' house is the Golden Fleece Inn (a name which reflects the past importance to York of the wool trade). Although the front of the building dates from the nineteenth century, much of the structure is at least as old as the middle of the sixteenth century and the house has been an inn for almost all of that time, making the Golden Fleece one of the oldest inns in York. The Golden Fleece was one of the town's coaching inns and behind the building the name Lady Peckitt's Yard survives as the narrow lane that is all that is now left of what was once the extensive courtyard. The houses on the part of Lady Peckitt's Yard which runs down the south side of Sir Thomas Herbert's house, are also noteworthy — these brick houses on the north side are late seventeenth century and are the earliest domestic use of brick as a building material in the town.

Number 17 Fossgate was bought by John Macdonald and Philip Thompson in

1947, and turned into a successful furniture retailing business. Prior to that it had been York's first electric cinema. The Electric Cinema, a neo-Grecian building faced with terracotta tiles, opened in 1907. The screen was at the front of the building and patrons entered by a door on Fossgate and made their way to the back of the hall.

The Black Swan Inn on Peasholme Green is interesting as much for the people who lived there before it became a public house as for the architecture of the building itself. The house which originally stood on this site was owned by the Bowes family (ancestors of Queen Elizabeth II). Sir William Bowes became Lord Mayor of York in 1417 and, eleven years later, Member of Parliament for the town. His grandson, Sir Martyn Bowes, became Lord Mayor of London (and is mentioned in connection with St Cuthbert's Church in Chapter Three, and Ouse Bridge, p. 119). Later still the present building was the home of Miss Henrietta Thompson before and after her marriage. Her son, General James Wolfe, died in 1759, in the act of successfully expelling the French governmental influence from Canada. (James Wolfe himself was born in Kent). The house itself dates from the late sixteenth and early seventeenth centuries.

There are numerous small medieval houses scattered throughout the town. The Bowes Morrell House, at the bottom of Walmgate, dates from the fifteenth century and was recently restored by York Civic Trust. A small hall, its present fine state owes not a little to Dr J.B. Morrell, one of the great figures of the city during the middle years of the twentieth century. Dr Morrell endowed the University of York (which he played no small part in founding) with its main library, which today bears his name.

(Our) Lady's Row, a short row of houses on the north-west side of Goodramgate, close to the junction with King's Square, was built in 1316 in part of the yard of Holy Trinity Church (behind the Row) where there had not been any burials. Contemporary with the nave of the Minster, the Row has remained almost unaltered, and is one of the oldest jettied buildings in the country (possibly *the* oldest). The cult of the Blessed Virgin was always particularly strong in York and these houses were built in order that the rents raised would pay the salary of a priest to attend a new chantry altar in the church, dedicated to St Mary from which the Row takes its name. (Four other parish churches in the city were given similar permission to build rows of houses in unused portions of their churchyards to endow altars to the Virgin, but only this Row survives.) The chantry was removed following the Dissolution, when the Row became the property of the Corporation, which now lets the houses as shops.

The old houses next door to All Saints' Church on North Street date from the fifteenth century. (The brick work is more recent, added in the eighteenth century.) These houses were occupied either by persons connected with the church or by those judged poor and needy.

On Micklegate, a group of half a dozen somewhat larger, three-storey houses with double overhangs, now used today as shops, date from the first half of the 1600s.

St Mary's Square, between Castlegate and Coppergate, is an example of the sensitive use of late-twentieth-century styles in architecture in the city. The square, adjacent to the medieval church of St Mary's, became available for development following the demolition of a redundant nineteenth-century sweet factory. It is a shopping area of subdued brown brick, and has been designed both to fit in with the character of the city and not to intrude. (Even a multistorey car park has been made to blend with imaginative fenestration.) Under St Mary's Square the site of an archaeological excavation of Viking York (carried out as a 'rescue dig' prior to the building of the Square) has been converted into a subterranean museum to life in the Viking city, known as the Jorvik Viking Centre.

Many of Yorks buildings are adorned with curious decorations, particularly coats of arms. For example, throughout the town one can find pairs of crossed keys, one of the city's coats of arms of the city. The two keys, the symbol of St Peter to whom the Minster is dedicated, should differ from each other — one representing the key to Heaven and the other to Hell. That they are frequently shown as the same in the Arms is a curious mistake. Two other Arms which are particularly common on buildings throughout the city. The official Arms of the city are the red cross on a white background — the cross of St George, together with five lions, crossed sword and mace, and the Cap of Maintenance. The lions were added to the cross of St George as the City Arms by William the Conqueror. They are memorials to five York men who, in the rebellion against the Normans in 1069 fought, according to William himself, like lions. The sword is the Sword of the City, presented to York by Richard II when he elevated the office of Mayor to that of Lord Mayor in 1389. The sword should be held and depicted point uppermost, except in the presence of the king — another not infrequent mistake around the town. The sword itself had belonged to Emperor Sigismund of Germany. The Emperor gave it to Richard who presented it to the first Lord Mayor, William de Selby. It disappeared in 1705 and the ceremonial sword used today was presented to the city by George V in 1915. The Cap of Maintenance, worn by the sword-bearer who precedes the Lord Mayor at official ceremonies, is medieval and its origins are obscure. Richard also presented the city with a cap at the same time as the sword.

The other coat of arms is the bishop's pallium. The symbol of office, presented to archbishops in the Church of Rome on their inauguration by the Pope. A ribbon-like vestment in the shape of a Y and embroidered with crosses, the pallium was discarded by the Church of England at the time of the Reformation and Dissolution in the sixteenth century. The Arms can still be found throughout the city on buildings with Roman Catholic associations.

Finally, the cats dotted around the town at various high places deserve a mention. Nobody seems to remember the origin of the two cats on Low Ousegate or the one on Gillygate, except that they were placed there 'to scare away the mice'. The rest are the personal motif of the contemporary York architect Thomas Adams. There is no connection between the Ousegate cats and Thomas Adams' beasts — Adams started signing his drawings with cats while studying at the University of Birmingham, and his cats are 'for fun, in an age when getting planning permission for an interesting building is all but impossible'. His first York cat is on the ridge of a shopping complex on Coney Street, overlooking the Ouse. The rest followed to the extent that they are now demanded by Adams' customers and are famous throughout the country. The pigeon being stalked with felonious menace above King's Square was added by Adams' client, Alan Black of Lawson Larg (who claims that it must be the most photographed pigeon in Britain).

There are many other buildings of aesthetic, architectural and historical interest around the town, too numerous to mention in the space available here. A vigilant walk around York is, however, its own reward.

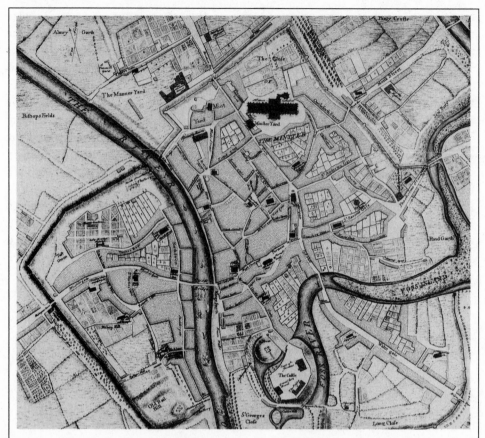

A plan of the City of York, 1750.

CHAPTER SIX

THE DERIVATIONS OF YORK'S STREET NAMES

The names of streets in York often arouse curiosity. Some of the more recent, and a few of the older street names in the city are of obvious origin and as such have not been included in this chapter. A number of streets which have been renamed are included here, together with their original names and the origins of these.

An American visitor once complained that much in York seems to be named in order to confuse — the streets are 'gates', the gates are 'bars' and the bars are 'pubs'. The Scandinavian word *gata*, meaning 'street', is found in its anglicized form throughout the areas of England colonized or settled by the Danes and Norsemen (including the City of London). York has more 'gates' than any other English town and the tradition of naming streets 'gate' has, to a degree, been retained to the present day. (The companion to 'gate' — *gail*, or *gayle* — which implies a narrow path and was once also common in the town, has been lost completely, and replaced by 'lane', its English equivalent.)

THE STREET NAMES OF INNER YORK
(IN ALPHABETICAL ORDER)

Aldwark means old fortification. In Norman times an eighty-yard stretch of the Roman wall remained standing to the north of Aldwark, to a height of twenty feet (unlike the rest of the Roman defences of the north-east side of the town). The Normans incorporated this into their rampart.

Bedern was the site of the dormitory of the vicars-choral who occupied St William's College in the fifteenth and sixteenth centuries. (The College is described in Chapter Two.) The street, however, takes its name not from a place of beds, as is often supposed, but from its chapel — a place of bidding, that is, prayer. The name is also found associated with colleges in Ripon and Beverley.

Bishophill Junior and **Bishophill Senior** are the sites of two churches, both dedicated to St Mary and both owned by the archbishop prior to the Norman Conquest. The older, which became known as Bishop's Senior, was recently demolished, but St Mary's, Bishop's Junior, still stands, in part the oldest building in the city.

Blake Street derives from the Norse *bleiki*, or 'bleached' and may have been a street paved with white stones, or possibly a street of white-washed houses.

Blossom Street derives from Ployhsuaingate c.1280, which became Ploxswaing-ate and means Ploughman's Street. It is said that it was the one street in York wide enough to allow a horse and plough to be turned around.

Bootham was an area where there was a village (*ham*) of small huts (*booths*).

Brownie Dyke is the staith on the Foss at Castle Mills Bridge. It derives from the Anglo-Norman *brun eau dyke*, a dyke of brown water — the muddy Foss.

Buckingham Street is named after George Villiers, Duke of Buckingham. Two George Villiers, father and son and each in turn Duke, lived close by in a house on Skeldergate that the elder duke bought from Sir Thomas Fairfax. (George Villiers, the first duke, got himself into trouble for making love to the Queen of France. His son was a Royalist at the time of the Civil War but recovered his confiscated lands by secretly marrying Thomas Fairfax's daughter.)

Burton Stone Lane was formerly called Chapel Lane and takes its name from the Burton family to whom the land adjacent to the north side of the lane passed at the Dissolution in November 1539. Prior to the Dissolution the land had been occupied by the hospital of St Mary Magdalene. The stone, a plinth that once carried a cross, stands on the corner of Burton Stone Lane and Bootham. An original stone probably marked the boundary of the hospital, but when boundary stones were made illegal in 1593 it must have been demolished. In 1604, plague hit York. Plague was an ever-present threat and there had been a severe outbreak in 1550 (in living memory of the oldest inhabitants of the city). The epidemic of 1604 was particularly severe (three and a half thousand people are said to have died). With containment in mind, stone crosses were re-erected just outside the town on the main thoroughfares. Here country traders would leave the vittels they wished to sell, to be collected by the townsfolk. In this way the country people need not enter and leave the town. The present Burton Stone is the base of the cross erected in 1604.

Carmelite Street cuts through the land occupied from 1295 to 1540 by a Carmelite Friary.

Carr's Lane used to be called Kirk Lane, but was renamed in honour of John Carr, the architect responsible for many of the best of York's eighteenth-century buildings. Carr settled in York in 1751, buying a house which stood at the bottom of the lane, on Skeldergate. He was twice Lord Mayor.

Castlegate, of course, leads to the castle along the line of Coney Street, Spurriergate and Nessgate. The name was once used for the whole of what since 1820 has been called Tower Street, various parts being referred to as Castlegate, Castlegate Lane and Castlegate Postern Lane. (See also TOWER STREET.)

Cherry Hill Lane once ran through a cherry orchard which occupied the land bounded by Bishopgate Street and Clementhorpe.

Church Street is so called after St Sampson's Church but was known, until 1836, as Girdlergate — the street of girdle makers. (See also PARLIAMENT STREET.)

Clementhorpe was once the parish of St Clement's Church (absorbed by St Mary, Bishophill Senior, early in the fourteenth century). The Norse *thorpe* means a small hamlet or village.

Clifford Street takes its name from Clifford's Tower, itself named after Robert de Clifford, Constable of the Castle during the fourteenth century. The Clifford family were (or at least claimed to be) hereditary constables of York Castle.

Coffee Yard takes its name from being the site of the first coffee-house in York which, in the early eighteenth century, stood on the corner of Coffee Yard and Grape Lane.

College Street refers to the college of priests, serving chantries in the Minster, founded during the fifteenth century and dedicated to St William of York. The College was housed in the fifteenth-century brick- and half-timbered building which now takes up most of what is left of the street. Until Deangate was created in 1903 College Street was known as Vicars' Lane. In the eighteenth century it was also referred to as Little Alice Lane — nobody seems quite sure why.

Colliergate was associated with charcoal burners or, more probably in a city centre crowded with houses built of tinder, charcoal sellers.

Coney Street is the Anglo-Norse *Kuningestrete* or 'King's Street'. It is one of only three streets to have retained the Anglo-Saxon *strete*, possibly reflecting its central role in the life of the town. (The other two are Blake Street and North Street.) As the street that ran along the (long gone) staiths of the Ouse, between the river and the front of the Roman fort, it has been York's most important street since the founding of the town. It has been suggested that it takes its name from having been the site of an imperial or regal palace in Anglo-Saxon times. More probably, *Kuningestrete* reflects its position in front of the Roman fort and its imperial *Principia* building, which in post-Roman times was taken over for use as a regal palace.

Coppergate was associated with carpenters, and is derived from the Old English *koppari*, meaning a turner or joiner. It occurs as early as the twelfth century and is not cognate with 'cooper' (which has often been assumed to be the origin of this street name).

Cromwell Road named after Oliver Cromwell is one of several streets in the Bishophill area of the town that commemorates leaders of the country during the Civil War. Previously Cromwell Road was known as Gaol Lane, after the King's Gaol which was in the Bitchdaughter Tower (the tower at the southernmost corner of the city wall).

Davygate is named after one David, the king's Lardiner during the reign of Henry II. In the fifteenth century the street was known as Davygatelardiner. The position of Lardiner in York was subsequently held by David's descendants (who were known by the surname of Davy). The Lardiner was an official responsible for the game for the king's table, hunted in the royal forest of Galtres to the north of York. In effect, the post meant responsibility for enforcing the laws of the forest, which comprised a large section of Magna Carta and were later excised into a separate charter — the *Carta de Foresta*. It has been estimated that more than one third of England was royal forest at the time of Henry II's reign, and thus fell under the jurisdiction of the Lardiners of the thirteenth century. Consequently the post was one with wide-ranging responsibilities, and the Lardiner would have been one of the wealthier men of the city. The duties of the Lardiner extended far beyond those of simply a policeman-grocer. For example, it was David who was charged with overseeing the rebuilding of the castle in York during the twelfth century. The Lardiners of York possessed the only prison in England for the exclusive use of persons transgressing the forest laws — the prison was Davy Hall, which stood in Davygate until the 1740s, on the site of what is now St Helen's churchyard on the south side of the street.

Deangate dates only from 1903 when it was created to relieve the pressure of traffic on Petergate. It is named from the site of the former Old Deanery, which stood between the end of Grape Lane and Deangate. It was demolished shortly before 1830.

Duncombe Place was named after Dean A.W. Duncombe when Little Blake Street, by which it was formerly known, was demolished and widened in 1859. It had become known as Little Blake Street only at the turn of the nineteenth century. For over five hundred years before that it had been referred to as Lop Lane, meaning the street full of fleas.

Earlsborough Terrace derives its name from the ninth-century stronghold of the Danish earls of Northumbria, which stood somewhere in the grounds of the later St Mary's Abbey, possibly between St Olave's Church and the river. A *burh*, (which later became 'borough') derives from the Old English verb *bergen*, to protect, and originally meant nothing more than a walled enclosure. The original Earls' *burh* was destroyed in 937 by the great Wessex king, Athelstan, following his suppression of a Norse army. (See also p. 100 and KING'S SQUARE.)

Elbow Lane which presumably takes its name from its crooked path has been known as such since at least 1575 and probably for much longer.

Exhibition Square. At the instigation of York School of Art, the city held an Exhibition of Fine Art and Industry in the grounds of Bootham Park Hospital between 24th July and 31st October, 1866. It was attended by over three hundred thousand people and was clearly a huge success — so much so that it was decided to hold another exhibition a decade later. For this a site of a little less than three acres in the north-east corner of St Mary's Abbey (then known as Bearpark's Garden) was leased by the Corporation. The Bird in Hand public house and a number of other buildings were demolished, and Exhibition Square was created. A permanent building was erected and the exhibition finally opened on 7th May, 1879. By the time of its closure in November it had attracted over half a million visitors. The profits were used to expand the nucleus of an art collection which was given to the city in 1882, and from 1890 the paintings were housed in this building, which became York City Art Gallery.

Fairfax Street is named after Thomas, Lord Fairfax, the great Parliamentarian General. Fairfax lived in a house he had built to his own design situated on Skeldergate, at the end of Carr Lane, a hundred yards from Fairfax Street.

Feasegate is derived from *feoh*, the Old English and Norse word for cattle (the root of the modern word 'fee') and *hus*, or house — that is, a street containing one (or perhaps more) cattle houses. (See also The Shambles in Chapter Five.)

Fetter Lane derives from Feltergayle — a lane occupied by felt workers.

Finkle Street was known as Finclegayle in 1356 and *Fynkullstrete* in 1370. It probably derives from the Scandinavian personal name Finnkell. In an attempt to improve the image of the area when a new market-place was created in 1836, the medieval name of Finkle Street was revived to replace Mucky Pig Lane, the label it had acquired by the eighteenth century through its association with the pig market which had been held in this area. (See also PARLIAMENT STREET and SWINEGATE.)

Fishergate leads to site of the former lake which used to be at the head of the Foss, created when the river was dammed in the 1070s to flood a moat around the castle. The cost of the moat was 120 acres of previously prime land upstream of the castle. This became shallow lake and swamp, dotted with islands. Subsequently the lake, owned by the Crown as part of the castle, was used for fish farming and became known as the King's Fishpool. Fishergate was presumably where the fishermen lived, and the name is recorded from almost immediately after the lake was created in the 1070s.

Fossgate obviously leads to the River Foss and Foss Bridge. During medieval times, the sea-fish market was held on Foss Bridge and the lower part of Fossgate was known as Fish Shambles.

Foss Islands Road runs across land which, until it was drained during the nineteenth century, was part of the King's Fishpool. (See also FISHERGATE.)

Friargate derives its name from its association with the Franciscan Friary which stood between the river and Castlegate.

George Street. This was originally the continuation of Fishergate, which formerly entered the walled city through Fishergate Bar (see Chapter Four). The part of Fishergate inside the walls was renamed St George Street early in the last century, after the church of that dedication which had stood here, and this became shortened to its present name. (The church was disused after 1586 and demolished before 1800.) Prior to the nineteenth century it was known as Nowtgail, meaning 'cow lane'.

George Hudson Street was created in 1841 and named after George Hudson, three times Lord Mayor of York during the 1830s and 1840s. Hudson was responsible for bringing the railway to the north-east, centred at York. Dubbed the 'Railway King', he was also a ruthless businessman and cruel landlord, much hated by many of the city's residents during his lifetime. On his bankruptcy and disgrace in 1849, George Hudson Street was renamed Railway Street. In 1971, the centennial anniversary of his death, time having numbed the memory of Hudson's less attractive qualities, Railway Street was again renamed George Hudson Street.

Gillygate is named after St Giles. A church dedicated to the saint stood here, opposite the end of Lord Mayor's Walk.

Glover Lane (Lund's Court), a small alley joining Low Petergate to Swinegate, was formerly Glovergail and was the lane occupied by the glovers of medieval times.

Goodramgate derives from the Danish name Guthrum, possibly (though perhaps improbably) the same Guthrum who led the Viking army which settled in York following its defeat by King Alfred of Wessex in May 878.

Grape Lane. Grape is derived from the Old English *grapian*, the root of the modern words 'grab' and 'grope'. In the fourteenth century the street was known as Grapcunt Lane. Grape Lane was known for its brothels. (See also Petergate in Chapter Five.)

Gregory Lane takes its name from the church dedicated to St Gregory which once stood on the north side of the lane. Formerly it was known as Barker Lane from the tanning industry which dominated this part of the town. (See also ST MAURICE'S ROAD.)

Groves Lane see PENLEY'S GROVE STREET.

Hampden Street named in memory of John Hampden, one of the five Parliamentary leaders who, in 1642, precipitated the Civil War.

Hornpot Lane. One of the oldest surviving Anglo-Saxon street names in York, Hornpot Lane used to be occupied by workers in horn. Today it is thought of as running from Petergate into the churchyard of Holy Trinity Church. In fact it winds its way through to St Sampson's Square. Before Church Street was created in the 1830s Hornpot Lane was an important thoroughfare.

Hungate appears in twelfth-century records as Hundegat in Mersch, that is, 'the dogs' street in the marsh' (the marsh being the edges of the King's Fishpool — see FISHERGATE). Hungate was the site of a public tip and dogs seem to have become associated with the place, particularly as a result of the butchers of The Shambles throwing away their waste bones etc., there. In 1411 a complaint was made by the parishioners of the Church of St John the Baptist, which stood here, against the smell of the site and the nuisance caused by the dogs. Prior to being known as Hungate the street was referred to as Dunnyngdykes from it being used as a dump for animal dung.

Jewbury was a Jewish burial ground. However, the name derives from before the burial ground, from Jew's *burh*, or Jewborough — the village of the Jews.

Jubbergate was, in the twelfth century, Brettgate, meaning 'the street of the Bretons', and was possibly where a number of affluent Breton traders had their houses (see also NAVIGATION ROAD). By 1280 it had become known as Joubrettegat, meaning Jewish/Breton street. By this time, Jubbergate and Coney

Street had become the home of a number of wealthy Jewish financiers and their families.

King Street, the continuation of Coppergate, takes its name from KING'S STAITH (see also). However, until the sixteenth century it was known as Kergate, meaning 'boggy street' — perhaps an indication of the poor state of the staith?

King's Square and **King's Court**, formerly Coninggate and Kuningsgarth, Anglo-Norse forms of King's Street and King's Court, was the site of the hall of the Viking kings of Northumbria (itself the land of those who lived north of the Humber). The north-east gate into the Roman fort was sited in King's Square and was still standing in Viking times. It has been suggested that parts of the Roman structure were utilized by the Danish earls as their palace. It was possibly after the destruction in 937 of their original palace (which stood where the modern Museum Gardens are today) by Athelstan, the King of Wessex, that the Danish earls moved their seat to King's Square. (Later the earls moved their palace back to its former site.) King's Square itself was only created in 1937 when Christ's Church was demolished. (See also EARLSBOROUGH TERRACE.)

King's Staith. The name King's Staith is associated with visits to York by kings Edward I, II and III in the thirteenth and fourteenth centuries, but did not come into general use until the Tudor times or later. Prior to the seventeenth century the staith was referred to as 'the pudding holes', from the Old English *pudd* meaning 'ditch'. The ditches, dug perpendicular to the river bank at the southern end of the staith, were places where members of the public could bring meat and clothes to be washed, and from the fifteenth century it was prohibited to dump waste into the river upstream of this point.

Lady Peckitt's Yard. In the fourteenth century the two parts of Lady Peckitt's Yard were known by different names. Bacusgail, that is, Bake House Lane, ran from Pavement right down to the Foss, while the lane from this through to Fossgate was known as Trichourgail — *Trichour* is thought to mean trickster. Alice Peckitt was the wife of William Peckitt, Lord Mayor of York 1701–2. William Peckitt gave the land behind Pavement to the city. This was then an open yard where the coaches to and from London and Edinburgh often stopped over for the night. The name was not adopted until after the deaths of both William and Alice and why Alice's name was chosen is not clear, but may be related to the York custom of referring to former Lady Mayoresses as 'Lady' for the rest of their lives. The Lord Mayor reverted to being plain Mr Smith, Jones or Peckitt at the end of his term of office of a year and a day.

Lawrence Street. During the town's boom years of the twelfth century the population grew rapidly and the suburbs spread. By the end of the century Walmgate had extended as far to the east as Green Dykes Lane, and the part outside the city walls was named after the twelfth-century Church of St Lawrence, built on the street at this time.

Layerthorpe may derive its name from its position on the edge of the forest of

Galtres — a royal forest immediately to the north of York. A *thorpe* is a hamlet, and carries the connotation of being a suburb. *Layer* is possibly the Old English *leer* or *layre* and is a hunting term referring to a place where deer congregate.

Leeman Road is named after George Leeman, arch-rival of, and successor to George Hudson. (See also GEORGE HUDSON STREET.)

Lendal is thought to be a contraction of 'Landing Hill', a name it acquired in the seventeenth century, a century after the dissolution of St Leonard's Hospital (see Chapter Five). The hospital used a staith along the Ouse below where Lendal runs, owned by the Austin Friary which stood here and with which the hospital was associated. The continuation of this below Lendal Bridge is still known as St Leonard's Landing. It was an important staith and it was here that the stone for building the Minster was landed after being brought by barges from Tadcaster. Prior to being known as Lendal the street was referred to as Aldeconyngstrete or Old Coney Street.

Little Shambles used to be known as Haymonger Lane when The Shambles was known as Haymongergate, and the name Haymonger Lane continued to be used for several centuries after The Shambles had become known by that name. Before the construction of Parliament Street in 1836 the lane connected The Shambles to Peter Lane. (See also The Shambles in Chapter Five.)

Lord Mayor's Walk. In the early eighteenth century the unmade track outside the north-east side of the city wall was widened, paved, lined with elm trees and renamed to create Lord Mayor's Walk — the town's first fashionable Georgian promenade. It was formally opened in 1718, with great ceremony, by the Lord Mayor, taking its new name from the ceremony. Prior to the eighteenth century the muddy path had been known as Goose Lane since at least the fourteenth century, and the ditch along this stretch of the city wall as Goose Dyke.

Marygate is associated with the Benedictine Abbey dedicated to the Virgin Mary, which occupied what are now the Yorkshire Museum Gardens and flourished until 1539. It is recorded as Seintemariegate as early as 1354.

Merchantgate takes its name from the adjacent Merchant Adventurers' Hall. It was created as recently as 1912.

Micklegate. Until 1863 Ouse Bridge was the only crossing over the Ouse, and Micklegate the only street into the city from the south and London. The name derives from the Old English word *mickle*, meaning 'great'. (In some Yorkshire dialects the word 'mickle' remains in use.) It was the site of much important trade, and from at least the seventeenth century the most prosperous area of town. The wholesale butter market for the north of England was held in front of St Martin-cum-Gregory, and the wine and bacon markets were also held on the street.

Minster Gates was the site of one of the four gates giving access to the Minster Close. It was the lane where book publishers traded and was known as Bookland Lane in the days before printing, and Book-binders' Lane by the sixteenth century.

Monkgate is recorded as Munccagate as early as 1080 and acquired its name from the monks who regularly used the street. The monks were associated with the pre-Conquest Minster and the name was already obsolete as a description of the street by the end of the twelfth century.

Museum Street. In the thirteenth century, Museum Street was known as Ffotlesgate, or 'Footless Lane' (referring to the cripples who lived at St Leonard's Hospital). By Tudor times it was known as Finkle Street, perhaps meaning crooked street for the same reason (but see also FINKLE STREET). In the seventeenth century it had become Back Lendal, and Little Lendal by 1782 when it was widened by demolishing much of what remained of St Leonard's Hospital. By the 1850s it was being referred to as Museum Street by association with the adjacent Yorkshire Museum (opened in 1830), but remained little more than a quiet lane until 1863, when it was turned into the major thoroughfare it is today, to accommodate traffic approaching the new Lendal Bridge (opened the same year).

Navigation Road was so named in the early 1850s from the Foss Navigation. This is the stretch of the Foss navigable by boats with more than the shallowest of draughts, as distinct from the King's Fishpool. (See also FISHERGATE.) The Foss Navigation was lined with staiths to which Navigation Road gave access from Walmgate. In the thirteenth century it was known as Little Brettgate — the street of the Bretons. That the Bretons, who would have been merchant sailors, are found living close to the staiths is not surprising. (The prefix 'Little' was to distinguish it from a more important Brettgate — see also JUBBERGATE.)

Nessgate leads to a ness, or headland. This is the spur of clay between the Foss and the Ouse which has grown over the centuries at the confluence of the two rivers, and is the site of the castle and St George's Field.

Newgate runs from King's Square down the north side of the market, to become Jubbergate. It was Le Newe Gate, that is, the new street, in 1336. Newgate Market, the present market-place, was created by the demolition of the houses that stood there (some of them very old) in 1955.

New Walk. Following the success of the newly opened Georgian promenade of Lord Mayor's Walk as a fashionable social meeting place, this second, broad, tree-lined promenade running southwards from the confluence of the Foss and Ouse, was newly opened in 1732.

North Street is recorded as Nordstreta as early as the late eleventh century and is one of only three streets in the city to have retained the Anglo-Saxon *strete* rather than adopting the Scandinavian *gata* or *gayle*. It was along the staiths of North Street and Skeldergate (now Queen's Staith) rather than at King's Staith opposite, that the majority of the goods imported into and exported from the city were loaded onto river barges and ocean-going boats. North Street used to refer not only to the present street, but also to what is now known as Tanner Row, at least as far as Barker Lane.

Nunnery Lane runs alongside the Bar Convent, just outside Micklegate Bar.

Until 1829 the land between the city walls and the convent, and continuing south to become Scarcroft, was undeveloped. The lane was then known as Baggergate, meaning the street of the pedlars (or, possibly but less likely, the street of the badgers).

Ogleforth is recorded as Ugel's Ford early in the twelfth century. Who Ugel was and what he was fording has long been forgotten (although there was an open ditch which ran between Ogleforth and the city wall).

Parliament Street. Originally there were two markets in the town. The food market was held on Tuesdays, Thursdays and Saturdays on Pavement, in the square at the east end of All Saints' Church. The hardware market was held in St Sampson's Square on Thursdays and Saturdays. Until 1818, St Sampson's Square (St Sampson's Church stands just outside the east corner of the square) was known as Thursday Market, and was entered by Feasegate, Davygate, Finkle Street or Silver Street — then all narrow lanes. In the early 1830s, Parliament was petitioned for permission for York to hold a larger combined market. The area joining the two market-places was then fully built up (apart from Jubbergate, which then ran from the site of the modern market-place to Coney Street, and Starkthwaite Lane which ran along the north side of where Parliament Street is today). As a result of an Act of Parliament passed in 1833, all the buildings between Pavement and Thursday Market, and on the north side of St Sampson's Square were razed. The new combined market-place was consequently named Parliament Street and the new street out of St Sampson's Square, Church Street. The first market was held in Parliament Street in July 1836, and to maintain the right to use the area as a market-place, markets are still occasionally held here.

Patrick Pool used to refer to the whole length of the street from Newgate to Grape Lane. Today only the short stretch leading from Church Street into the modern market-place is still called Patrick Pool and the rest is now Swinegate (see p. 161). First recorded as Patricpol at the end of the twelfth century, the origin of the name is a bit of a puzzle. Patrick probably refers to a church dedicated to the saint, possibly standing where St Sampson's stands today. The pool, it is thought, refers to the old Roman bath, part of which can today be seen inside the Roman Bath public house in St Sampson's Square. It has been suggested that perhaps a collapse of overlying medieval ground exposed the lost pool (which is known to have extended from St Sampson's Square to under what is now Swinegate). There are records of the lane being flooded in the mid-thirteenth century — in 1249 the street was so boggy as to be impassable. Early in Tudor times it was known as a good place to pick herbs, suggesting a persistently damp place, and towards the end of the sixteenth century there were moves to drain the lane. Interestingly, almost under the middle of the street there are the remains of a large vaulted Roman sewer, in a state of remarkably good preservation.

Pavement is the former site of the vittels market, which used to be held in the square at the east end of All Saints' Church. (See also PARLIAMENT STREET.) As such it is referred to in the Domesday Book as Marketshyre, a *shyre* being one of the seven divisions of the city, similar to the modern wards. In the early fourteenth century, Marketshyre became one of the first of the town's medieval streets to be paved, and from that time has been called Pavement.

Peasholme Green was a green river meadow (the Old English *holm*) beside the Foss, where peas were grown. During the eighteenth century Peasholme Green was the site of the important wool market.

Penley's Grove Street derives from Paynlathcrofts. *Lath* is Old Norse and means an area of land. The street name thus implies crofts with their own land associated. *Pay* may just refer to an area (as the French *pays*).

Peter Lane was formerly Le Kyrk Lane and ran alongside the church of Peter-the-Little which stood on the east side of the lane. The church became disused in 1586 and the parish was united with that of All Saints' Church a few yards away.

Petergate is the Roman *Via Principalis*, or principal street. It is recorded as Petergate at the beginning of the thirteenth century, taking its name from the dedication of the Minster to St Peter.

Piccadilly was created between Fishergate and the Foss in 1840, and named after the Piccadilly in London. The land upon which it was built was newly reclaimed as a result of the draining of what had been the King's Fishpool. The bridge over the Foss was built, and the road extended to Pavement, in 1912 (for which a number of medieval buildings in the way were destroyed).

Priory Street runs across the south side of the site once occupied by the Benedictine Priory of Holy Trinity. The great main gate of the priory stood here but was demolished when the street was created in 1855.

Queen's Staith is presumably named by association with King's Staith opposite. (See also NORTH STREET.)

Rougier Street was created in 1841 and named after the Rougier family who sold the land to the city. The family owned much of the land in this area (having made their fortune manufacturing combs).

St Andrewgate contains St Andrew's Church. During medieval times it was sometimes also referred to as Ketmongergate, meaning the street of the meat sellers, a name also associated with St Saviourgate. (It was not uncommon in medieval times for a street to be known by two names; less common for two streets to share a name.)

St Helen's Square was created in 1745 out of St Helen's churchyard, to allow access by carriages to the new, fashionable Assembly Rooms on Blake Street.

St Leonard's Place is named after the medieval hospital of St Leonard which used to occupy the whole of this corner of the walls. Prior to 1835 it was known as Mint Yard, the Royal Mint having been housed here for periods during the sixteenth and seventeenth centuries.

St Maurice's Road takes its name from the Church of St Maurice which stood near the west end of the road. The church was demolished during the nineteenth century. St Maurice's Road was formerly known as Barker Hill — a street of tanners and parchment makers (from their use of tree bark as a source of the preservative tannin). The city rampart, at its widest here, was known as Herlot Hill as early as 1340 and as late as the eighteenth century as Harlot Hill. In the 1300s, *herlot* merely implied beggar. However, by the eighteenth century both the word and the area had acquired their modern meanings. Euphemistically, a path which ran from St Maurice's Road to Monk Bridge, between Monkgate and Foss Bank, was known as Love Lane in the seventeenth century. Like Grape Lane, the area was not considered fashionable amongst the gentility of the town.

St Sampson's Square is named after St Sampson's Church which stands close by in Church Street. (See also PARLIAMENT STREET.)

St Saviourgate, which contains St Saviour's Church, is recorded under its present name in the middle of the fourteenth century. Prior to that it was known as Ketmongergate, or the street of the flesh-sellers, before the majority of the town's butchers moved to The Shambles from here. (See also ST ANDREWGATE.)

Shambles, The The middle English word *shambel* derives from the Latin *scamellum* and means a bench, particularly a bench supported on trestles. In the thirteenth century, when the butchers' market was in St Saviourgate, the street was known as Haymongergate, the street of hay sellers. By the fifteenth century it was occupied by butchers and known as the Flesh Shambles, to distinguish it from the Fish Shambles — see FOSSGATE. (See also The Shambles in Chapter Five.)

Silver Street takes its name from being, from 1837, the place where the fish market was held.

Skeldergate. There is a widely held belief in York that Skeldergate takes its name from being a street of the shield makers (the Norse for shield being *skjöldr*). However, this seems unlikely, and there is no evidence, documentary or otherwise, of shield makers working here. In fact, this was one of the most important streets in the city as it was along the staiths of Skeldergate and North Street that much of the city's business was loaded onto and off-loaded from trading boats. It seems much more likely that it takes its name from the Norse *skelde*, meaning 'shelf' and referring to the street and its staith sitting below the Roman terracing on which the town above was built. (A further possible derivation from the Scandinavian personal name Skjöldr has also been suggested.)

Spen Lane comes from *ispen*, or aspen — a lane lined or overgrown by aspen trees.

Spurriergate means the street of spur makers and once contained the workshops of the lorimers of York.

Stonebow was called Staynebow in the thirteenth century, meaning a stone arch. What the stone arch was is unclear. It has been suggested that it might have been a Roman gateway, or the remains of a Roman sewer like that found between

Church Street and Swinegate. A street of the same name in Lincoln refers to the southern gateway to the walled city. Stonebow ran along the side of the Carmelite Friary, which in 1295 moved to the land between Stonebow and the river, and for a while it was known as Whitefriar Lane. The old name was readopted when the present street was created in 1955, out of what had been a small lane connecting Pavement to Peasholme Green.

Stonegate has possibly been paved with stone since Roman times, but is more likely to have taken its name from the Roman *Porta Praetoria* — the great gate into the Roman fort, which was a large and imposing gritstone structure which still stood in Viking times in what is now St Helen's Square.

Swinegate first recorded in the middle of the thirteenth century as Swyngaill, once contained pig houses that were, until 1605, the site of the pig market. It acquired the name only in the late sixteenth century, prior to which it was known as Patrick Pool (as its continuation on the other side of Church Street still is). (See also FINKLE STREET and PATRICK POOL.)

Tanner Row, Tanner Street and **Tanners' Moat** reflect the leather industry which once dominated that area of the town.

Toft Green merely means a street of small dwellings (or *tofts*) sited on a green. The area used to be known as Kingestofts and was once the site of a church dedicated to St Mary Magdalene endowed by Henry III as a gift to the Dominican order. The king's gift allowed them to found a House in the city, and the tofts belonged to the friary. Toft Green was one of the places around the town where the medieval mystery plays were performed, and at one time was known as Pageant Green.

Tower Street runs alongside Clifford's Tower. There used to be a gate in the city wall (now demolished) on Tower Street, to the the west of the castle and known as Castlegate Postern (from the Latin *posticum*, a back door). Tower Street was then known as Castlegate Postern Lane and ran between the castle moat and the wall of the Franciscan Friary on the banks of the Ouse. In a garden on Tower Street, just outside Castlegate Postern, the ducking stool was sited to be used 'for common skoulders and punyshment of offenders' in a stagnant pool in the ditch around the castle.

Victor Street used to be known as St Mary's Road (when it led to the now demolished Church of St Mary's on Bishophill Senior). Before that it was called Lounelithgate. *Lounelith* means a hidden gateway, and as the name dates from at least the twelfth century it predates the medieval stone walls and must refer to a cutting through the earthen rampart. When Victoria Bar was constructed in 1838 just such an obscure, narrow cutting was found.

Walmgate is corrupted from the name of one Walba who probably lived during the second half of the eleventh century.

Whip-ma-Whop-ma-gate. The derivation of the name of the shortest street in the town (with the longest name) is uncertain, lost in the mists of time, although there have been a number of suggestions made, some more fanciful than others. The most probable derivation is that it is from a combination of the Yorkshire *whitna* and its Lancashire equivalent *whatna* both meaning 'what kind of'. Whip-ma-Whop-ma-gate then means, derisively, 'what a street!', perhaps on account of its short length. Later this may have acquired the connotation of whipping by association with a nearby house of correction in St Anthony's Hall.

AUTHOR'S NOTE

Eboracum — *or the History and Antiquities of the City of York* by Francis Drake, published in 1736, was the first accurate and comprehensive history of the city to be published. It remains a fascinating book, an important source of much information, and is very readable. A more recent compilation is the *History of Yorkshire* in the Victoria County History series, particularly the fifth volume devoted to the town of York itself, published in 1961. For those with an interest in the city's buildings, the six volumes which make up the inventory of the town, compiled by the Royal Commission on Historical Monuments, are the best starting point for detailed information. Perhaps more accessible is the excellent little book *The Architecture of York* by Eric Gee. Unfortunately, it is currently out of print and is difficult to find. The definitive history of the Minster is *A History of York Minster* by G.E. Aylmer and R. Cant.

The general history of York has been catalogued by Charles Brunton Knight and published in 1944 in his *History of the City of York*. This remarkable and invaluable book is a year by year chronology of the city through the centuries. In addition, there are a number of excellent studies dealing with specific periods of the town's past. One in particular, *The Great and Close Siege of York, 1644*, by Peter Wenham, describes this interesting period in York's history in an eloquent and easy style. With the close of Wenham's book, the close of the civil war, came the close of York's central role in the political life of England.

During the course of the three years which it took to compile and collate the information in this book, I have become indebted to the generosity of a great many people who have given their time and expertise freely and with enthusiasm. I hope they will accept a blanket expression of my gratitude. However, there is one person who displayed considerable patience, gave continuous encouragement, contributed a great deal of work herself and bullied me into working when necessary. She is Catherine Walton. Without Cathy's contributions this book would never have been finished. It is to her that I dedicate this work.

INDEX

164